# JESUS OUR LORD

T0323831

## OTHER WRITINGS BY JOHN PHILLIPS

*Bible Explorer's Guide*
*Introducing People of the Bible*
*100 Old Testament Sermon Outlines*
*100 New Testament Sermon Outlines*
*Only One Life: A Biography of Stephen Olford*
*The View from Mount Calvary*

### THE EXPLORING SERIES

*Exploring Genesis*
*Exploring the Psalms*
*Exploring Proverbs*
*Exploring the Love Song of Solomon*
*Exploring the Book of Daniel*
*Exploring the Minor Prophets*
*Exploring the Gospel of Matthew*
*Exploring the Gospel of Mark*
*Exploring the Gospel of Luke*
*Exploring the Gospel of John*
*Exploring Acts*
*Exploring Romans*
*Exploring 1 Corinthians*
*Exploring 2 Corinthians*
*Exploring Galatians*
*Exploring Ephesians and Philippians*
*Exploring Colossians and Philemon*
*Exploring 1 and 2 Thessalonians*
*Exploring the Pastoral Epistles*
*Exploring Hebrews*
*Exploring the Epistle of James*
*Exploring the Epistles of Peter*
*Exploring the Epistles of John*
*Exploring the Epistle of Jude*
*Exploring Revelation*
*Exploring the Future*
*Exploring the Scriptures*

# JESUS OUR LORD

*24 Portraits of Christ Throughout Scripture*

## JOHN PHILLIPS

Kregel
*Publications*

*Jesus Our Lord: 24 Portraits of Christ Throughout Scripture*

© 2007 by John Phillips

Published by Kregel Publications, a division of Kregel, Inc., P.O. Box 2607, Grand Rapids, MI 49501.

All Scripture quotations are from the King James Version of the Holy Bible.

ISBN 10: 0-8254-3374-6
ISBN 13: 978-0-8254-3374-0

Printed in the United States of America

07 08 09 10 11 / 5 4 3 2 1

# CONTENTS

## CHAPTER 1

# THE CHILD IS BORN
*Isaiah 9:6*

1. His absolute Godhead
2. His abundant gifts
   a. In a very troubled world, He is the wonderful Counsellor
   b. In a very tiny world, He is the mighty God
   c. In a very transient world, He is the Father of the future
   d. In a very tense world, He is the Prince of Peace
3. His abiding government

ISAIAH WROTE THE NINTH CHAPTER OF HIS prophecy during a dark age for the nation of Israel. The rebel northern kingdom, comprising ten of the tribes, had pursued an errant and erratic course toward disaster under a succession of guilty and godless kings. It wasn't much better in the southern kingdom of Judah, where wicked King Ahaz sat on the throne. Far to the north, the armed might of the dreaded Assyrians was mobilizing for a devastating southward march of conquest. The warnings of Isaiah, the statesman-prophet, fell on deaf ears in both Israel and Judah. To dramatize the situation, Isaiah had just given his newborn son a significant and prophetic name that encapsulated a warning of the impending siege and sack of Samaria (Isa. 8:1–4). The constant threat to Judah caused by the alliance of Israel and Syria was about to end, but this would be small comfort for the southern kingdom. The incursions of the Syro-Ephraimitic War were about to be replaced by the plague of an Assyrian invasion.

Then, suddenly, the prophetic impulse again seized the great prophet. He saw another birth! A birth that was far, far beyond the birth of his own son, Maher-shalal-hash-baz. He saw the birth of one who would solve all the world's problems. He saw the birth of the Messiah. Beyond that, borne on the wings of inspiration into an age even further removed, he saw the Battle of Armageddon and the subsequent reign of the Prince of Peace. Thus Isaiah's ancient prophecy is tremendously relevant to us today. It gives us both a Christmas theme and a contemporary theme as well, taking us back to Bethlehem and forward to days yet to come.

The prophet highlights three important aspects of the Lord Jesus: His absolute Godhead, His abundant gifts, and His abiding government. "Unto us a child is born, unto us a son is given" (Isa. 9:6). Here we see *His absolute Godhead,* as it would one day be manifested at Bethlehem. "His name shall be called Wonderful, Counsellor, the mighty God, the everlasting Father, the Prince of Peace" (v. 6). Here we see *His abundant gifts.* He has all that it will take to subdue and rule the earth. "And the government shall be upon his shoulder. . . . Of the increase of his government and peace there shall be no end" (vv. 6–7). Here we see *His abiding government.* He is to set up an empire on this planet the likes of which the world has never seen, but an empire that it has yearned and longed for these six thousand years.

## 1. His absolute Godhead

"Unto us a child is born, unto us a son is given." That simple statement was in truth a lighted fuse that burned away for some 750 years until it exploded with a roar, a massive, earthshaking, history-changing, mind-boggling concentration of spiritual high explosive laid down by God on this planet in a small Judean town called Bethlehem.

The statement in itself does not look like much. A child born? A Son given? But those seemingly innocent phrases carry within themselves the great truth of the incarnation of God in Christ. They tell us that the one who was born at Bethlehem was both God and man. He was a person whose advent into time is absolutely unique in every sense of the word. That little bundle of humanity, wrapped in swaddling clothes, rocked in a young woman's arms, and laid to rest on a bed of hay in a manger in a dirty, smelly Judean barn, was none other than God himself clothed in human clay, entering this world to achieve a purpose planned in eternity past.

Who would have thought that so simple a statement could convey so much? But that is exactly what it does, and the gospel record bears it out.

Matthew and Luke both set before us the fact that Jesus was the Child born.[1] Both take us back to the manger and deal with events surrounding Christ's birth. Matthew shows Christ's connection with the *Hebrew* race. He underlines the fact that Jesus was the true Messiah, the son of David, and the promised King. Luke shows us Christ's connection with the *human* race. He underlines the fact that Jesus was a true man.

Matthew traces the ancestry of Jesus through His foster father, Joseph, the husband of Mary. He follows the main ancestral line back through some twenty kings to David. He traces the Lord's lineage back through Solomon to show that Jesus was *legal* heir to David's throne. He tells how Joseph was prepared for the event by being told in a dream that Mary had indeed conceived miraculously and was to give birth in due time to the incarnate Son of God.

Luke traces the ancestry of Jesus through the Virgin Mary. He follows a subsidiary line of descent, forgotten but unbroken, back to Nathan, another of David's sons. He shows that Jesus was *lineal* heir to David's throne. He tells how Mary was prepared for the unprecedented event and of her natural and spiritual reactions. Luke does not stop his account of Christ's lineage with David, however; he traces back through Abraham to Noah and to Adam.

But both Matthew and Luke are agreed. Jesus was "the Child born," as foretold by the prophet Isaiah. He was born of the Virgin Mary, conceived of the Holy Spirit. Around that amazing event countless carols have been sung. For the meaning of Christmas, after all, is not "here comes Santa Claus." It has nothing to do with "Rudolph the red-nosed reindeer." These nonsense rhymes are travesties on the truth—deliberate attempts by the enemy to dilute and distort the true significance of the Advent season. Christmas and Calvary are two of God's hammer blows directed at the Evil One. Christ's coming and Christ's cross are two signature blows from which Satan never will recover. So then, "unto us a Child is born."

John shows us the Son given. He does not take us to the manger. In fact, he stays clear of Bethlehem altogether. That part of the story had been well covered by Matthew and Luke long before John wrote. John instead takes us back not to Christ's earthly birth, but back to the very beginning: "In the beginning was the Word, and the Word was with God, and the Word was God. . . . All things were made by him; and without him was not any thing made that was made . . . and the Word was made flesh, and dwelt among us" (John 1:1, 3, 14). That is how John begins his gospel. He shows us the Son given. "For God so loved the world, that He gave His only begotten Son that whosoever believeth in Him should not perish but have everlasting life" (3:16).

When we put the two together—the Child born and the Son given—what do we have? Deity in humanity! We have one who was both man and God. We have the greatest mystery in the universe. We have man and God perfectly blended into one single, fully adjusted, unique person. Never before has anything like that happened. Jesus stands apart from all others. So then, we have His absolute Godhead. "Unto us a child is born, unto us a son is given."

## 2. His abundant gifts

As we might expect, one who combined deity and humanity would be unique, replete with a unique array of gifts and abilities. Yet, the Lord Jesus was not odd or unbalanced or peculiar. He was a very real human being. He grew up like other people. He went to school and asked questions. He knew what it was to be hungry, thirsty, and tired. He appreciated friendship and fellowship. He was a true human being.

At the same time, He was God, upholding the entire universe even as He was rocked in His mother's arms. He could still a storm, change water into wine, cast out demons, raise the dead, cleanse a leper, give sight to the blind. He called God His Father with all the assurance of fact.

When Jesus walked the earth, his gifts were displayed and employed for the benefit of other people. Throughout eternity, they will be employed on a much vaster scale. Isaiah caught a glimpse of the Messiah's abundant gifts, as reflected in the list of attributes he ascribes to the coming Child: He would be called *Wonderful Counsellor*, the *mighty God*, the *everlasting Father*, and the *Prince of Peace*.

### a. In a very troubled world, He is the wonderful Counsellor

Science evidently does not have the answer to this world's problems. On the whole, science has given us more problems than it has solved. Along with space technology it has given us intercontinental ballistic missiles. Along with atomic energy it has given us the hydrogen bomb, the cobalt bomb, and the neutron bomb. Whereas men once waged war with swords and arrows, they now have at their disposal apocalyptic weapons. Science has given us the Salk vaccine, open-heart surgery, and increasing skill in transplants, but it has also opened a Pandora's box of potential genetic nightmares for the future.

Much of modern medical research, for example, is made possible by the invention of powerful tools for the study of living things. Chief among these is the electron microscope, which can magnify as much as a million times. It lays bare structures far beyond the capacity of old-fashioned light microscopes. Medical science now has available, as well, various remarkably subtle and powerful methods for delineating the various components of complex biological mixtures. For instance, the various parts of human and animal cells can now be identified. More, the various types and sizes of molecules can be recognized. In most biological laboratories today, machines work day and night, tirelessly making measurements and recording them and calculating results from them.

These breakthroughs in science have also been made possible by the growing sophistication of chemistry. We can now explain many of the incredibly complex sequences of reactions within the cells of the body, as well as those that may take place in the blood, the lymphatic system, and elsewhere. Biochemistry has become virtually a separate discipline. Beyond all that, biophysics has emerged with even more precise and accurate tools.

In short, biology has moved into a phase of accelerated development. Many of the new developments can be misused, resulting in new dimensions of horror for mankind. In *The Biological Time Bomb,* Gordon Taylor discusses a wide range of current biological research, including research into life's origins, mood and memory control, genetics and heredity, transplants, viruses, and life from chemicals. Taylor titles his closing chapter, interestingly enough, "The Accursed Scientist." He writes, "One is forced to the conclusion that some knowledge is too dangerous to possess."[2]

Science evidently does not have the answer to the world's problems, and neither does philosophy. Much human philosophy boils down to what J. B. Phillips, in an inspired moment, called "intellectualism and high-sounding nonsense" (Col. 2:8).

Government does not have the answer. We have witnessed the rise and fall of totalitarian governments that were able to harness all the resources of a nation to catastrophic ends. We have watched democratic forms of government seesaw back and forth, only to deadlock.

Religion does not have the answer. More blood has been shed over religion than over any other single issue in the history of mankind.

Psychiatry does not have the answer. A successful psychiatrist friend of mine told me years ago, "Every psychiatrist needs a psychiatrist."

Every attempt by mankind to forge its own answers to the world's problems has come up empty. Only Jesus, the Wonderful Counsellor, has the answer. He proved it when He was here the first time. We still marvel at His teachings. Even those who deny His claims would acknowledge that His parables are miracles in words. His prophecies were far-reaching, foretelling what the last days would be like with scientific precision. The Sermon on the Mount is a piece of legislation that towers in monumental splendor over all the Magna Cartas and constitutions ever devised. His knowledge of human behavior has never been surpassed. We read, "He knew what was in man" (John 2:25). His creedal statements took the sublime edicts of Old Testament law and translated them into peerless, pragmatic, and pungent precepts of faith.

And, best of all, He is coming again! Coming to solve the problems of this world; coming to bring all the genius of His omniscience to bear on the follies and failures of this troubled world. He is the Wonderful Counsellor.

*b. In a very tiny world, He is the mighty God*

Who among us has not stood and stared into the vast immensity of space on a clear, bright night and wondered about the vast, countless worlds that sparkle so brightly up there? At such moments, we are reduced again to little, staring children.

> Twinkle, twinkle little star,
> How I wonder what you are;
> Up above the world so high
> Like a diamond in the sky.

At such moments, we feel how tiny and insignificant and puny we are; in the vast immensity of things, we feel how microscopic our little world is.

Some astronomers have concluded that the earth does not occupy any particularly privileged position in the sky, that the universe has no boundaries, that the galaxies are receding from each other faster and faster, and that out there, on the remotest fringes of space, are galaxies so remote that they are fleeing outward at almost the speed of light.

Those galaxies, traveling away from our standpoint in the universe at such enormous speeds, can never be seen by us because their waves of radiation would be red-shifted by an infinite amount and thus would be undetectable on Earth. Were there astronomers on some of the other galaxies, they would be able to see these fleeing galaxies because they would be closer to them, and they would be able to see the Milky Way, the galaxy we call our own, but even these celestial astronomers would have undetectable horizons of their own. There would be galaxies receding from them at the speed of light, beyond the cosmic horizon. Likewise for possible astronomers on yet other galaxies. Playing center to a different region of expansion, each galaxy would have a different horizon beyond which were more and more horizons they could never detect. Such is the vastness of space.

We live on a very tiny world. Light, which can travel around Earth's equator seven times in one second, takes one hundred thousand years to cross from one end of our galaxy to the other.

But, small as our planet is, it is a world that is absolutely without peer in the universe. For this little world of ours was home to Jesus Christ, the mighty God incarnate in human flesh, for thirty-three-and-a-half years, or about 12,235 days. This fact alone makes our world of great cosmic importance. It makes it the center of everything. In a coming day, this same Jesus is coming back. There is to be a new heaven and a new Earth. Christ himself will dissolve all the suns and stars and satellites of space, including the planet on which we live. He will then remake them. It would seem likely that planet Earth will be the center of the new creation—the focal point for billions upon billions of worlds. This is a proposition that many cosmologists rule out completely as they try to predict the future of the universe. It is a proposition, however, quite in harmony with the fact that the mighty God has visited this planet again and again, and with the fact that He has fully declared His intention of coming back to rule it in the person of His Son.

### c. In a very transient world, He is the Father of the future

Everything is running down. Within the past few decades, we have become acutely aware that we are depleting the resources of this planet at an alarming rate. Ecologists tell us we are running short of oil, we are ripping off the seas, we are running short of fresh water.

The world's population is multiplying, and its deserts are expanding. Weather experts even hint that another ice age might be on the way. We are living in a very transient world.

Moreover, our own sojourn on this world is briefer still. Seventy years, or perhaps a decade or two more, at best, and then the countdown is over and we die. Every living soul comes with a built-in time fuse. Some fuses burn slowly, others more quickly, but every birth signals the beginning of a countdown that ends in death. Yet daily we shrug our indifference. Each night we yawn in God's face, roll over, and go to sleep while our fuses burn ever closer to the end.[3]

One night in 1912, in the cold Atlantic, a grim countdown ensued when the supposedly unsinkable luxury liner *Titanic* struck an iceberg and sank. But the fuse had been lit sometime earlier: perhaps at high noon on April 10, 1912, when the *Titanic* was tugged out from her Southampton berth; or perhaps it was on May 31, 1911, at the Belfast shipyards of Harland and Wolff, when the ship was launched; or perhaps even earlier when the ship was on the drawing board, or when its concept was first conceived in the boardroom of the prestigious White Star Line; but at some point between the time she was suggested and the time she sailed, the countdown for the *Titanic* began. Her maiden voyage was her only voyage, and she never made it to port.

We are living on a *Titanic* in space—a very transient world with even more frail and fleeting people aboard. Into this transient world comes one who is called in our English text "the everlasting Father." That seems a doubtful translation because the context is talking about God the Son. However, the phrase can be also rendered "the Father of eternity," or "the Father of the future." Either way, we see the Lord Jesus as one who has conquered time. He has put an end to the transient nature of this world. He offers us everlasting life. He plans a permanent, significant position for Earth in the new creation.

The Father of the future! The unborn ages are His. He makes them, He fills them, He controls them. Well might we pray with the hymn writer:

Swift to its close ebbs out life's little day;
Earth's joys grow dim, its glories pass away;
Change and decay in all around I see;
Oh, Thou who changest not, abide with me![4]

So, then, we are living in a very troubled world (a world with more problems than solutions). We are living in a very tiny world (a world that is lost amid a bewildering multitude of stars in space). We are living in a very transient world (a world in which our innermost beings call out for permanence only to find that old age is creeping down on us, and a world that itself is beginning to creak and groan from abuse and advancing years).

### d. In a very tense world, He is the Prince of Peace

We are living in a world that is increasingly bearing witness to the truth of Christ's warnings about the last days. He said, "Ye shall hear of wars and rumours of wars" (Matt. 24:6). And so there are. For if there is one thing that man cannot achieve on this earth, it is peace. The United Nations, launched with such a flourish of hope by the world's statesmen at the close of Word War II, has become a monumental symbol of man's utter inability to avert war. It became for years a tool of Communist imperialism, so much so that many thoughtful Americans felt we should get the United States out of the United Nations and get the United Nations out of the United States.

World War I brought a change in man's approach to warfare. Up until that time, it had been a matter of army against army. With the coming of the Great War, the prediction of Jesus came into focus. War ceased to be a matter of army against army and became a matter of nation against nation. Sir Winston Churchill, in his war memoirs put it like this:

It was not until the Twentieth Century of the Christian Era that war began to enter into its kingdom as the potential destroyer of the human race. The organization of mankind into great states

and empires, and the rise of nations to full collective consciousness, enabled enterprises of slaughter to be planned and executed
upon a scale and with a perseverance never before imagined. All
the noblest virtues of individuals were gathered to strengthen
the destructive capacity of the mass.[5]

Churchill wrote these words as a footnote to World War I, years
before World War II eclipsed it in scope, ferocity, and duration.
Then came the nuclear standoff. There are nations now armed with
intercontinental ballistic missiles, which have a horrifying potential
for chemical and germ warfare. Outer space is a potential arena of
conflict. Technology keeps on adding new and frightful weapons of
destruction to the world's arsenals. Worse still is the increasingly hor-
rific possibility of international terrorists acquiring nuclear capability
from rogue nations.

What the world needs is a Prince of Peace. And, in Christ, God
sent the world just such a Prince. When Christ was born, the angels
sang, "Peace on earth, goodwill toward men." Within a generation,
however, men flung that great peace offer back in God's face. They
ploughed the Lord's back with a Roman scourge, crowned Him with
mocking thorns, and spiked Him to a tree.

But He is coming back! Coming back as the Prince of Peace, coming back to deal with the tensions and terrors that increasingly stalk
this globe. He has abundant gifts. He is the Wonderful Counsellor,
the mighty God, the Father of the future, the Prince of Peace. He is
absolutely God. He is the sole hope of mankind.

## 3. His abiding government

"The government," he says, "shall be upon his shoulder. . . . Of the
increase of his government and peace there shall be no end. . . . The
zeal of the Lord of hosts will perform this." When Christ returns, the
world will be engaged in the final horrors of the battle of Armageddon. East and West will be locked in a titanic struggle to decide the
final fate of the world.

The warring nations will look up. They will see in the sky the signs of the coming of the Son of the living God. They will call a halt to their mutual slaughter, patch up their differences in the face of this overwhelming threat from outer space and, deluded by the Devil, they will turn their arsenals on the descending Lord of hosts. In a moment, the armies of Earth will be annihilated.

Jesus will come and He will set up His kingdom on Earth. At last, the prayer the church has breathed now for two thousand years will be fulfilled: "Thy kingdom come. Thy will be done on earth, as it is in heaven" (Matt. 6:10). As Isaiah says, "The zeal of the Lord of hosts will perform this." The stone that Daniel saw—a stone, cut without hands, that descended with devastating force from on high to smite the feet of the image of latter-day world government—the stone the builders have rejected, that stone will descend. It will shatter in pieces the kingdoms of this world. It will grow and spread and become a great mountain that will fill the earth. And then, as the old hymn puts it:

> Jesus shall reign where'er the sun
> Doth His successive journeys run.
> His kingdom stretch from shore to shore
> Till moons shall wax and wane no more.[6]

He is coming again. He is coming as certainly and as surely as He came before. He came once to fulfill scores upon scores of Bible prophecies that all centered on God's plan of salvation. He is coming back to fulfill the rest of the prophecies still slumbering in the womb of time—prophecies that all center on the sovereignty of God. The destiny of the world is wrapped up in Him. And so is ours—now and for all eternity.

## CHAPTER 2

# THE ADVENT OF JESUS CHRIST

*Matthew 1*

1. The archives of Judah
   a. Abraham
   b. Jacob
   c. Tamar
   d. Rahab
   e. David
   f. Solomon
   g. Rehoboam
   h. Ruth
   i. Athaliah
   j. Hezekiah
   k. Manasseh
   l. Jeconiah
2. The anxiety of Joseph
   a. His dilemma
   b. His dream
   c. His deed
3. The arrival of Jesus

TO RECORD THE COMING OF CHRIST, God begins a new book. He does not merely turn over a new page. He begins a new book. It is called "the book of the generation of Jesus Christ" (Matt. 1:1).

That statement turns us back to the beginning of the old book, to read again what is recorded about Adam, "This is the book of the generations of Adam" (Gen. 5:1). Note the difference. The book of the *generation* of Jesus Christ; the book of the *generations* of Adam.

Poor old Adam was a total failure. All kinds of families have sprung from him, and they have all ended in dismal failure. God had to begin again and again and again with Adam's family. It was one generation after another. Each successive generation was reaped off the earth by death. As Paul so expressively put it, death reigned from Adam to Christ.

But, when Jesus came, God began to write names into a new book. He records the generation of Jesus Christ. All of us who are saved by His blood and who have been put in the family of God are all of the same generation. It is a deathless, eternal, never-ending generation. It is a generation that will outlast the suns and stars of space. It is a generation that lives in the power of endless life. It is a generation born, not of corruptible seed, but of incorruptible seed by the Word of God, which lives and abides forever. It is a generation that shares the life of Christ. It is a generation that laughs at the grave, for the portals of the tomb are simply the portals of life forevermore.

When we were born, our names were written into the book of the generations of Adam. Death and decay began to work on us at once. When we were born again, our names were written into the book of the generation of Jesus Christ. "The book of the generation of Jesus Christ" is a notable way to start the New Testament.

What we have in this chapter is the descent of God's eternal Son from heaven to earth; out of eternity into time; out from the bosom of the Father to rest in the bosom of His mother, Mary. There are three notable things in this chapter. We have set before us here *the archives of Judah,* which underlines God's grace; *the anxiety of Joseph,* which underlines God's goodness; and *the arrival of Jesus,* which underlines God's greatness.

## 1. The archives of Judah

We have enough material in the first dozen-and-a-half verses of Matthew's gospel, in the names alone, to preach scores of sermons. And, in preaching those sermons, we would preach our way clear through the Old Testament. While that is so, the primary purpose of this fascinating chronology is to show us what kind of human roots the Lord Jesus had. As we select a sample here and there from this list, we will marvel at *God's grace*. In the ancestry of Jesus, for instance, we have the following notable figures:

### a. Abraham

The Bible sets Abraham apart from everyone else by giving him the title "the friend of God." He was the first of a race of spiritual giants. He is called "the father of all them that believe." He was the founder of the Hebrew race. Without him there would have been no Jews and no Messiah. It is a noble start to Christ's earthly ancestry, but not everyone we'll see is as upstanding as Abraham.

### b. Jacob

Jacob lied and cheated his way through most of his life. He cheated his twin brother. He lied to his blind old father, telling him five lies on one occasion in a single breath. He did his best to cheat his uncle Laban. His boys, for the most part, were as bad as he was. Finally, at the Jabbok, we see that Jacob was a man whom God had to break physically before he could bless him spiritually.

### c. Tamar

Tamar did not hesitate to play the harlot to get what she wanted, namely a child who would be in the Judean line. Certainly she was entitled to this child, and Judah had to acknowledge as much in the end, to his own disgrace, but Tamar's name was nonetheless sadly stained.

### d. Rahab

Rahab was a professional Canaanite temple prostitute. Surely it was simple grace that saved her from Jericho's doom, and sublime grace that placed her in the royal line of Christ's ancestors.

### e. David

Not even the great David escaped scandal. There is more space given to David in the Bible than to anyone else, except the Lord himself. Yet David lived a checkered life. He seduced a neighbor's wife, and when he discovered she was pregnant tried to cover up his paternity. When his efforts along that line failed, he discreetly but deliberately had the woman's husband murdered so he could marry her himself.

### f. Solomon

Solomon made a mistake right from the start. When he first ascended the throne, God asked him to choose what he would like to have bestowed on him. Solomon asked God to make him wise. It is a pity he did not ask God to make him good. Solomon proved to be so lacking in spiritual discernment that he imported scores of foreign women into Israel in order to marry them and indulge his lusts. He allowed the Holy City to become the breeding ground for vile and disgusting pagan idolatries and well nigh turned Jerusalem into Babylon. The Hebrew nation did not recover from the damage Solomon did until after the Babylonian captivity.

### g. Rehoboam

Rehoboam was a pompous idiot who tossed away ten of the twelve great provinces of his kingdom just to indulge his childish temper.

### h. Ruth

Ruth was a Moabite woman, a foreigner cursed under Mosaic Law until her tenth generation. It was grace that found her—a poor, lost pagan woman—and made her a wife to Boaz, a prince of the tribe of Judah, which put her in the royal line to David and to Christ.

### i. Athaliah

She is not even in the genealogy, but she was in the royal line. Athaliah was the granddaughter of Omri, a powerful Israelite king (2 Chron. 22:2). She was also the daughter of the pagan Jezebel. She married Jehoram, son of Jehoshaphat, the good Judean king. She debauched Judah just as her mother had debauched Israel. Her marriage was a deliberate attempt by Satan to destroy the line by which "the seed of the woman" was to come. Jehoram began by killing off all his brothers (2 Chron. 21:4). When Athaliah's son Ahaziah died, she murdered all of his sons, except for the infant Joash, who was rescued by Ahaziah's sister.

### j. Hezekiah

Hezekiah was a good king. When he was told he was about to die, he wrung from God the promise of another fifteen years of life. During those added years, he brought into this world a son, Manasseh, who was to be the worst and most wicked king ever to sit on the throne of David.

### k. Manasseh

This king, the vile son of a godly father, was so filthy-minded and so permissive that he transformed the nation of Judah into a pornographic society in which sex, spiritism, and sodomy became the accepted lifestyle. He gave equal rights to sex perverts in defiance of the law of God, and he so undermined the moral and spiritual fiber of the Judean monarchy that it never recovered.

### l. Jeconiah

Jeconiah was so destitute of spiritual life that, because of him, God broke off the royal line to Christ through Solomon. The prophet Jeremiah decreed that henceforth no seed of Jeconiah's should ever sit on David's throne. Yet down through all these long years, God's grace prevailed.

Such was the royal line. As we look at the archives of Judah, we can write one word over the whole gloomy record: *grace!* Remember that preserved in this ancestry in the gospel of Matthew is the human ancestry of Christ. Only one word explains why God did not abolish the line from the start: *grace!* Here, as the hymn writer puts it, we see "sovereign grace o'er sin abounding." There is nothing here, in this sad list of names, that savors the human merit. If Christ is to come to earth, He must descend from a line of lost and guilty men and women.

So tragic is the story of the line of Judah through Solomon that the Holy Spirit must go back to the beginning, in the gospel of Luke, and trace another line, starting with a new root altogether. The lineage in Matthew records the ancestry of Jesus from David through Solomon to Joseph, Christ's foster father. Jesus, of course, did not descend physically from the line recorded in Matthew. He became a part of that line only because of Joseph's later marriage to Mary. The record of failure and folly in the royal line as recorded in Matthew was all too open and evident and shameful.

But while Satan was concentrating his heavy artillery on the line of Solomon, spitting on it, polluting it, making it a mockery and a shame, God was working away in secret on another line! This line led to Jesus through Nathan, another of David's sons. Like Solomon, Nathan was born to David by Bathsheba, but the details of his life are not recorded in the Bible. Through Nathan, wending its way secretly down the bypaths and back alleys of history, ran a hidden and unnoticed Davidic line. It terminated in the Virgin Mary, of whom Christ was born. Mary, like Joseph, was a lineal descendant of David. Jesus had a *legal* claim to the throne through His mother and a *regal* claim through adoption into the family of Joseph. Thus God's grace operated in secret for a thousand years, from David to Christ. So, whichever way we look at it, the archives of Judah spell out the grace of God.

## 2. The anxiety of Joseph

Joseph was a carpenter. The royal line of David through Solomon had fallen on such hard times that its last rightful claimant to the throne had to labor for his bread as a poor working man. He wielded not a scepter but a saw. He lived not as a prince but as a peasant. His home was not in David's royal city but in distant and despised Nazareth. His mother tongue was not the Hebrew of the prophets and the princes of Israel but Aramaic, and even that he spoke with a thick north-country brogue you could cut with a knife—the kind of accent that brought sneers to the lips of the sophisticated aristocrats of Jerusalem and Judea. Let us note three things about the anxiety of Joseph: his dilemma, his dream, and his deed.

### a. His dilemma

Joseph was engaged to be married to a pure-minded, spiritually enlightened, morally impeccable young woman by the name of Mary. He had no doubts as to the moral character of this girl. She was not perfect, of course. The only person ever to live a sinless life on this planet was the matchless one who would one day spring from her womb. But she was about as good and as pure a person as one could ever hope to meet in this sin-cursed world. And Joseph was engaged to be married to her.

The day of this betrothal was a great day for him. He could have sung:

Heav'n above is softer blue,
Earth around is sweeter green!
Something lives in every hue
Christless eyes have never seen.[1]

He was going to marry Mary! Beautiful, beloved, blessed Mary! The girl who, in all this world, was closest to an angel that a mortal maid could be.

Then came the shock. Mary had taken off suddenly for Judea, and when she came back she was evidently pregnant. And she made no attempt to hide it. When questioned about it, she willingly told her story. She was with child by the Holy Spirit. Joseph was stunned.

What should he do? He had never known Mary to be anything but pure and good. He had never known her to tell lies. It was unthinkable that she should be guilty of such a gross, moral sin. It was even more inconceivable that, in her condition, she should have run off to the home of her cousin in Judea. For her cousin's husband was a priest. In those days, the penalty for sexual sin was death, and a priest was to be the first to invoke the law against her, kin or not. Yet, it was even more inconceivable to Joseph that an angel should have appeared to her, as she said, and that she should be carrying in her womb the Son of the living God. The Bible prophesied something of the sort, but in the hard, pragmatic, everyday world where people live, that kind of thing does not happen. That was Joseph's dilemma.

### b. His dream

Poor Joseph tossed and turned on his bed. Should he, himself, denounce Mary to the local synagogue? That was clearly his duty as a loyal son of the law. But then Mary would be stoned and he himself would have to throw the first stone. That was impossible. Unthinkable. But, if he did not, then all the world would accuse him of being Mary's accomplice, the partner of her sin. And he too would face the stones. But that would be a blessed relief.

Oh! Mary! Mary! Why? Why? Why? Why this, of all things? No,

he could never expose her to such public shame. He simply could not and would not make a public example of her. One thing he could do was go ahead and marry her, turn a deaf ear to the gossip and slander of the town, and hope the law would not be invoked. Or he could quietly and privately annul the betrothal. This, at last, was what he decided to do. After all, there were others involved besides himself. He had to protect the good name of his family. He would just quietly put her away.

Then came a dream. The angel of the Lord appeared to him, as he had appeared to Mary. "Marry her," he said, "and call the child's name Jesus—Jehovah the Savior!" We can well imagine with what joy and delight Joseph sprang from his bed that morning. All his doubts dissolved like the morning mist before the rising sun. He must hurry over to Mary's house. He must ask her to forgive his doubts, as indeed he asked God to forgive him now, devoutly on his knees. He must hurry up the wedding. He must tell Nazareth and the world that he too had been granted an audience by an angel of God. Sure, the world would laugh and scoff and call him a liar. But so what? Mary was to be the mother of the Messiah! And God had chosen him to be the foster father and the lifelong guardian of His eternal Son.

### c. His deed

We read that "Joseph being raised from sleep did as the angel of the Lord had bidden him, and took unto him his wife" (Matt. 1:24). That was prompt, complete obedience to the known will and revealed word of God. Joseph's anxiety was over.

## 3. The arrival of Jesus

We read of Mary that she "brought forth her firstborn son: and he [Joseph] called his name Jesus" (Matt. 1:25).

> There is no name so sweet on earth,
> No name so sweet in Heaven;

The Name, before at His wondrous birth
To Christ the Savior given.[2]

"Thou shalt call his name Jesus," said the angel, "for he shall save his people from their sins." The arrival of Jesus marked one of the great turning points of time. It marked the moment when God interfered directly, decisively, and dramatically in human affairs to deal with the age-old problem of human sin.

That is the sole reason why Jesus arrived on this planet. He did not come on a state visit, so to speak. He came to grapple with sin, the monster that brings every unhappiness that hell can devise into human hearts. What an arrival! Unsung by men, but heralded across the skies and throughout the universe by chanting angel choirs.

Let us think what the arrival of that little Babe of Bethlehem meant to this world. In one of his books, F. W. Boreham directs our attention to the year 1809, a year in which the whole world was thinking of battles. The empire of Napoleon sprawled all across Europe. His legions had marched into almost every capital on the continent. England was locked in a life-and-death struggle against this seemingly invincible conqueror. The year 1809 fell midway between the battles of Trafalgar and Waterloo. Trafalgar was where Lord Nelson dealt the final deathblow to the French navy, and Waterloo was where the Iron Duke of Wellington pulverized the enemy's armies.

The whole world, says Boreham, was thinking of *battles;* God was thinking of *babies.* In that one year, a whole host of remarkable babies stole unnoticed into the world. They arrived singly, one here and one there. Those babies would grow up to change the world, for better or for worse.

In 1809, William Gladstone, destined to be one of Britain's greatest and godliest prime ministers, was born at Liverpool. Alfred Lord Tennyson, who would become one of the great poets of the world was born at Somerset rectory. Oliver Wendell Holmes was born in Massachusetts. Charles Darwin was born at Shrewsbury. Abraham Lincoln was born in Old Kentucky. Fredrick Chopin was born at Warsaw. Felix Mendelsohn was born at Hamburg.

In similar anonymity, nearly two thousand years ago, the most astonishing, remarkable baby ever born of a woman arrived on the scene. The world yawned. A few shepherds came to see him, some wise men arrived from a far country, and there was a brief stir of interest, laced with hostility in the Herodian palace. That was all.

Meanwhile, all heaven watched with bated breath the historical arrival of God's Son on our planet. They watched with awe and amazement as the throne of God in glory was vacated by one of the eternal, uncreated, self-existing persons of the Godhead. They watched as the Son of the living God was contracted to the span of a virgin's womb. They counted the days to that momentous, unparalleled fragment of time when He would be born.

Then the day dawned. For nine months, in the unseen world, they had massed a vast honor guard over the virgin mother. They now drew up in orderly ranks, undiscerned by men, rank upon endless rank, crowding around a tumbledown inn at Bethlehem and peering with bated breath into a cave that served as a cattle shed. They watched the little bundle of humanity stretch his tiny limbs upon the straw and yawn and open his wondrous eyes upon the light of day.

We can almost hear Gabriel, the herald angel say to Michael, the archangel, "There! Mike! Did you see that? He smiled and He has dimples in His cheeks." And the sons of God shouted for joy, and all the angels of glory awoke the echoes of the everlasting hills with their hymns and hallelujahs, as they had when the universe was born.

But men on earth went about their business as if nothing had happened. Caesar went on collecting his taxes, Herod went on executing his high-handed crimes against God and man, the priests kept on jockeying for office, and the common people scarcely heard that Christ had been born, that God had visited man, and that Immanuel had come.

"Call his name Jesus: for he shall save his people from their sins." That is what His arrival meant. It meant that God's plan of salvation for sinful men had now found its full and complete focus. It meant that scores of Old Testament prophecies, which had slumbered for ages in the womb of time, could now leap forth in life and proclaim that their fulfillment had come. God did not send a soldier into the world, He did not send a scholar into the world, He did not send a statesman into the world. He did not send a salesman or a scientist. He sent a Savior.

For man does not need any more battles or any more books. He does not need any more bills in Congress. He does not need to be pressured to buy something. He does not need to wrest any more secrets from nature, for he cannot handle the ones he already has. What man needs is a Savior. Man is a sinner. He is born in sin. He is a sinner by birth, by practice, and by choice. And he cannot save himself. He needs a Savior. And that is exactly what God sent. That is exactly what arrived on earth that day, two thousand years ago. A Savior.

What man needed two thousand years ago, he still needs today. I need a Savior. You need a Savior. We all need a Savior, one who can save us from our sins, from their penalty and from their power. And that is exactly the Christmas gift God has given to the human race—a Savior.

We must accept Him. Come Christmas morning, we receive presents from our family and friends. We will take each one in turn, untie the string, take off the wrappings, and say, "Thank you!" We must accept God's gift the same way by personally, deliberately, and thankfully receiving the gift of Jesus Christ into our lives.

## CHAPTER 3

# THE WORD MADE FLESH
*John 1:1-4, 14*

1. The infinite Creator (vv. 1–3)
   a. His unique person (v. 1)
      (1) He is eternally God
      (2) He is equally God
      (3) He is essentially God
   b. His universal power (vv. 2–3)
2. The incarnate Creator (vv. 4, 14)
   a. His translation to humanity
   b. His transfiguration of humanity

MATTHEW, MARK, AND LUKE HAD PUT down their pens a full thirty years before the aged apostle John decided to take up his. John wrote in Greek, but his style is Hebrew and his words are few. In the original text, there are only about six hundred words in John's vocabulary—the vocabulary of a seven-year-old. His vocabulary is concise, but the effect of his words is far-reaching. He may not have many coins in his grammatical purse, but what he does have are like the golden coins in a rich man's pocket. John is not a wordy writer, but he is certainly a weighty writer.

John tells us why he put pen to paper; however, he does not hang the key to his gospel by the front door, but way round at the back door. We have to read the book all the way through before he comes out and tells us what we have already found out: He is writing to show that Jesus is God.

There is no genealogy, no birth account, no boyhood, no baptism, no temptation, and no Gethsemane in John's Gospel. With strict economy, everything is directed to prove his main point that Jesus is God. There are no scribes, no lepers, no publicans, and no demoniacs. John does not record a single parable, and five of the eight miracles he records are found in his gospel alone. Again, everything is intended to demonstrate that Jesus is God.

In the first chapter of his gospel, John sets Jesus before us in two ways: as the *infinite Creator* (vv. 1–3), and as the *incarnate Creator* (vv. 4, 14).

## 1. The infinite Creator (vv. 1–3)

John's first proposition is that Jesus is, absolutely, unquestionably, sovereignly, and eternally *God*—in every sense of the word. As a Palestinian Jew, who would be horrified by any form of blasphemy, John did not make this proposition lightly. He was not a learned man. He was not a philosopher or a theologian. He was a very ordinary man, a working man. But he was also a businessman. Moreover, he had spent three-and-a-half years in the personal company of Jesus of Nazareth, and for some fifty or sixty years he had thought things over. It was his mature, unshakable conviction that Jesus of Nazareth was God.

To demonstrate Christ's deity, John approaches the theme along two lines. In verse 1 he talks about *the unique person* of Jesus, and in verses 2 and 3 he talks about *the universal power* of Jesus.

### a. His unique person (v. 1)

John begins with the words, "In the beginning was the Word, and the Word was with God, and the Word was God." That is quite a statement! It declares that Jesus was *eternally* God; that He was *equally* God; and that He was *essentially* God. All that God is, Jesus is also. All the attributes that belong to God also belong to Jesus. God is omnipotent, omniscient, and omnipresent. Jesus is omnipotent, omniscient, and omnipresent. He is eternally, equally, essentially God.

### (1) He is eternally God

"In the beginning *was* the Word." Let us begin our discussion with the noun used to describe Jesus: *the Word.* At first blush, the term appears somewhat abstruse, pedantic, and vague, but let us put it back into the context of the day and age in which it was written. The Greek word used by John, *logos,* is the common Greek expression for "word." It is used of Jesus because just as a word gives form and expression to an invisible thought, so the Lord Jesus gave form and expression to the invisible God. One cannot know what another person is thinking until he expresses himself in words. Our words clothe our thoughts in such a way that they can be communicated to others in an understandable form.

In Greek philosophy, the term *logos* was familiar enough. It referred to the whole realm of thought, to the abstract concept lying at the back of everything concrete. In Plato's philosophy, the *logos* was ideal and abstract. In English, the Greek idea is best expressed in the word *wisdom.* Greek philosophy recognized wisdom as preceding all works.

John, however, did not get his concept of Jesus from Greek philosophy. He was not influenced by Greek philosophy but by Hebrew philosophy. When he uses the Greek word *logos,* he does so in a Hebrew sense. The Hebrew philosophers would say, "If things require thought; then thought requires a thinker." So when John describes Jesus as the Word, the *Logos,* he is describing Him as the Thinker whose omniscient genius lies behind every law known to science in the vast and complex universe.

But there is more to it than that. The noun *logos* points to the person who thinks the thoughts that issue in every law being explored today in every branch and discipline of science. Whether in chemistry, astronomy, or genetics, Jesus is the original Thinker behind the universe.

In our understanding of verse 1, the verb is just as vital: "In the beginning *was* the Word, and the Word *was* with God, and the Word *was* God." This statement is much more arresting in the original text. The tense in the Greek is in the imperfect case in every instance. The imperfect suggests not something past, present, or future, but something continuous. The verb translated "was," then, suggests a continuous state. What John describes in his opening statement is not a *start* but a *state*. In the beginning *was* the Word—a continuous fact. The Word *was* with God—a continuous fact. The Word *was* God—a continuous fact. The imperfect tense describes a form of existence that cannot be measured by what we call time. Time is simply a pragmatic way of marking off of a portion of eternity to help finite beings like us manage our daily affairs. The verb as employed here by John takes us into the realm of the timeless.

In other words, the person described here as the Word, the *Logos*, the Thinker behind the universe, lives in a dimension where time does not count. He never had a beginning. He will never have an end. That boggles our imagination. We are so bound by time and space that we cannot conceive a form of existence that does not have a beginning. We are quite comfortable going back in time one hundred years. We do not mind going back five thousand years. We can even allow the geologist to go back in time a million years and the astronomer to go back billions of years. But to go back to no beginning at all is beyond us. When we think of Jesus, however, that is exactly where we must begin. We must begin in a dateless, timeless past—in eternity. We must conceive of Him as never having had a beginning. He is *eternally* God.

### (2) He is equally God

"In the beginning was the Word, and the Word *was* with God." In other words, in the Godhead, there is more than one personality and more than one person. The ancient Hebrews had a glimmering of this. Their great creedal statement—"Hear O Israel: The Lord our God is one Lord" (Deut. 6:4)—declares the unity of the Godhead. Yet the very first verse in the Bible refers to the *plurality* of the Godhead: "In the beginning God (*Elohim*—plural) created (singular) the heaven and the earth." For, although God is consistently referred to in the plural form throughout the Old Testament, the plural noun is constantly accompanied by singular verbs and adjectives. To be consistent in our use of grammar we should read, "*We* are your Elohim." Instead we read, "I am your Elohim." Thus, planted and embedded firmly in the Old Testament is the idea of the Trinity: one God, three persons. Not three Gods, but one God in three persons. Expressed mathematically the idea would not be $1 + 1 + 1 = 3$, but $1 \times 1 \times 1 = 1$. This profound revelation of God as being one God, yet existing in three persons, now comes into clearer and sharper focus. "In the beginning was the Word, and the Word was with God."

The three persons of the Godhead are known to us as God the Father, God the Son, and God the Holy Spirit—three persons but one God. Admittedly, this is a difficult concept to grasp, but let us consider a few simple illustrations.

The electricity that runs into our homes provides three things: heat, light, and power. It is still electricity whether it manifests itself in one way or the other. Three forms of manifestation, one electrical current.

The universe everywhere bears testimony to the fact that its Creator is a triune God. It consists of space, matter, and time—a simple triunity. *Space* exists in three dimensions—length, breadth, height. *Matter*, too, is a triunity—energy, motion, and phenomena. Every material entity in the universe is made up of atoms. At the center of the atom is energy. That energy is transformed into motion. That motion is revealed as phenomena. *Time* is yet another triunity—past, present, and future. All of time relates either to one or the other, no more, no less. A simple triunity.

The interrelationships among all these are very profound, and each, to a greater or lesser degree, mirrors the triunity of the Creator.[1] Take, for example, the relationship between past, present, and future.

Time has its source in the future. Let us take a definite date—today, for example. For a long time, this day was far in the future. Then it was next year, next month, next week. Then it was tomorrow. Then it became today. Soon it will recede into the past. It will become yesterday, then last week, last month, last year—receding further and further into the past. The present is the living instant, the flashing reality through which the vast oncoming future flows into the endlessly receding past.

Let us take these four words—*time, past, present,* and *future*—and state their interrelationships. As Dr. Nathan Wood points out, the future is the source. It is both unseen and unknown, except as it embodies itself and makes itself visible in the present. The present is what we see, hear, and know. The present perpetually reveals the future, hitherto invisible and unknown. The future is logically first, but not chronologically first, because the present exists as long as time exists and was there in the very beginning. Time acts in and through the present, and it is by means of the present that time and the future enter into human experience. The past proceeds from the present, though the present is not the source of the past. The future is the source of both past and present. The past acts invisibly. It continually influences us with regard to the present and casts light on the present. That is its great function. It helps us to live in proper relation with the present, which we know, and with reference to the future, which we expect to see.

Now, if we take the entire previous statement, with its carefully detailed description of the various relationships of past, present, and future, and rewrite it substituting only four words, we get a perfect description of the Trinity as revealed in the Bible. If we substitute the word *God* for "time," *Father* for "future," *Son* for "present," and *Holy Spirit* for "past," here is how the paragraph would read:

The Father is the source. He is both unseen and unknown except as He embodies himself and makes himself visible in the Son. The Son is who we see, hear, and know. The Son perpetually reveals the Father, hitherto invisible and unknown. The Father is logically first, but not chronologically first, because the Son exists as long as God exists and was there in the very beginning. God acts in and through the Son, and it is by means of the Son that God the Father enters into human experience. The Holy Spirit proceeds from the Son, though the Son is not the source of the Holy Spirit. The Father is the source of both the Son and the Holy Spirit. The Holy Spirit acts invisibly. He continually influences us with regard to the Son, and casts light on the Son. That is His great function. He helps us live in proper relation with the Son, whom we know, and with reference to the Father, whom we expect to see.

We are not so concerned here with the astonishing fact that our universe so exactly and minutely mirrors the triune nature of God as God is revealed in the New Testament. Instead, our aim is to demonstrate that Jesus is equally God. He is as much God as are the Father and the Holy Spirit. "In the beginning was the Word, and the Word was with God," John says. The Word, the Son, was with God as equal, as a member of the Godhead, as the second person of the Trinity. When we speak about the Lord Jesus Christ, we are speaking of *God,* over all, blessed for evermore.

### (3) He is essentially God

Jesus is God, in His essence; in what He actually is; in His actual, real, and ultimate nature; in His attributes; in His actual entity. "In the beginning was the Word, and the Word was with God, and the Word *was* God." He is partaker of the divine nature. All the characteristics of deity are His. Everything God is, everything God does, everything God has, Jesus is, Jesus does, Jesus has. He is God. Does God exist in His own right, independent of any creature, without beginning or ending of days, self-existing, uncreated? Jesus exists in His own right, independent of any creature, without beginning or ending of days, self-existing, uncreated. Does God have the wisdom and the power to create a universe? Jesus has the wisdom and the power to create a universe. He is essentially God.

So then, He is the infinite Creator. This is true as to His unique person. All that God is eternally and essentially, Jesus is.

*b. His universal power (vv. 2–3)*

When we describe God, we usually begin in terms of His ability to create. Jesus possesses this same power. We read, "All things were made by Him; and without Him was not any thing made that was made. In Him was life; and the life was the light of men." The Greek word *panta*, translated "all things," means exactly that. But it recognizes "things" separately, in the infinite variety and endless detail of creation, not just in its sum totality. Each individual thing was made by Him.

With a good radio telescope, we have a range of about five billion light years. That is, we can look out into space and see galaxies on the frontiers of the universe whose light has been traveling toward us for that long. How far from us these universes are, we simply cannot conceive. Light travels 186,273 miles per second. A light year is the distance that light travels in one year. In one second, it can encircle the earth seven-and-a-half times. In one year, it can travel six trillion miles. Our sun is only eight "light minutes" away. Light from the sun takes only eight minutes to reach us. But there are suns and stars out in space whose light, astronomers tell us, has taken four billion light years to reach us. That is how long they have been there, pouring out their light into space. Jesus made them all. Every single one of them, and every atom of stardust in between.

Jesus not only made the infinitely vast worlds explored by astronomers, He also made the infinitely small worlds explored by atomic scientists. Atoms are only 150 millionths of an inch in diameter, and every one of them is a whirling powerhouse of inconceivable energy. Each is a universe comparable to the universe of space. Moreover, the distance between the nucleus of an atom and the paths of its whirling electrons is actually, in proportion, emptier than space. If the molecules in one drop of water could be converted into grains of sand, there would be enough sand to build a concrete highway, one-half mile wide and one foot thick from New York to San Francisco. Jesus made every single one of those atoms and molecules. Such is His universal power.

This man we know as Jesus of Nazareth is also the infinite Creator, unique in His person, and universal in His power. But there is more to it than that. As the infinite Creator, He is farther removed from us than the remotest star. The glorious news of the gospel, the happy message of the Christmas season, is that the infinite Creator has become the incarnate Creator.

## 2. The incarnate Creator (vv. 4, 14)

"And the Word was made flesh, and dwelt among us (and we beheld his glory, the glory as of the only begotten of the Father,) full of grace and truth." He is that great, "almighty Word, chaos and darkness heard, and took their flight." But that Word was unintelligible to us, so God translated it into humanity for us. Usually, when we translate from one language to another, something is lost in the process. Translate the Bible from Hebrew and Greek into English and something is lost. Sometimes words in English are not the exact equivalent of the Greek or Hebrew. Some idioms cannot be translated exactly. But when God translated the Eternal Word into human flesh and blood, not the tiniest inflection was lost. Jesus was at once both perfectly God and perfectly man. God translated deity into humanity without losing anything of the deity or distorting anything in the humanity. That, in itself, is a miracle.

John, who knew Jesus so well, draws our attention to two monumental facts concerning this miracle: the coming of Jesus into a body of flesh and blood confronts us with the miracle of His translation into humanity, and the miracle of His transfiguration of humanity.

### a. His translation to humanity

"The Word was made flesh, and dwelt among us." The words *was made* do not refer to the beginning of something new. They refer to something that already existed but that is now made manifest in a different form. In this, the birth of the Lord Jesus was absolutely unique. The birth of a baby marks the beginning of a new life, the creation of a new personality, the coming into existence of someone who never existed before. When Jesus was born, however, it was not the creation of a new personality at all. It was the coming into this world of a person who had existed from all eternity. The birth of Jesus was something new, different, and unique in the history of the universe. No wonder the angels crowded around the cradle to see the mighty miracle of God, manifest in flesh! Then, having entered into human life in such a lowly way, by way of a virgin's womb, the great, eternal Son of the living God "dwelt among us." The word for "dwelt" literally means "to pitch one's tent." The Lord Jesus pitched His tent among us. Or, to employ a word that has rich meaning to anyone conversant with the Old Testament, He *tabernacled* among us.

Thus John describes the Incarnation. Luke uses twenty-five hundred words to describe the event. John uses only four. That little baby, wrapped in swaddling clothes and lying in the manger, was the eternal God. That little toddler, taking His first steps in a human form, hanging tightly onto Mary's hand, was the eternal God. That busy little boy, running here and there around that Nazareth home, watching eagerly at the well, playing with shavings and sawdust in Joseph's shop, busy learning His ABCs, was the eternal God.

> A Child He was, and had not learnt to speak,
> That with His word the world before did make.
> His mother's arms Him bore, He was so weak,
> That with one hands the vault of heaven could shake.
>
> See how small room my infant Lord doth take
> Whom all the world is not enough to hold,
> Who of His years, as of His age hath told?
> Never such age so young, never a child so old.[2]

### b. His transfiguration of humanity

The Lord Jesus took common, human clay and glorified it forever. John said: "(We beheld His glory, the glory as of the only begotten of the Father,) full of grace and truth." Think for a moment of the word

John has already used to describe Christ's descent into bodily form. He *tabernacled* among us. Now think of the Old Testament tabernacle pitched by Moses in the wilderness. It was all glorious within, but its glory was a hidden glory. There was nothing very beautiful about the outside. The outside furniture was common brass or copper. The outside curtains were made of ordinary linen bleached in the sun. The outside coverings of the tabernacle were unadorned animal skins. There was nothing very distinctive or attractive about its outward appearance. There was no particular beauty about the tabernacle to attract the eye of the curious, the passerby. It was just another tent, spaced off from the others, but just an ordinary tent.

When the tabernacle was moved from place to place, every piece of furniture from the inner Holy Place and from the Holy of Holies was covered up so that profane eyes might not gaze at them. In like manner, the glory of the Lord Jesus was a covered glory. When He came to earth, He did not lay aside His deity, but He did lay aside His glory. Only once did it blaze through and then it was seen only by John, James, and Simon Peter.

But inside the tabernacle, everything was glorious. The inner hangings were of rich colors—scarlet, blue, and purple. All the furniture was of acacia wood overlaid with purest gold. It was this inner beauty of the Lord Jesus that John and the other disciples so clearly saw in their three-and-a-half years of close acquaintance with Him. "(We beheld His glory, the glory as of the only begotten of the Father,) full of grace and truth," says John.

"Ah!" John exclaims, "We lived with Him, we walked with Him and talked with Him. We tramped the dusty highways of life with Him. We observed Him closely. We saw Him in a thousand situations. And always there was a perfect balance, a God-like perfection—always grace and truth in perfect proportion and balance.

"We saw God living and breathing, laughing and crying, eating and drinking, coming and going, telling parables the likes of which have never been told, and doing miracles the likes of which the world had never known. We saw Him in private and in public. We saw Him when He was hailed as Messiah and when He was derided as a malefactor.

We saw Him when He was confessed and when He was cursed. We saw Him when He was consulted and when He was contradicted. We saw Him when He was acclaimed and when He was crucified. He was unquestionably God manifest in the flesh."

It only remains for John to ask one simple question. What will we do with Jesus? Our response should be that of the poet:

> What can I give Him, poor as I am?
> If I were a shepherd, I'd bring a lamb;
> If I were a Wise Man, I would do my part;
> Yet what can I give Him: give my heart.[3]

## CHAPTER 4

# JESUS AS A BOY

1. The truth of God
   a. The place
   b. The period
2. The temple of God
   a. What He asked the rabbis
   b. What the rabbis asked Him
3. The timing of God
   a. His human family
   b. His heavenly Father

IN THE GOSPEL ACCOUNTS, WE SEE Jesus as a baby. We see him again as a grown man at the Jordan taking that great step of obedience as He is baptized by John. We see Him only once in between, at twelve years of age, going up to Jerusalem, perhaps for the first time.

We can picture the little cottage where He lived. A little house with a white, flat roof with vines running up the walls and with doves sunning themselves on the ledge that ran around the roof. We can peer inside and see mats or carpets lying along the walls. We can see the little oil lamp that hangs in the center of the one main room. In a recess, perhaps, is a chest, painted with bright colors, in which are kept the family's few books or other prized possessions. On a ledge, running around the wall, and within easy reach, are the neatly rolled-up quilts that serve as beds. And, on the same ledge, the earthen vessels for everyday use. Near the door stand the large, red clay water pots with a few twigs or green leaves or fragrant shrubs surrounding them to keep the water cool.

We can picture mealtimes in that humble abode. A painted wooden stool is placed in the center of the room. A large tray is placed on it. In the center of the tray stands a dish of rice and meat. The family sits around and each one dips into the common bowl. Before and after the meal, the youngest member of the family pours water over the hands of each one from a brazen vessel.

Such was the daily life of Jesus. Simple, humble, uneventful. When Joseph decided to settle in Nazareth, he knew that the family was going into seclusion. There, hidden away in that little town, buried in a little amphitheater of hills, sometimes thought to be the crater of an extinct volcano, they would be safe.

Nazareth was the Lord's home for all but three or four years of His life. It stood in the region of Galilee. The name *Galilee* comes from a Hebrew word that means "a circle." It was originally applied to the twenty cities that Solomon gave to Hiram, king of Tyre, for his services in transporting timber for the temple. The Phoenician king was not impressed with the gift. He gave the circle of towns the contemptuous name Cabul, which means "disgusting." This always seems to have been the fate of Galilee. From early days it had a mixed population. The Jews sneeringly called it "Galilee of the Gentiles." Phoenicians and Arabs lived there, and also numerous Greeks.

For thirty years, Jesus lived in complete obscurity in a Galilean village. He lived not only in a conquered land, but also in its most despised province and in its most disregarded valley and town. There He lived a quiet life as a young boy, a teenager, a young man, the village carpenter; for Jesus, as man, did not come into the world endowed with infinite knowledge. He gradually advanced in wisdom. Nor was He, as man, clothed in infinite power. He arrived as a baby, dependent for every human need on the tender care of Mary and the kindly provision of Joseph. He was God. Never for a moment did He cease to be God. But at the same time He grew up just like a normal, human boy. Except for sin. He was wholly free from sin.

Outside of Nazareth was the hill on which the city was built. Certainly there could have been no boy of Nazareth, in that day, who did not climb that hill. Jesus must have climbed it too. It rises about six hundred feet above sea level. Some four hundred or five hundred feet below is "the happy valley." With his feet among the wildflowers of the hill and with the breeze lifting His hair, Jesus must often have stood there watching the eagles in the blue, unclouded sky. Every field and farm, every garden and glen, every house and shop would be familiar to Him. He would single out in the village the humble abode of the carpenter. Home! His hideaway.

Until He was twelve. At the age of twelve a boy became a man. He was required by the rabbis to learn a trade. He became Ben Ha-Torah, "a son of the law." Up until this time he was called "little." Now he was "grown up." He was presented in the synagogue. His larger education began. At five, he was to study the Scriptures; at ten, he was to study the Mishna; at thirteen, the Talmud. At eighteen, boys were to marry; at thirty, acquire strength; at forty, become prudent.

When He was twelve, Jesus was taken to Jerusalem for the annual celebration of the Feast of Passover. It was possibly His first glimpse into the great outside world. It was a trek of eighty miles from Nazareth to Jerusalem. In spite of the hostility of the Samaritans, the caravan probably took the most direct route, which lay through the old tribal territory of Manasseh and Ephraim. The pilgrims would descend the flower-bordered limestone path into the great plain of Jezreel, where past and future armies fought. Since Passover was in the spring, the country would be wearing its best robe of green, embroidered like a high priest's robe with innumerable flowers of blue, purple, and scarlet. Past the departed glory of royal Jezreel. Past bare and dewless Mount Gilboa. Past Megiddo, with its Roman military camps alive with soldiers with helmets and shining breastplates and golden standards. On to En-Gannim, where they would make the first night's camp.

The next day would take them up the mountains of Manasseh,

across meadows and through olive groves and fig orchards. On past
the hills which, in the day of their splendor, had been the pride of
Samaria. Until they came to Jacob's well in the beautiful vale between
Ebal and Gerizim, the mounts of blessing and cursing.

The third day would take them past Shiloh and Gibeah of Saul,
past Bethel to Beeroth, where they would encamp again, now only a
short, easy stage to the first sight of the towers of Jerusalem.

And as they went, they would sing the fifteen psalms that follow
Psalm 119. Among the Arab tribes they would sing, "Woe is me that
I sojourn in the tents of Kedar." When they were clear of Samaritan
ground, they would sing, "My soul has escaped as a bird out of the
snare of the fowler." When they tramped along in cheerful good fellowship, they would sing, "Behold, how good and pleasant a thing it
is for brethren to dwell together in unity." Jesus would sing along with
them all, entering heart and soul into the meaning of the sacred songs.
Then, when Jerusalem at last came in sight, they would exclaim, "I
will lift up mine eyes unto the hills. From whence cometh my help?
My help cometh from the Lord."

And so, at twelve, Jesus came to Jerusalem. We get just this one
glimpse of Him. We see Him standing in the center of *the truth of
God*, in the center of *the temple of God*, and in the center of *the timing
of God*. Let us look at these three circles of interest.

## 1. The truth of God

The truth of God is suggested to us by two things: the place (Jerusalem) and the period (Passover).

### a. The place

Jerusalem! Ten thousand times ten thousand biblical memories
would fill Christ's mind as He stood there. His mind would go back
to the beginning. He would think of Melchizedek, king of Salem,
priest of the Most High God, who met Abraham, spread before that

pilgrim patriarch the emblems of Calvary, and received tithes from his hand. Whoever Melchizedek was and whatever Melchizedek was, Jesus entered Jerusalem that day as its true King-Priest.

He would think of Jerusalem and its links with the lives of David and Solomon, of the good and bad kings of Judah down to its destruction by Nebuchadnezzar. He would think of the prophets who had preached in this city, of Zerubbabel and Ezra and Nehemiah. He would think of how the city had been rebuilt in troublesome times. He was standing on sacred soil, surrounded by truth. This was the Holy City. This was the city of God. This was His Father's city, now trodden down by the Gentiles, now the center of faction and strife. This was the city to which, one day in the distant future, He would return to rule. He was standing in the center of truth. The very stones of that place cried out to Him.

### b. The period

It was Passover time! The feast lasted a week, a week of deep emotion and sacred memories. Into each and every one of them the mind of that twelve-year-old boy would enter. The taking of the lamb, the tethering of the lamb, the slaughter of the lamb, and the supper it provided. It all pointed back fifteen hundred years to the very beginning of Hebrew history, to the night of the Exodus, to the night when God sheltered His people behind the shed blood of the Passover lamb so that the angel of wrath might pass over the people. And it pointed forward another twenty years to the time when Jesus himself would become the Passover Lamb, not just for Israel but for all mankind. He would be "the Lamb of God, which taketh away the sin of the world." What thoughts flooded His mind? His first and last visits to Jerusalem were at Passover. The first time He came, the foreshadowing of it all loomed up in His holy mind. The last time He came, the fulfillment of it all was upon Him. So we see Him standing there at the age of twelve, in the center of the truth of God. We see Him also standing in the center of God's temple.

## 2. The temple of God

The temple! It drew Him like a magnet. It was His Father's house. We do not know exactly when it was that Jesus, as man, entered into the full knowledge of His essential and eternal deity. We do know that He knew God to be His Father at the age of twelve. How He must have haunted those temple precincts during that one, short week He was in Jerusalem! How He must have stood and stared at the sacrifices.

The wonderful week in Jerusalem came and went. Then the party, heading back north to Nazareth, reassembled and set out. The road would be enlivened with mirth, with conversation, with singing, with the sound of drums and timbrels. The pilgrims would pause for refreshment—dates and melons and cucumbers, water from the water pots filled at every bubbling spring. Among such a sea of excited human beings, how easy to lose track of one young boy.

A whole day elapsed before Joseph and Mary discovered their loss. Then came the hasty search among the various relatives, the wider enquiry in the ranks of their friends, then the urgent call to the whole camp. He was not there.

Back they went to Jerusalem. They had lost the Christ of God. The road was dangerous, even ominous. The country was in a wild and unsettled state. The ethnarch Archelaus, after ten years of cruel and disgraceful rule, had been deposed and banished by the emperor in Rome. The Romans had annexed the province. They had introduced a new system of taxation. And that had kindled widespread revolt. Judas of Gamala and Zadoc the Pharisee had wrapped the whole country in a storm of sword and flame. Without the shelter of the caravan, Joseph and Mary must have had a scary journey back to Jerusalem.

And yet they could not find Him! How strange it is that they did not go straight to the temple. They might have known that they would find Him there. Had He not haunted the temple grounds? Had He not asked ten thousand questions about the temple? At last they went there, and sure enough, there He was. He was sitting, perhaps, in the Hall of Squares, or in one of the spacious chambers assigned to the teachers. There He sat at the feet of the learned doctors of biblical and Talmudic law. Joseph and Mary found Him in the temple of God.

It would be interesting to know who the rabbis were at whose feet Jesus sat that day. It is possible that the great Hillel was there, a man the Jews regarded as a second Moses, though his hair would have been white with the snows of well-nigh a hundred years. His grandson was almost certainly there, the refined and liberal Gamaliel, at whose feet Saul of Tarsus was later to sit. Annas might well have been there, the man who was later to be His judge. Boethus was probably there, the father-in-law of Herod. Maybe Joseph of Arimathea was there, and the timid but earnest Nicodemus. All learned men. But Jesus was there, that is what made the difference to this particular assembly of the scholars of the nation. Their Messiah was there and they did not know it. They were so wrapped up in their traditions and their endless wrangles over the finer points of the law that they did not know Him. Jesus was "in the midst," as He is "in the midst" today wherever people gather, and they did not have the eyes to see Him, nor the ears to hear Him, nor the heart to accept Him. We could wonder what He asked the doctors of the law, and what the rabbis asked Him.

### a. What He asked the rabbis

We are told that Jesus was both listening and asking questions. He had a mind unblunted by sin. He must have swiftly detected the shallowness of their teaching. He had a mind saturated, through and through, with the Word of God. He must have seen through the trivialities that obsessed them.

The Jewish rabbis had evolved a theory that, at Sinai, God had given Moses the written law and also an oral law. Their tradition had arrived at the point where it placed the oral law above the written law. For instance, God said in the written law, "Remember the sabbath day, to keep it holy." The rabbis claimed they had the right to determine the exact boundaries of that command and to clarify it by setting out its myriad ramifications. They made the Bible of no effect by all their useless verbiage.

The Sabbath was intended by God to be a day of rest, a day when the Hebrew people relaxed, enjoyed each other's fellowship, and luxuriated in the love of God. The rabbis made the Sabbath an intolerable burden of petty restrictions. Alfred Edersheim tells us that through some sixty-four or sixty-five folio columns in the Jerusalem Talmud, and through some 156 double pages in the Babylonian Talmud, the rabbis haggled over minutia so utterly puerile and trivial that one could scarcely imagine a sane intellect would seriously entertain.

For instance, the rabbis decided that if a person were in one place and his hand, filled with fruit, stretched into another, and the Sabbath overtook him in this attitude, he would have to drop the fruit, because if he withdrew his hand from one locality into another, he would be carrying a burden on the Sabbath. The rabbis decided that "a burden" meant the weight of a dried fig. A tailor might not walk out of his house with his needle, nor the scribe with his pen. Clothes were not to be examined by lamplight. A teacher might not allow his pupils to read if he himself looked at the book. Shammai, who was a rival of Gamaliel's and had even more disciples, was possibly also present when Jesus stood that day in the temple. Shammai preached that it was forbidden to make any mixture the ingredients of which would not be wholly dissolved and assimilated before the Sabbath. More! Wool might not be dyed if the process was not completed and the wool dried by the Sabbath.

The rules went on and on. A woman must not look in a mirror on the Sabbath, because she might discover a white hair and attempt to pull it out, which would be profaning the Sabbath. A person must not throw hot water on himself on the Sabbath, because the vapor might spread or because the falling drops might clean the floor. If a parent picked up his little child on the Sabbath and the child happened to have a stone in his hand, the parent would have violated the Sabbath because picking up the child involved the labor of carrying the stone. If one had an earache and had some cotton batten in his ear and it fell out on the Sabbath, he must not put it back in again. Even to pluck a blade of grass was a sin.

What must have been the look on Jesus' face as these gray-bearded and venerable men, the leading intellectuals of His nation, sat around in their sober circle and solemnly discussed these things. They would quote all the appropriate rabbinical authorities for these astonishing conclusions. What kinds of questions did Jesus ask them?

"Yes, venerable rabbi," Jesus might have said, "but what saith the Scripture? How does the Torah rule on the matter of the Sabbath?" "My son," the venerable Gamaliel or learned Shammai might reply, "understand that these things are in the oral law. We sit in Moses' seat. We are his spiritual heirs. To us has been entrusted the elaboration of the written law." "But sir, can you show me in the Torah where it is written that God entrusted an oral law to Israel?" We wonder what He asked them. We wonder, also, what the rabbis asked Him.

### b. What the rabbis asked Him

The Holy Spirit says that the rabbis were "astonished at His under-standing and answers." So evidently they questioned Him. Did they try out any of their famous theological chestnuts on Him? As they looked at Him, at His lovely face, so pure, so intelligent, so eager, so absolutely irresistible, they might say, "Young man, suppose a man died and left a widow. Suppose the man had six brothers. Suppose that, according to the Mosaic law, the widow was married by her husband's nearest brother. Then he died. Supposing, in that way, she was married to all the brothers. Suppose, too, she had no child by any of the brothers. Now whose wife would she be in the resurrection, seeing that they were all legally married to her? Would it be the one who had her first? Would it be the one who had her last, the one to whom she was still married when she died? Would it be the one she liked the best of them all? Whose would she be?"

We know how He answered that in later years. We know, too, they would have been astonished at his answer even at the age of twelve. His was a mind that had been drilled in the Scripture since His earliest days. We see Him, then, standing in the center of the truth of God, and standing in the center of the temple of God. We also see Him standing in the center of God's timing.

## 3. The timing of God

We read that Jesus went down to Nazareth with Mary and with Joseph "and was subject unto them." By now He knew who He was—the eternal, uncreated Son of the living God; Israel's Messiah; Israel's Prophet, Priest, and King; the Creator of all the stars and suns of space. But He was still a boy of twelve. And, as a boy, He still had a lot more growing up to do. He went down to Nazareth and was "subject unto them," to Joseph and Mary. What a magnificent statement! He was standing in the very center of the timing of God. It was not yet time to teach. It was not yet His time to perform miracles. It was not yet time for Him to reveal to the world who He was. He had another eighteen years before He could begin His work. Luke tells us of two things in this connection. He makes mention of Jesus and His human family, and Jesus and His heavenly Father.

### a. His human family

The scene shifts to Mary and Joseph and their frantic search for the missing Christ. We see them supposing and seeking and scolding. We see them in their utter desperation. It had suddenly come home to them just exactly how life would be without Him. It was not He who was lost. It was they who were lost.

For, to be without Christ is to be lost indeed. They supposed Him to be in the company. Could anyone make a greater mistake? We must not just suppose. We must make sure.

This is particularly relevant to those who are brought up in Christian homes, who have been used to having Jesus as part of the background of their lives. It is particularly relevant to those whose parents have surrounded them with Christ. His was one of the first names they learned to say. The stories of Jesus were the first stories they ever heard. Long before they heard of Little Red Riding Hood or Little Bo-Peep or Jack and the Beanstalk or Tom Thumb, they heard about Jesus.

Some have been to Sunday school and church as long as they can remember. They know all about Him. Maybe once, long ago, they made a profession of faith. But they have just been "supposing" Him to be in the company. Many a young person has lost Him at college, when confronted with an agnostic professor. Others have lost Him on the job, when mocked by a sneering coworker. They have lost Him. Probably they never had Him. Or perhaps He never had them. They would be wise never to stop seeking Him until they find Him. "They sought Him sorrowing." Those who have lost Him would do well to be desperate about this search.

They found Him in the temple. Strange, they did not go there first of all. A person, of course, might find Jesus anywhere, but they are most likely to find Him in the house of God.

### b. His heavenly Father

"Wist ye not," He said, "that I must be about my Father's business?" (Luke 2:49). They should have known that. Mary should have known it. She knew who His Father was. His Father was not Joseph; His Father was God. His Father's business was not the work of a carpenter, even though for a number of years Jesus dutifully toiled at the carpenter's bench in Nazareth. What magnificent furniture He must have made!

See Him take the saw and adze into His capable hands. See Him measure off the wood and make His cut. Every line perfect, every joint perfect. See Him take the gouge to add some decoration. Look at those olive leaves, that cluster of grapes. Look at the final finish He puts on that table, that chair, that corner cabinet. Never had the world seen a craftsman like Him. But just the same, His Father's business was not the work of a *carpenter*. It was the work of a *cross*.

He had been to the altar. He had watched intently each step of the ritual in the slaughtering of the lambs. He had watched people bring their offerings, their sin offerings and their trespass offerings. He had shuddered in His soul. He had watched them bring their peace offerings and their burnt offerings. He had watched the flash of the knife, the dying gasp of the lamb. He had watched the fire do its dreadful work. He had come into a full understanding of why He had come into the world, just what, indeed, His Father's business was on this sin-cursed planet Earth.

As a boy of twelve, Jesus set His face firmly toward the completion of the work now being made known in all its heights and depths to His soul.

He came! He came to die! He came to die for you, for me! Surely the least we can do is trust Him. Surely the least we can do is to give Him back the life we owe. Surely we can accept Him as Savior. Surely we can say to Him, "And now, Lord Jesus, Your Father is our Father." We, too, must be about our Father's business.

## CHAPTER 5

# THE LORD'S BAPTISM
*Matthew 3:13-4:11*

1. The exercise that preceded it (3:13–15)
   a. A controlling exercise (3:13)
      (1) Controlled His movements (3:13a)
      (2) Controlled His motives (3:13b)
   b. A convicting exercise (3:14)
   c. A continuing exercise (3:15)
2. The experience that accompanied it (3:16–17)
   a. The anointing of the Spirit (3:16)
   b. The approval of the Father (3:17)
3. The exploit that followed it (4:1–11)

PURELY AND SIMPLY, BAPTISM IS AN ACT of obedience. Jesus said, "If ye love me, keep my commandments" (John 14:15). He also said, "Go ye therefore, and teach all nations, baptizing them in the name of the Father, and of the Son, and of the Holy Ghost: teaching them to observe all things whatsoever I have commanded you" (Matt. 28:19–20). It is a proclamation to the world that we have passed through death and burial with Christ, that we stand in Him on resurrection ground, that He is our Savior and our Lord, and that we intend to obey Him.

In many countries, baptism is an act of singular courage. It does not cost most of us much to be immersed in a private tank, in congenial surroundings, amid the approval and encouragement of our Christian friends. It might cost us more if the service were to take place in a public place before our neighbors and work peers. In some countries, it is a death sentence.

When a believer steps down into the waters of baptism, he is simply following where the Lord has already led the way. The Lord was baptized by John the Baptist, whose baptism was one of repentance. Christ's baptism was an event of national significance. It was a preparatory act designed to give public witness to the Jewish people by believing individuals that they had repented of their sins and were ready for the coming of Christ. The Lord had no sins of which to repent. Moreover, He was the Christ. His baptism, therefore, was an act of identification. It was intended to identify Him with the people He had come to save. It was a foreview of the more dreadful baptism with which He closed His life on earth. He began His ministry by being baptized in water, in the chilly waters of the Jordan. He ended it by being baptized into the icy waters of death. The one baptism anticipated and illustrated the other.

Let us follow Jesus to the Jordan. Then, if we have not already done so, let us follow Him in simple obedience into the waters of baptism ourselves. A study of the Lord's baptism, as recorded by Matthew, reveals a threefold movement: the exercise that preceded it, the experience that accompanied it, and the exploit that followed it.

## 1. The exercise that preceded it (3:13–15)

The Lord did not rush lightly into His baptism. Before He presented himself to John at the Jordan, there were months and years of careful spiritual exercise that led up to it. When He was a boy of twelve, he bore testimony to the principle that controlled his whole life. He had been to the altar and witnessed the offering of the morning and evening sacrifices. He had seen the blood flow and the fire burn. Those lambs were mere types. He was the Antitype. For the first time it is recorded that He called God His Father. He said, "I must be about my Father's business." His Father's business led Him to the Jordan and then on to Calvary.

Before anyone can be baptized scripturally, a like relationship with the Father must be established. We must go in spirit to Calvary. We must contemplate the enormous cost of that one great sacrifice that took away the sin of the world. We must accept Christ as personal Savior and enter into a new, personal, eternal relationship with God. He must become our Father. Just as Jesus entered into the human family by being born at Bethlehem and thus became a partaker of human nature, so we must enter into God's family by being born again and thus become partakers of the divine nature. Until that new relationship is established, baptism is a meaningless ritual.

There came a time in the human experience of the Lord Jesus when He, who ever was, from all eternity, uniquely the Son of God, realized that He was the Son of God, and He confessed that fact in His first recorded utterance. So, there must come a time when we, who never were the sons of God, accept Christ as Savior and thus become sons of God and confess it before others.

The time came in the life of the Lord Jesus when He had to publicly declare himself before the world as the Son of God. The way He chose to do it was by means of baptism. In this, as in all things, He walked in obedience to the will of His Father. We note three things about the exercise that immediately proceeded His baptism. It was a controlling exercise, a convicting exercise, and a continuing exercise.

### a. A controlling exercise (3:13)

Christ's baptism was the kind of exercise before God that resulted in deliberate, step-by-step obedience to what He knew God's will to be. God's will controlled His life. Thus, this exercise controlled His movements and his motives.

### (1) Controlled His movements (3:13a)

"Then cometh Jesus from Galilee to Jordan." It is generally believed that Jesus was baptized at a ford of the Jordan River east of Jericho. It is the same section of the river that parted for the passage of the children of Israel in the days of Joshua. It is also the same part of the river that opened up for Elijah and again later for Elisha. This ford was some seventy or eighty miles from Nazareth.

In those days, travel was either by foot or on the back of a mule. No journey was undertaken lightly. Any journey in Palestine involved a long, arduous tramp uphill and downhill in the burning heat of the Mediterranean sun or in the snows of winter.

The Lord Jesus was far more aware than we are of the importance of being just where His Father wanted Him to be at any given hour of any given day. The fact that He undertook this journey indicates His consciousness that it was God's will for Him to go. The psalmist said, "The steps of a good man are ordered by the Lord" (Ps. 37:23). If David could find this true, how much more the Lord? As the Shechinah-glory cloud paced out each step of the wilderness journey for Israel of old, so the Lord moved only in obedience to that still, small, inner voice of God. He set out on this journey, then, conscious that God was leading Him every step of the way. Thus this exercise controlled His movements.

### (2) Controlled His motives (3:13b)

"Then cometh Jesus from Galilee to Jordan unto John to be baptized of Him." His sole reason for going to the Jordan was to be baptized. He did not go to hear John preach or to see firsthand the great crowds that followed the Baptist. He did not go to congratulate John on the success of his ministry or out of curiosity to see a revival in progress. He went because it was God's sovereign will for His life. Nobody had to persuade Him to go. He was convinced it was God's will. That was all.

All too often, we do something because someone has high-pressured us into doing it. People have gone to the mission field because they have responded to a high-powered missionary talk followed by an impassioned emotion-packed appeal. Such missionary candidates rarely last.

People sometimes give to the Lord's work under the impulse of high-pressure appeals. I remember hearing the founder of a well-known mission use every kind of emotional appeal to get people to give. First some little Asian orphans sang in phonetic English. They had learned the correct sounds but had no idea what they meant. It was very cute and appealing. Many of the little ones were half Asian, half American, the offspring of casual liaisons between active-duty American servicemen and local women. Unwanted by the soldiers, the little ones had been abandoned by their mothers.

Next, we were shown an emotion-drenched film about a pastor who was martyred by the Communists because he would not deny the faith. It was a true story and it wrung our hearts and consciences.

Then came a brief message intended to make everyone feel guilty because they ate three meals a day and drove a car to work while the rest of the world starved and suffered. It was as if we were personally responsible for all the heartache and suffering in the world. Much of what was said was true. The appeal, however, was entirely to the emotions. It was a clever psychological setup for an offering.

And then the offering was taken as appeal after appeal was given. All the emotionally tender spots were cleverly pounded anew by the preacher until checks and large bills and faith-promises of generous amounts were squeezed out of the crowd.

That kind of thing is not spiritual at all, it is merely psychological. God does not want us to be motivated along such low lines. He does not want anyone to be high-pressured by man into doing His will.

The Lord Jesus came to Jordan to be baptized of John, not because John had persuaded Him to come, not because He felt pressured to go, but because He was emotionally controlled by the will of God. So then, His exercise was a controlling exercise. It controlled His movements and His motives.

### b. A convicting exercise (3:14)

"But John forbad him [would have hindered Him], saying, I have need to be baptized of thee, and comest thou to me?" The presence of the Lord Jesus, walking in perfect obedience to the Father, brought John himself, great prophet-evangelist that he was, under personal conviction of sin.

John was a good man, a godly man. People from all over the country flocked to his revival. Thousands of them, some of them the worst people in the nation, had come under conviction of sin and had publicly repented at his preaching. So far as he knew, John was walking in obedience to God, and God was blessing his ministry. However, confronted with the superior goodness and absolute godliness of Christ, John felt himself to be a sinner as vile as anyone who had ever come forward at his meetings. And mark this, Jesus had said nothing about sin.

There was something about a life lived in such close communion with God that wrought conviction even in a good and a godly man. That is one of the great values of baptism. It is a step of obedience, and a step of obedience by a truly exercised person always speaks loudly to others. Most of us can think of one or two people whose lives have been a challenge to us. We have observed their obedience and been made aware of our own shortcomings, failures, and reservations. A life of obedience always convicts.

### c. A continuing exercise (3:15)

"And Jesus answering said unto him, Suffer it to be so now: for thus it becometh us to fulfill all righteousness. Then he suffered him." John's baptism was not part of the law of Moses. But it was of God. John himself claimed that God had instructed him to baptize his converts (John 1:33).

There was no human necessity for the Lord Jesus to be baptized by John, because John's baptism was a baptism of repentance and Jesus himself was sinless and therefore had no need to repent. But His Father had told Him that He should be baptized of John, so baptized He was. It was an act of implicit, unquestioning obedience to the known will of God for His life.

Some people have doubts and difficulties with baptism. This is not surprising since numerous errors have grown up around the ordinance like weeds around a tree. But whether we can explain all its implications or not, it is a clearly revealed command of the Lord Jesus that we be baptized. That reduces it to a matter of simple obedience.

The Lord Jesus refused to be turned aside from His objective. A good man, a godly man, questioned what He was about to do. He questioned it honestly, sincerely. He tried to turn Him aside from obeying God in this way. The Lord's exercise was a continuing exercise. He refused to be deterred.

A girl once applied to the elders of her church for baptism. They thought she was too young to know what she was doing. They questioned her carefully and she answered to the best of her ability. They told her she would have to wait until she was older. The child was wise beyond her years. She refused to be turned aside. She had a continuing exercise before God about this matter, young as she was. Finally she turned to the elders and said, "Very well, will you promise to baptize me before the Lord returns?" They baptized her at once.

We should not allow anything to hinder us from being baptized. Jesus did not allow even John the Baptist to stand in his way. People allow all kinds of things to come between them and simple obedience to the Lord. Sometimes people plead ill health or old age. It is said, in this connection, that Charles Spurgeon had a standing offer to pay the funeral expense of anyone who died as a result of being baptized. So we note carefully the godly spiritual exercise that preceded the Lord's baptism.

## 2. The experience that accompanied it (3:16–17)

No act of outright obedience to God goes unrewarded. Luke tells us the Lord Jesus was praying at the time of His baptism. Entering into the very act of baptism in a spirit of fervent prayer will not only make it a more meaningful spiritual experience but will also prevent it from being a merely mechanical ritual.

Two experiences accompanied the Lord's baptism. There was an anointing of the Spirit and there was an announcement from the Father. While these were unique in His experience, they have a parallel in ours.

### a. The anointing of the Spirit (3:16)

"And Jesus, when he was baptized, went up straightway from the water [was coming up out of the water]: and, lo, the heavens were opened unto him, and he saw the Spirit of God descending like a dove, and lighting upon him." The Lord's actual position is worthy of notice. He was coming up out of the water. This was no mere sprinkling. This was baptism by immersion. He had been down into the water. Now he was coming up out of the water. Baptism is a type of death, burial, and resurrection. In baptism, a person takes his stand in an element that spells death to him as a natural man. He is thus put in the place of death, symbolically buried, and then raised again out of the watery grave. This is the spiritual significance of baptism. The Lord thus signified His death for us in the waters of the Jordan. We thus signify our death with Him in the waters of baptism.

As Jesus was coming up out of the water, the Spirit of God came down and alighted on Him. Ever since the fall of man, the Spirit of God has hovered over this world seeking a place to alight and make his home. As Noah, after the Flood, opened the window of the ark and sent forth a dove that flew to and fro across the face of the waters and found no place to rest and thus returned to the ark, so the Spirit of God. As at last the dove found an olive leaf and brought that back to the ark, so the Spirit of God. As finally the dove went forth upon the face of a new earth, cleansed by the waters of judgment and there found its home, so too the Spirit of God.

The Spirit of God brooded century after century over the restless, surging seas of tempest-tossed mankind. He found no home. At last He came down and alighted upon God's Ark, the Lord Jesus Christ, and found a home in Him. He has brought back the olive leaf, glorious token of the new life now available to all in Christ. The judgment is past. The Lord braved the storm. New life can be ours. And then He alighted as a dove upon the church, in a way never known in Old Testament times. It is in the church and in each believer's heart that the Holy Spirit, the Dove of God, now makes His abode on earth. This was hinted at when the Dove of God came down to the Jordan and alighted on the Lord Jesus.

But there was something more. By alighting on the Lord Jesus, the Holy Spirit anointed Him for the tremendous years of ministry that lay ahead. It is significant that He did not utter a single word or take a single step in His ministry until He was thus anointed by the Spirit of God.

There never was a time when the Lord Jesus was not *filled* with the Spirit. In the power of that filling He lived the marvelous hidden life between His birth and His baptism. But He was not *anointed* with the Spirit until now. In the power of this anointing, He went forth to be the Messiah of Israel in evident manifestation.

In the Old Testament, three classes of people were anointed with oil, and thus, symbolically, anointed with the Spirit. Israel's priests were anointed, the prophets were sometimes anointed, and the kings were anointed. Jesus was now going to show himself to Israel as God's Prophet, Priest, and King. Hence His anointing.

There are three ministries of the Holy Spirit for the believer that are often misunderstood.

There is the baptism of the Spirit, which is primarily mystical. It is the ministry of the Holy Spirit that takes a believer in the Lord Jesus Christ and makes him a member of Christ's mystical body, the church. The Lord Jesus was never baptized with the Spirit, but every born-again believer is automatically baptized with the Holy Spirit at the time of his conversion. Apart from the Spirit's baptism it is impossible to be linked to Christ's mystical body.

There is the filling of the Spirit, which is primarily motivational. It is the ministry of the Spirit that makes it possible for us to live the Christian life. When a person is saved, the Holy Spirit takes up His residence in his body, making that body His temple. When a person is filled with the Spirit, the Holy Spirit begins His reign in that believer's life and makes his heart His throne. As He is given access to all the mainsprings of the believer's life, He begins to motivate and empower and make possible the living of the Christian life. Thus the Christian life is a supernatural life. It can only be lived in the power of the Spirit of God and only in the measure in which He is allowed to fill and control.

Then there is the anointing of the Spirit, which is primarily ministerial. In the Old Testament, anointing was for service in the official capacity of a prophet, a priest, or a king. In Christ's life, it was for service. Today it is also for service. The anointing (sometimes called unction) of the Holy Spirit enables a believer to use the Word of God in power so that its message reaches the hearts and consciences of sinners and saints alike.

The Lord's anointing took place at His baptism. At the time of our baptism, if the step is taken with an exercise and an attitude of surrender and obedience to God similar to that of the Lord, there surely should be a fresh experience of the Spirit of God in one's life. We may not receive an anointing, but we surely should receive a fresh filling.

So the first experience that accompanied the Lord's baptism was a fresh experience of the Holy Spirit, which made it possible for Him to enter into the great redemptive work for which He had come to earth. It was an amazing transitional point in His life.

### b. The approval of the Father (3:17)

"And lo a voice from heaven, saying, This is my beloved Son, in whom I am well pleased." The anointing of the Spirit looked forward to the future, to the next three-and-a-half years to be spent in ministering to the needs of mankind. The announcement of the Father looked back over the past thirty years that Jesus had spent in the seclusion of Nazareth. It was God's public endorsement of those hidden years. It was God's "Well done!" on nearly eleven thousand days lived in absolute holiness and victory. As a tiny baby in swaddling clothes, as a toddler hanging on to Mary's robes, as a little boy playing with His toys, as a youth at school, at home, at play, with brothers and sisters, family and friends, as a young man at the carpenter's bench. God's all-seeing eye scanned the years and pronounced the verdict: "This is my beloved Son." It was the absolute, unequivocal blessing of God on a superb life scrutinized and approved by His Father in heaven.

Certainly a person coming forward for baptism should be able, in some measure, to exhibit a life that wins the approval of God. That is one reason why only a saved person can be baptized. God can never put His stamp of approval on a sinner's life. If God looks at us and sees Christ, then He can say of us as He said of Him, "This is my Son." If He looks at us and sees Christ being lived out in our lives, then He can say of us as He said of Him, "This is my son. I am well pleased."

### 3. The exploit that followed it (4:1–11)

Strange to say, the exploit that followed the Lord's baptism was not in the area of spectacular service at all. He did not go away from Jordan to astound Jerusalem with amazing miracles. On the contrary, He was driven by the Spirit into the wilderness to be tempted by the Devil. The morrow after some great spiritual experience is always fraught with peril. Satan always counterattacks a spiritual victory.

The tremendous thrill of baptism was followed by the tremendous threat of temptation. The temptation was fierce, prolonged, deadly, and comprehensive.

The Lord Jesus had already met and mastered all the temptations of ordinary, private life. That is why the Father set the seal of approval on those silent years. But now Christ must meet the Devil face-to-face. He met that foe in all His strength. It is reasonable to suppose that He never before encountered such a concentrated attack. After this experience, His attitude toward Satan and all his demon powers was that of the victor toward the vanquished. Driven by the Spirit into the wilderness, the Lord Jesus now forced the enemy to stand out clear from all secondary causes and to enter into direct combat with Him in His role as "the second man." That is not Satan's normal way. Satan likes to put something else between himself and the one he would tempt. Jesus dragged him out into the open. The Devil challenged the first man, Adam. The second man, Christ, challenged the Devil.

The temptations came along the old line of the lust of the eyes, the lust of the flesh, and the pride of life. They were answered, in each case, by an appropriate quotation from the Word of God. The Lord Jesus took into His holy hands the identical weapon He has put into ours, the sword of the Spirit, which is the Word of God. With that sword, He cut each temptation to shreds.

The first temptation had to do with hunger. It was not a sin to be hungry. It was God's will that He be hungry. God created the need but there was no provision for that need to be satisfied. Now mark the subtlety of the foe. "You are hungry, act on your own initiative. Command these stones to be made bread." The subtlety of the temptation lay in the fact that the Devil suggested that the Lord satisfy a perfectly legitimate craving. The evil of the suggestion lay in the fact that he suggested that a legitimate craving be satisfied in an illegitimate way. He suggested that the Lord use the privileges of His sonship for violating its responsibilities.

The second temptation went behind the bulwarks that had thwarted Satan in the first. Behind the failure of the first temptation lay the Lord's unshakable confidence in God. "It is written . . ." The Lord preferred to suffer hunger in the divine will rather than satisfy a necessity of life by deviating from the will of God. The Devil now goes behind that confidence and suggests that the Lord use it in a wrong way.

He took Him to a wing of the temple overlooking a giddy gorge far below. You have confidence in God, he said, so cast yourself down and demonstrate your confidence by doing a daring thing. Do an unusual, spectacular thing for God. Prove to everyone how much confidence you have in Him. What could be more fitting than that you prove your trust in God by going out on a limb, by doing some daring thing, by taking some great risk. Do something adventurous, do something magnificent, do something out of the ordinary. Demonstrate your faith. Christ's weakness in the physical realm had been tested, so now His strength in the spiritual realm was tested.

Finally, Satan sought to ruin Jesus along the line of His specific mission. He showed Him all the kingdoms of the world, together with their power and their glory, and he offered them to Christ for a price. Satan suggested that Christ might gain all these things without having to go to Calvary. He offered Him the crown without the cross.

Again and again Jesus triumphed. The world, the flesh, and the Devil hammered at the citadel of His soul in vain. He triumphed gloriously. The whole secret lay in His submission to the will of God, a submission that manifested itself in obedience to God's will that He be baptized; a submission that made possible a fresh work of the Holy Spirit in His life; a submission that put the Devil to flight.

As James says, "Submit yourselves therefore to God. Resist the devil, and he will flee from you" (4:7).

## CHAPTER 6

# THE TEMPTATION OF CHRIST
*Matthew 4:1–11*

1. The preparation
2. The provocation
   a. Along the line of God's provision: The promise of instant food
   b. Along the line of God's protection: The promise of instant fame
   c. Along the line of God's program: The promise of instant fortune
3. The proclamation

ACCORDING TO TRADITION, THE SCENE of our Lord's temptation was a mountain to the south of Jericho. It was a long, tiring ascent up the mountain, and with every step upward, the Jordan Valley looked more and more terrible. Even at the top, the climber is still two hundred feet below sea level. The mountain is "naked and arid like a mountain of malediction, rising precipitously from a scorched and desert plain, and looking over the sluggish, bituminous waters of the Sodomite sea."[1] The whole scene was a wilderness, a fitting stage upon which to enact this great drama. The waste and desolate places of the earth are the legacy of fallen man. The wastes and wilderness of the world simply echo the desolation that sin has wrought in the human heart.

So the stage was set. Two men, in the history of the world, have been exposed to a fierce, face-to-face encounter with the Prince of Darkness. The circumstances, however, were poles apart. Adam met his temptation in paradise, a garden planted by God, a place of pristine beauty and one subservient to his will. Jesus Christ, the Last Adam, met his temptation on the desolate hillside.

In each case, there was a perfect man. In the first instance, a man created by God; in the second, a man conceived by God. The first Adam surveyed a scene where all was beauty and bliss; the Last Adam looked upon a scene of barrenness and blight, where hunger and danger stalked.

Mark tells us that Jesus was "with the wild beasts," for the lion and the jackal lurked there. They came to pay homage to their Maker, to acknowledge the second man, in all His perfection, and to lie at his feet as tame as lambs.

Alone, except from these wild companions, with no food to eat, with no agenda to fulfill except to be where God wanted Him to be, the Lord and Creator of the Universe, tabernacling now in human flesh, felt the progressive pains and pangs of starvation. He was alone with a ruined world, with wild animals, with His memorized Bible, and with God. Such was the setting for the temptation of the man, Christ Jesus.

What did He do for the long period of forty days that He waited in the wilderness? Some think that He was tempted throughout the whole period and that the three temptations actually recorded in the Gospels came as the climax at the end. It is equally as likely that the whole period was simply one of preparation. Moses stayed on Sinai for forty days. Elijah sojourned in the wilderness for forty days. We can well believe that the Lord needed the time afforded to Him in that waiting period to hone his heart for the onslaught to come when, after a forty-day fast, he would be at the end of all his physical resources.

The Lord dealt with all the enemy's attacks by quoting from the Bible. By quoting, in fact, from one book of the Bible, the book of Deuteronomy. Perhaps He spent the entire period of waiting going through the Pentateuch again and again. Perhaps He spent five days doing a survey of that portion of the Bible, a book a day—Genesis on one day, Exodus on another day, Leviticus on the third day, Numbers on the fourth and ending with Deuteronomy on the fifth. Then with thirty-five days left, He would have five weeks to go back over the same ground, this time taking a book a week. We do not know. But it is possible.

In any case, when the temptation came, He was more than ready. He had at His hand the one weapon the enemy feared most: the Word of God, sharper than any two-edged sword, a critic of the thoughts and intents of the heart.

"Thy word have I hid in mine heart, that I might not sin against thee," said the psalmist (119:11). Jesus took His stand on the same ground. One suspects that Satan was none too keen for this encounter. He must have been appalled to see the Son of Man waiting for him, sword in hand.

The Devil had won such an easy victory over Eve by robbing her of her Bible. Indeed, she quoted it three times, but each time she made a mistake. Twice she subtracted from it and once she added to it. As a result, she ended up with a rough-and-ready paraphrase that Satan easily struck to the ground. In his very opening statement to Eve, he showed what he was after. "Yea, hath God said . . . ?" he began. Well he knew that so long as Eve had recourse to the Word of God in spirit and in truth, he was through.

As for Adam, he made no attempt at all to wield the Word of God against the temptation that engulfed him. Eve bungled her handling of God's Word, but Adam abandoned it altogether, substituting his own will in disobedience to God's will without the slightest trace of a struggle. Not so the second man, the last Adam. Satan appeared and found Him armed and ready.

## 1. The preparation

This encounter had been a long time in preparation. Satan had observed, with loathing and dread, the walk of God's Son on earth over a period of some thirty years. He had watched this one who had declared, "Lo, I come: in the volume of the book it is written of me, I delight to do thy will, O my God" (Ps. 40:7). Satan knew how truly Jesus could say, "I do always those things that please the Father." He had watched, for thirty years, a man on earth—man as God always intended man to be, man inhabited by God, filled with the Spirit of God, delighting in the Word of God, living the life of God, obedient to the will of God. He had watched Him since He was a baby, and there was never such a baby, absolutely free from any trace of self or sin. He had watched Him as a boy, perfectly natural, perfectly normal, and by the time He was twelve, fully aware of who He was and what He was: God, manifest in flesh, the only begotten, well-beloved Son of God.

Satan had watched Him as a man. He had sifted and studied His years as the village carpenter for just one wrong move. He had scrutinized Him in the home. He had kept an eagle eye on Him in the synagogue and, we can be sure, did his best to provoke some response, out of the will of God, for the kinds of things being taught by the rabbis. He had watched Him on high days and holy days. He had watched Him on His annual pilgrimages to Jerusalem. He had watched Him on His periodic visits to kinfolk at Capernaum. He had watched Him in His contact with the Jewish authorities, with the Roman authorities, with the citizens of his hometown, a town with an unsavory reputation, and he had watched Him in His contacts with the ragtag and bobtail crowds of Gentiles that passed through on the caravan routes.

Until at last we can envision a scene like that that confronts us in the book of Job. God might well have said to Satan, "Hast thou considered My Servant, Jesus, that there is none like Him in all the earth?" on one of the occasions when the sons of God came to present themselves before Him and when Satan came from walking to and fro on the earthly trail of God's Son.

"Considered Him?" we can hear Satan say. "Considered Him? I have done nothing but consider Him these past thirty years. Hast Thou not put a hedge about Him? There are great barricades and bulwarks between Him and me. You have twelve legions of angels, with drawn swords, that march as His honor guard everywhere He goes. You have Michael, the archangel, constantly at His side. You have Gabriel forever running to and fro between earth and heaven with reports. You have cherubim and seraphim. You have thrones and dominions. You have so hedged Him about that I cannot get anywhere near Him. Just take that hedge away. Let me get at Him, like I got to Adam and Eve, and there will be a different song to sing."

So the hedge was taken away, bit by bit, over forty days of fasting in the wilderness, and now Satan has his chance. All heaven and all hell watched with bated breath.

## 2. The provocation

When the last bit of the barricade was down, Satan came. In what guise, we wonder, did he come? Surely not as the old serpent. That guise had worn somewhat thin. Surely not as a roaring lion. Jesus was a Lion himself, the great Lion of the tribe of Judah. Satan came as an angel of light, perhaps, or as the god of this world, or as the prince of this world, or as the prince of the power of the air. Perhaps he switched from one guise to another as it suited him. It made no difference, after all. That "terrible, swift sword" in the hands of Jesus turned this way and that, stripping away one guise after the other as fast as they were assumed.

Jesus was ready and waiting. They were old acquaintances, of course. Jesus knew who he was. And though He was going to meet and master the Evil One simply and solely as man, nevertheless, He was God, and as God He knew Satan from of old.

He had been there when Satan had come demanding that he be allowed to put Job to the test. He had been there when judgment had been pronounced on the Serpent in the presence of fallen, naked, and wretched Adam and Eve. He had, indeed, pronounced the prophecy that had haunted the evil one for four thousand years about the coming of the seed of the woman. He had been there, in a dateless, timeless past, when this same Evil One had been known as the anointed cherub, as Lucifer, Son of the morning, when he had been arrayed in glory and beauty and was loved and honored as the choirmaster of heaven.

Oh yes, He knew who he was. He might have rightly said what Ahab so mistakenly said to Elijah, "Hast thou found me, O mine enemy?" (1 Kings 21:20). Well, of course, He had always known that this hour would come. It was to be the opening round, on earth, of a battle that will end with Satan banished forever to the lake that burns with fire.

Satan now surveyed the Son of God in His robe of perfect humanity. He had seen Him many a time in a glory that outshone the sun. He had seen Him as the mighty Creator hurling galaxies into space. He had seen Him on the great white throne of God, bathed in a light unapproachable, above the waters of the crystal sea. He had seen Him hailed and heralded by angels and the theme of seraphic song. Now he saw a man. And what a man! A man reduced to life's extremity by a forty-day fast. A glorious man, arrayed in absolute goodness, but gaunt and weary and worn down almost to the door of death. He had some hope then, perhaps, that after all he might succeed.

Satan attacked along three lines. He attacked along the line of God's provision. He attacked along the line of God's protection. He attacked along the line of God's program. As he looked at this man, Christ Jesus, he saw one who, to all outward seeming, had *no food, no fame,* and *no future.* This is what thirty years of the most perfect and rigid obedience to the Word and will of God had brought Him. Or so it seemed. Encouraged, the Evil One began.

### a. Along the line of God's provision: The promise of instant food

We can almost hear Satan say, "Well! Look at You! So this is what you get for serving God! He drives you by His Spirit into the wilderness, commands you to stay there since that is His good, and acceptable, and perfect will for your life, and then He leaves you to starve. What a God of love!

"You are hungry! You are desperately hungry! Your whole body cries out for food. You are at the extremity of physical exhaustion. Another day or so of this starvation and you will be dead! And then what will it all have come to?

"What kind of a God is He anyway, who would sit in silence and watch you slowly die of hunger? A few weeks ago, I was down there by the Jordan. You are not the only one I have been watching, you know. I have had my eye on that fellow John the Baptist for some time. One of these days, I'll get my hands on him too.

"Just the same, he does have some kind of reputation as being a prophet. But what kind of reputation do you have? People know you only as 'the carpenter's son!' I saw John baptize you in the river. I thought that was very silly. And I saw and heard what he saw and heard. I heard that voice from heaven announce that you are the Son of God. So, that is what you want people to believe, is it? Well! Go ahead and prove it! If Thou be the Son of God, command that these stones be made bread.

"*If!* You certainly don't look much like a God to me. If you were indeed the Son of God, you would be able to turn water into wine; you would be able to still the storm; you would be able to walk upon the waves; you would be able to multiply loaves and fishes in your hand; you would be able to turn these stones into bread. If you are God, act like God! Listen to me and you can have instant food. See what listening to your God has done for you. Now listen to me."

It was a temptation to act independently, to act in self-will, to act outside the will of God. It was a temptation to mistrust God and misuse a gift.

Jesus was ready for him. It was not for nothing He had been pondering the Pentateuch and dwelling in Deuteronomy for the past forty days. "It is written," He said, "man doth not live by bread alone, but by every word that proceedeth out of the mouth of the Lord" (Deut. 8:3). The Lord's appeal was not just to the spoken Word, but also to the written Word. Job, in his extremity, had said, "Though he slay me, yet will I trust Him" (13:15). Jesus was quite prepared to do the same. He knew that He was not going to starve to death. He had come into this world to die, that had been settled in heaven from before the foundation of the world, before ever Satan inaugurated the "mystery of iniquity" in the universe, but He had not come down here to die by starvation. He knew that, because as God He had been there, in the council chambers of eternity, when the decision had been made. And He knew it because, as God, He knew Psalms 22 and 69; Isaiah 53; and Zechariah 13:6. So Satan was defeated on that count. But he tried again.

### b. Along the line of God's protection: The promise of instant fame

"Ah!" the Devil said, "so that's it, is it? You are going to stick to the Word of God! You are going to throw Bible texts at me, are you? Well, I know the Bible too.

"You have been here for thirty years. Whatever have you been doing? You are supposed to be the Son of God! You seem to have been wasting both your time and your talents. Hardly anybody knows you. There is your family, but what do they amount to? They are just a handful of Galilean peasants. There is that fellow John the Baptist. True, he has a following, but he keeps hanging around in the wilderness, of all places. And now he has Herod and Herodias mad at him. He won't last long, I can tell you.

"You are going about things the wrong way. You need to do something spectacular, some kind of a publicity stunt, to get people's attention. I have a great plan for you. Just come with me." The Devil transported Christ to the temple in Jerusalem and set Him down on what is called "the pinnacle," most likely the southern wing of the temple, made magnificent by Herod's royal portico. Standing on the eastern edge of that portico, one could look down a sheer drop into the Kidron valley far below. It was a dizzying height.

"Now then," said the Devil. "What you need is instant fame. All you have to do is cast yourself down. You will be quite safe. You have quoted the Bible to me; I will quote it back to you. It is written: 'He shall give his angels charge concerning thee: and in their hands they shall bear thee up, lest at any time thou dash thy foot against a stone.'"

The quotation was a misquotation. It came from Psalm 91:11–12, and the Lord knew it by heart. He also knew that Satan had not quoted from the original Hebrew text but from a translation, from the Septuagint, the Greek version, because that rendering of the text came nearer to the emphasis he wanted to put upon the words. Moreover, he deliberately misquoted the passage. He left out the phrase "to keep thee in all thy ways," and added "at any time." And he had stopped short of the next verse, which foretold his own doom. But that is how the Devil quotes Scripture.

We look at the Lord Jesus, then, standing on the pinnacle where, of all places, He was in the public eye. Then Satan urged Him to cast himself down. For, with all his cunning and craftiness, Satan could not push the Lord down. Satan can persuade, but he cannot push.

In effect, he said to the Lord, "You are evidently determined to go by the Book. Well! Here is what the Book says. Now then, do it! You will have instant fame. After all, the world is waiting for a man who will really dare to take God at His word. Go ahead! Do something spectacular. Put God to the test. It is as simple as that. Instant fame."

Out came the Lord's sword again. "It is written," He said, "Thou shalt not tempt the Lord thy God" (Deut. 6:16). "You shall not put God to the test." It is only when we *doubt* a person that we make experiments to see how far they can be trusted. Foiled again, the Devil tried one more time. He had tried the Lord along the line of God's *provision* and along the line of God's *protection*. Now he presented a temptation along the line of God's program.

### c. Along the line of God's program: The promise of instant fortune

"If you listen to me," Satan said, "I will give you an instant fortune. I will set you on the throne of the world." We read, "Again, the Devil taketh him up into an exceedingly high mountain, and showeth him all the kingdoms of the world, and the glory of them; And saith unto him, All these things will I give thee, if thou wilt fall down and worship me."

Satan is the prince of this world; that is one of his titles. He was not given the principalities of this world by God, he seized them from Adam. As a result, he rules this world as its prince. In the spirit world, he sets up his "principalities and powers," the rulers of this world's darkness and wicked spirits in high places (Eph. 6:12) to supervise his plans and plots. On earth, he installs kings and rulers over the various nations and empires. The Lord Jesus did not dispute for one single moment the Devil's claim to be able to dispose of this world's kingdoms as he willed. The Lord had come to put an end to that very sovereignty in due course.

So we see Satan spread this world's vast kingdoms and empires out before Christ. "I have given these empires to various ones, down the long course of history," we can hear him say. "I gave them to young Alexander the Great, but he drank himself into an early grave. I gave them to Julius Caesar, but he dilly-dallied with the idea of becoming a king and was murdered. Right now, I have let one of this world's empires fall into the hands of a besotted fool named Tiberius. He is just one of my jokes. I can soon get rid of him.

"You are the kind of man I have been looking for. You are a better man than Alexander and a bigger man than Julius Caesar. You have great gifts and tremendous talents. Trust me, and I will put you where you can put your gifts to good use. I will put you on the throne of the world. Thereafter, you can put your own program into effect. All I ask is that, for just one moment, you bow your knee to me. Surely that is not much to ask for the throne of the entire world. Just a pinch of salt, as it were, on Caesars altar, and the world is yours. No cross! No conflict! No contest!"

In the hands of Christ, the mighty sword of the Spirit flashed again. "It is written, Thou shalt worship the Lord thy God and him only shalt thou serve" (Deut. 6:13). The battle was over and the war was won. All the way through, though He was indeed the *Son of God*, as Satan had twice mentioned, yet each time He met and mastered Satan as the *Son of Man*. It was as man that He was tempted; it was as man that He triumphed.

## 3. The proclamation

"Get thee hence, Satan!" Jesus said. He himself ended the affair. Satan was summarily dismissed by the triumphant man, Christ Jesus, and he departed, thoroughly beaten. From this moment on,

Satan became the conquered foe of our race. He had met his match. Though he used other tactics during the remaining three-and-a-half years of the Lord's earthly life, though he vented his rage at Calvary, his power had been broken, once and for all. Henceforth, throughout the Gospels, whenever Jesus had occasion to address those under Satan's sway, it was always in terms of His own absolute, sovereign authority and power.

When Satan comes our way, let us remember that we are not ignorant of his devices. He has but three cardinal temptations of offer. He may package them in different ways, but they are all that he has. They are the three temptations he offered to Christ.

There is the *lust of the flesh,* as offered to Christ in the first temptation; that He gratify His physical hunger contrary to the Word of God. There is the *lust of the eye,* as when Satan spread before Christ all the kingdoms of the world in all their glory. There is the *pride of life,* as when he suggested to Christ that, in vainglory and spiritual pride, He throw himself headlong from the temple crown. Moreover, we have the same mighty sword that Jesus wielded. Satan dreads and fears that sword as much today as he did when he ventured into Eden's grassy glens, and when He found his way to where a starving man awaited him in the wilderness.

## CHAPTER 7

# THE SERMON ON THE MOUNT
*Matthew 5:1–7:39*

WHEN MOSES RECEIVED THE LAW, and Israel's constitution, on Mount Sinai, it was amid scenes of terror and fear. There was a great sound of a trumpet. The whole mountain seemed to be on fire. The ground shook and quaked. The people cowered afar off in terror. Moses himself was terrified.

But that was a long, long time ago. Some fifteen hundred years had passed and a new age had dawned. The King had come, the King promised for so long. Not that He really looked like a king. There was none of the usual insignia of royalty. True, He could trace His lineage to David both through His mother, Mary, and His foster father, Joseph.

But there was no throne, no crown, no golden orb, no jeweled scepter, no imperial guard in burnished brass. There was just Jesus. Many of the people had known Him for years. He had grown up among them. They had known Him as the carpenter's son.

But He was the King, the last and only rightful heir to David's throne. Moreover, He had come to establish a kingdom that would last for all the ages of eternity. But not in the way the people expected. They sought and desired a king who would sally forth and smash the power of Rome, make Jerusalem the capital of a new world empire, and establish the Jews as head of all the nations of the earth. If there were to be new laws, then they should be given with all the proper pomp and ceremony. The place to issue such laws was Jerusalem. Mount Zion should be retaken. A palace should be built to outrival that of Solomon. The edicts should be accompanied by fanfare and cheering. But it was not like that at all. There He sat, in a homespun robe, surrounded by a handful of fishermen, a tax collector, and a few nondescript nobodies. He sat in the sunshine, overlooking a placid lake. Little children played around His feet. And He called for a standard of behavior that took one's breath away.

No such laws had ever been proposed. "Wholly impractical!" some would say. "Quite out of touch with reality." "He is just a visionary! As if anyone could live like that!" The fact, of course, was that He himself had lived like that for thirty years.

These laws have been hotly debated. Some think they are dispensational—that they belong to a future time, to the day when the Lord comes back to sit on the throne of His father David and rule from the river to the ends of the earth. They think these laws are millennial. Others are equally convinced that they are for today, that they set forth heaven's minimum standard of behavior, and that they can and must be lived by regenerated men and women indwelt and empowered by the Holy Spirit. There is probably truth on both sides of the issue: that they are for here and now, and for then and there. Let us look at them in broad perspective.

## 1. The contented man (5:1–12)

We call the opening paragraph of this sermon the Beatitudes. "Blessed," He says. "Blessed!" "Blessed is the man, woman, boy, or girl who does not do this, that, or the other, but who instead does thus and so."

The public ministry of the Lord Jesus, as recorded in Matthew's gospel, begins with nine beatitudes (chap. 5). It ends with eight curses (chap. 23). By the time the Lord put these precepts and principles into practice publicly, it was evident that nobody was ready for them, either in the capital or in the countryside. The nation, under its appointed leaders and in its religious, cultural, and political establishments, rejected them root and branch.

The word *blessed* means "happy." We are familiar with it from the Old Testament, especially from the book of Psalms. That is how the first psalm begins, "Blessed is the man that walketh not in the counsel of the ungodly . . ." The word is always in the plural. It means "happy, happy, happy is the man!" That is where the Lord begins. But what an extraordinary collection of things to make us happy. He does not say, "Happy is the man who has plenty of money in the bank." Or, "Happy is the woman who has a new wardrobe every season." Or, "Happy is the person who enjoys good health and who has a peaceful home." On the contrary, He says, "Happy are the mournful, the meek, and the merciful. Happy are the poor in spirit and the peacemakers, the pure in heart and the persecuted." Surely these things do not make us happy. This is a collection of the very things we spend our lives trying to avoid.

The beatitudes underline a basic fact of the kingdom that Christ's contemporaries never seemed to grasp. He told the bare truth to Pilate when He said, "My kingdom is not of this world" (Matt. 18:36).

He is, of course, going to establish a millennial kingdom in this world, but not until He has the right kind of people to put into it. That is why He starts as He does. He must first get some new men before He can build a new monarchy. He needs a race of people who are just like Him, the kind of people who have been made all over again into His image and after His likeness. Contented people, not because they like being poor and patient and peacemakers, and so on, but because they know that what the Lord is after is a new quality of life altogether. He wants us to have a life based on higher and holier principles than those found in the Old Testament law, a life made possible by the Spirit of God.

## 2. The conspicuous man (5:13–20)

He is the salt of the earth. He is the light of the world. He is a city set on a hill which cannot be hid. This is not carnal pride or even religious pride. This is not pride at all. This is simply a man, woman, boy, or girl being so much like Jesus in character, conduct, and conversation that he stands out from the ordinary rank and file of mankind.

Such a man was Henry Drummond, whose book on love, *The Greatest Thing in the World,* is a Christian classic. Sir George Adam Smith said that you might as well try to describe a perfume as attempt to describe Henry Drummond. Ian Maclaren said, "He was a singularly handsome man. But the distinctive and commanding feature of his face was his eye. No man could be base or mean or impure before that eye." Dr. Marcus Dods said that he was the most widely known, the best loved, and the most influential man of his time. D. L. Moody said, when he heard of Drummond's death, that the prospect of heaven had become invested with a new charm. Britain's great prime minister, William Gladstone, tried to get Drummond to enter Parliament. Lord Aberdeen, when appointed governor general of Canada in 1893, begged Henry Drummond to go with him because he was so very much like Jesus.

The story is told of a poor woman whose husband lay dying. Late one Saturday night she rang the bell at Henry Drummond's door. "My husband is dying, sir," she said. "He is not able to hear you, but I would like him to have a breath of you about him before he dies." He came about as close as any man of whom I have ever read, to actually live the Sermon on the Mount.

## 3. The consecrated man (5:21–48)

We see a man living beyond the demands and dictates of the Mosaic Law. The law of Moses represents heaven's minimum demands on the human race; and, even at that, setting forth a standard of behavior beyond all human hope of fulfillment. The Lord Jesus now took that law, lifted it from earth to heaven and said, "There! That is what the law is really all about." "Ye have heard . . . but I say unto you."

"Ye have heard!" The Lord was referring to the teaching of the rabbis who took the law of Moses, passed it through the prism of their minds, and broke it into an immensely cumbersome and burdensome body of trivia. Lethal trivia, however.

The rabbis debated for years a simple Mosaic precept: "Thou shalt not seethe a kid in his mother's milk" (Deut. 14:21). By the time they had finished, they had succeeded in filling the average Jewish kitchen with ritualistic booby traps. They called for separate pots for this, different pans for that, and woe betide the housewife who accidentally used the wrong dish for the milk or for the meat! The Lord Jesus consigned all such exegetical nonsense to the rubbish heap. Instead, He passed the law of Moses through the prism of His own holy intellect and showed its spiritual nature of perfection. Murder was a capital offense. True! But He traced murder to the anger that spawned it. Adultery was a capital offense. True again! He denounced the lustful look that resulted in adultery.

He called for a degree of consecration utterly and absolutely impossible to any unregenerated man or any carnal and worldly Christian. He called for absolute perfection—and then lived that life to demonstrate that He, as man inhabited by God, could take the law in His stride. The genius of the gospel lies in two great facts. First, Jesus gave His life *for* me. Now, Jesus gives his life *to* me. It is the great work of the Holy Spirit to live this impossible life in us as He lived it in Christ.

## 4. The concealed man (6:1–18)

It should be evident to all that there is no explanation for the believer's life except God. At the same time, there are some aspects of our lives as believers that should be kept secret. We are to pray—but in secret. We are to fast—but in secret. We are to give to the needy—but in secret. If we do these things in order to be seen of men and in order to receive the applause of men, as the Pharisees did, then we already have our reward. If we do them in secret, God will one day reward them openly.

In one of His parables, the Lord held up for inspection the kind of man who makes a public display of his devotions. He told the story of the Pharisee and the publican. The Pharisee struck an attitude and proceeded to boast to God of his own goodness. He fasted. He gave tithes. He was a very fine fellow indeed. He was thankful that he was not as other men are. He was certainly not like the publican, who was standing over there beating his breast and calling on God to be merciful to him because he was such a sinner. Jesus simply says that the publican "prayed with himself."

But, when we do seek out the secret place, how should we pray? What should we say? The Lord gave us the model prayer. We begin by addressing ourselves to "Our Father." What a marvelous thing that is—Our Father! God is not the Father of all men. He is the creator of all men, but He is only the Father of those who have been born into His family. The name *Father* is the greatest name for God in the Bible. In the Old Testament, God was known as *Elohim*, as *Jehovah*, and as *Adonai*. He was known as *Jehovah-Jireh, Jehovah-Nissi, Jehovah-Shalom,* and *Jehovah-Tsidkenue.* He was the God of Creation, the God of Covenant, and the God of Command. It was Jesus who taught us to pray: "Our Father."

Then we occupy ourselves in prayer with where He is and who He is. He is in heaven and He is holy. His Name is a hallowed name.

Next, we align ourselves with His great purposes. We lay siege to His throne for the speedy coming of His kingdom—the true answer to all this world's spiritual, social, and secular needs. We implore Him that His will might be done on earth as it is in heaven. The book of Revelation was written to show us how and when God will answer that prayer.

Only then do we ask something for ourselves. We ask for food and for forgiveness. We make known to him our physical needs and our spiritual needs. We ask Him also to deliver us from evil.

Then we come back to the things that lie so near to His heart. We conclude with: "Thine is the kingdom and the power and the glory for ever. Amen."

## 5. The carefree man (6:19–34)

Many of life's worries come to us because of our concerns about money. Those who have money are worried lest they lose it. Those who do not have money are worried because they need it. The Lord brings such mundane, material matters into focus.

There is the problem of *prosperity*—not that most people would think that to be a problem. Most people think that having plenty of money is the answer to most of life's problems. The trouble with money is that it can buy almost everything, except happiness and holiness. Moreover, it has a way of disappearing. One wrong investment is sometimes all it takes to wipe out a person's life savings. A sudden downturn in the economy, a crash on Wall Street, and disaster looms. The Lord has the answer to all that. Invest in heaven! As a preacher friend of mine says, "If you want to have treasure in heaven, it is a good idea to give some money to someone who is going there!" The story is told of a man who gave away large sums of money to the Lord's work. Then he lost his business. Someone said to him, "Don't you wish now you hadn't given so much away?" "Oh, no," he said, "That is all I really have."

There is also the problem of *poverty*. The rich man worries about what to do with his money. The poor man worries about what to do without any money. The Lord Jesus knows all about being poor. He was born into a poor family and knew the pinch of poverty. He had not where to lay His head at times. He knows the anxiety, the privation, the special problems of the poor. "Look at the birds! Look at the flowers!" He advised. "They are miraculously provided for by their heavenly Father." The world's wealthiest millionaire could not afford to feed all the birds in the world for a single day. God does it with effortless ease. So, why worry? We are of much more value to him than birds, yet He attends the funeral of even a sparrow. How much more He knows and understands our needs.

## 6. The compassionate man (7:1–5)

"Judge not, that ye be not judged," Jesus said. This, of course, has nothing to do with the careful weighing of a man's doctrine. We are to judge that. Nor does it mean, surely, that we are not to take note of a man's conduct. There are some teachings and some practices that call for punishment.

What the Lord means here is that we should not judge a person's motives. Nor should we be hasty in our judgment; maybe we do not have all the facts. The book of Job is a classic biblical example of judging a man wrongly simply on the basis of circumstantial evidence.

Likewise, when Aaron and Miriam criticized Moses for marrying a woman of whom they did not approve, Miriam was smitten with leprosy for her presumption and Aaron escaped only because he was the high priest. In any case, it was necessary (both in the case of Job and Moses) for the injured and insulted party to act as mediator.

The Lord tells us that we should look at ourselves before passing judgment on other people. We may be trying, He says, with a touch of irony, to extract a splinter from a brother's eye when all the time we have a rafter in our own.

There are times when judgment is necessary, but it needs to be exercised only after heart searching and after a consideration of all the facts. And, even then, it is to be tempered with mercy.

## 7. The confident man (7:6–11)

"Ask, and it shall be given you; seek and ye shall find; knock, and it shall be opened unto you." Heaven opens up before us. Paths are made clear to our feet. Doors swing open to us. All, of course, in the will of God.

The whole question of prayer and guidance is introduced here. We do not have to grope along in the dark. God sovereignly controls all the factors of time and space. He sees the end from the beginning. He plans wisely and wonderfully for us. We are to be in touch with heaven, so far as all our decisions and desires are concerned. God's plans and decisions are always best. When Israel marched out of Egypt, it would have seemed that the best way to get to Canaan, the shortest and the quickest way, was along the coast road. But then, Israel would have arrived in the land wholly unprepared for battle. So God took them all down around the Sinai Peninsula. He decided that, for Israel, the longest way around was the shortest way home.

Similarly, the apostle Paul, on his second missionary journey, kept finding his way blocked. It was puzzling to him. He had his eye, for example, on the busy and strategic city of Ephesus. God kept on closing doors. But once Paul came to Troas, all at once the way was made plain. He must cross over into Europe and evangelize Greece. Only after that was done did God open the way for Paul to go to Ephesus. God had not said, "No!" He had simply said, "Later!"

And so it is in all of life's decisions, great and small, if we let the Lord lead us. The key, of course, is our daily quiet time when, Bible in hand, we say with the young lad Samuel, "Speak Lord; for Thy servant heareth" (see 1 Sam. 3:9).

## 8. The Christlike man (7:12)

"Therefore all things whatsoever ye would that men should do to you, do ye even so to them: for this is the law and the prophets." There was a provision in the law, for example, that stated that if a man came across his enemy's cow wandering away, he must take it back to him. That was the law of love. That was the Golden Rule. That was designed to disarm enmity and turn a foe into a friend.

There was the time, for example, when the king of Syria sent a detachment of troops to seize the prophet Elisha—but, instead, Elisha captured them (2 Kings 6:8–23). He smote them with blindness and led them into the heart of the city of Samaria. When their eyes were then opened, they saw their peril. The Israelite king rubbed his hands and said to Elisha, "My father, shall I smite them? shall I smite them?" "Of course not?" in effect snapped the prophet. "Feed them. Sit them down to a banquet and then send them back home to Syria." The Holy Spirit adds, "So the bands of Syria came no more into the land of Israel." That is the way to disarm an enemy. Show him the kindness of God.

The Lord summed it all up. "Do unto others what you would like them to do unto you." He himself, of course, is the greatest example of that divine principle. People say that Christianity has failed. It would be more true to say that it has rarely been tried.

## 9. The cautious man (7:13–23)

The Lord tells us to beware, for there are false paths and there are false prophets. We need to look for the strait gate and for the narrow way. We need to look out for wolves in sheep's clothing. We are in a hostile world. Satan has his Doubting Castles along the way and has his Vanity Fairs. We are to beware of Mr. Worldly Wiseman and of Madam Bubble and of Mr. Legalist and all that great cast of characters that John Bunyan has created for us to warn of the perils on the way home. There is Bypass Meadow, there is Forgetful Green, and there is the Slough of Despond.

We need to be cautious. There is one infallible way to test a man's teachings. A good tree brings forth good fruit; an evil tree brings forth evil fruit. "By their fruits ye shall know them," Jesus said.

Our beliefs always affect our behavior. That is the basic principle behind nearly all of the Pauline Epistles. Invariably, Paul devotes the first half of a letter to what we should believe and the second half to how we should behave.

I knew a man some years ago who held the most pernicious views on the person of Christ. He was an absolutely charming individual. I stayed in his home before I knew what secret thoughts and designs he harbored. He was well-to-do, charming, gentlemanly, hospitable, and popular. He was a respected elder of his church. His family was exemplary. He satisfied himself, for years, with entrenching himself in his position and occasionally dropping a cautious hint as to what he really believed. When he was finally confronted, it was by a young, first-term missionary back from the foreign field. Before it was through, a score of churches were split down the middle over the issue. Those who understood their Bibles took a stand against him.

Many, deceived by his charm and reputation for godliness, thought he must be right. Churches were split. Families were split. The man's heretical views were carried to the mission field and took root there. The man was a wolf in sheep's clothing. "By their fruits ye shall know them," Jesus said. Some people looked at the man's morally blameless life and at his personal charm and thought that was the fruit. Oh no. The fruit was there to be seen in split churches and divided families. My father saw through him years before others did and sought to warn me against him.

## 10. The conscientious man (7:24–39)

The Lord brings us back to His Word, to the inspired Word of God. He told the story of the two builders; the one who built his house on the sand, and the other who built his house on the rock. The difference between the two men, as Jesus interpreted the parable, lay in the fact that the wise man both heard and heeded the Lord's teaching. The foolish man built on something else. He heard but did not heed, and all his work came to nought in the end.

## CHAPTER 8

# THE MYSTERY PARABLES
*Matthew 13*

1. The parables spoken publicly
   a. The sower: The message of salvation—the dispositional aspect of things
   b. The tares: The malice of Satan—the diabolical aspect of things
   c. The mustard seed: The myth of supremacy—the dispensational aspect of things
   d. The leaven: The mystery of subversion—the doctrinal aspect of things
2. The parables spoken privately
   a. The treasure: A national postponement—the Hebrew people
   b. The pearl: A new possession—the heavenly people
   c. The dragnet: A necessary process—the heathen people

THESE ARE PARABLES OF THE kingdom of heaven. First it must be noted that there is a difference between the kingdom of heaven and the kingdom of God. The kingdom of God is eternal; the kingdom of heaven is temporal. The kingdom of God is eternal, immutable, and infinite; the kingdom of heaven relates to God's purposes in time and in relation to this earth.

The kingdom of God is eternal. It is from everlasting to everlasting. It embraces both human and heavenly hosts. The psalmist caught the idea when he said, "Thy throne, O God, is for ever and ever" (Ps. 45:6). Nebuchadnezzar also caught a glimpse of it. He said, in a remarkable state document, "I praised and honoured him that liveth for ever, whose dominion is an everlasting dominion, and his kingdom is from generation to generation" (Dan. 4:34). Jesus taught us to pray, "Thine is the kingdom, and the power, and the glory, for ever" (Matt. 6:13). Indeed, the expression "forever and ever" is one of the key expressions in the Apocalypse, and it should be traced out and underlined. Such is the kingdom of God.

The kingdom of heaven is temporal. It relates to a period of time, carved out of eternity, during which God intends to set up a kingdom on planet Earth. This planet, we must remember, flies the flag of rebellion in the face of the universe. God, therefore, either has to annihilate it or subdue it. It has always been His purpose to subdue it. The story of this planet's rebellion against the throne, the might, the majesty, and the authority of God in heaven is a very long one indeed. It goes back beyond the creation of Adam and Eve and the beginnings of the human race. The "mystery of iniquity" is far older than mankind. Sin did not begin on Earth, it began in heaven. Its author was not the federal head of the human race, but a being of great power and authority in the universe long before the creation of humanity.

The original statement of creation is given in Genesis 1:1: "In the beginning God created the heaven and the earth." The statement draws our attention to two focal centers—heaven and earth. It ignores all the galaxies and super-galaxies. It concentrates on two locations: heaven, where God is undisputed Sovereign, and Earth, where His sovereignty is denied.

It seems evident that, between the statement in verse 1 and the statement in verse 2—"and the earth was without form, and void"—something went wrong. However, the Holy Spirit tells us elsewhere that it was not created that way (Isa. 45:18). Some Hebraists agree that the verb *was* can be translated "became." "The earth became without form and void." In other words, this planet of ours was the scene of a catastrophe long before the creation of the human race.

The state of affairs described in Genesis 1:2 must have had a cause. It may well have had something to do with the fall of Lucifer (Isa. 14:9–14; Ezek. 28:12–15). It may well have been that our solar system was once included in Lucifer's sphere of rule. Perhaps a pre-Adamic race inhabited Earth at that time. The fall of Lucifer and the chaotic state of the planet may have occurred simultaneously. If there was a prehistoric race of people on this planet, it would explain the existence of demons. Unlike angels, which have the power of assuming bodily form at will, demons crave the bodies of living people. That would suggest that they are disembodied spirits, who haunt the scene of their existence, lusting after bodies through which to express themselves. In the Gospels, we read of one wretched man who was invaded and inhabited by a legion of them.

The account of "creation" in Genesis would seem, rather, to be an account of the restoration of this planet, by divine decree, as a place suitable for human inhabitation. It was restored by God and blessed by Him to be the home of a new order of creation—the human race.

Having renovated the planet, God created its new overlord, Adam. He gave him dominion (Gen. 1:26–30) and crowned him with glory and honor (Heb. 2:6–8). The rule of the kingdom of heaven began. Earth was a subsidiary of heaven. That "the heavens do rule" was the great principle that both Nebuchadnezzar and Belshazzar had to learn (Dan. 4:25; 5:21).

We do not know how long it was before Satan, fallen Lucifer, made his move. We can only surmise the rage, envy, and malice with which he viewed the human race. If Adam had not sinned, he would have soon extended his rule from the Garden to the globe, and eventually, no doubt, from the globe to the galaxy.

However, Adam surrendered his sovereignty to Satan. Satan at once set up his kingdom, the kingdom "of darkness," on this planet (Col. 1:13). He ruled as "the prince of this world" (Matt. 4:8–9; John 16:11) as well as "the prince of the power of the air" (Eph. 2:2). He set up his angels as overlords of this planet, so that, to this day, the

various nations of the world are under the rule of Satan's overlords
in the spirit realm. We are up against these unseen invaders from
outer space whenever we engage in prayer or in Christian work. They
are called "principalities and powers"; "rulers of the darkness of this
world"; "wickedness in high places" (Eph. 3:10; 6:12).

In the process of time, God began all over again with a man called
Abraham. When He called him, He promised to make of him "a great
nation" (Gen. 12:1–3). In essence, He brought into being a new nation over which Satan had no prince. Instead, God put Michael, the
archangel, over the nation of Israel, which developed from Abraham's
seed. Michael is called "the prince that standeth for thy people" (Dan.
10:21; 12:1; Rev. 12:1–10). God entered into a treaty relationship with
Abraham and the nation developed through him. Israel, indeed, is
the only country on earth that enjoys a treaty relationship with God
(Gen. 12:1–3; 13:14–18; 15:1–21; 17:1–22).

Despite all of Israel's failures as a nation, that treaty relationship
holds solid for the simple reason that it was absolutely unconditional.
Israel was to be a theocratic kingdom under the direct rule of heaven.
It was raised up and ordained to bear witness to all the other nations of
the world of the nature, character, wisdom, love, and power of God.

In time, the kingdom purposes of heaven in relation to earth
were advanced by the enthronement of David as Israel's king and the
founding of a dynasty that, in time, would produce the Messiah, the
Son of God himself (2 Sam. 7:16).

Much of the history of the monarchy is taken up with the dismal
failure of Israel's and Judah's kings to even approximate the divine
ideal. Nevertheless, God pursued His purpose of bringing His own
Son into the world as part of David's line—to be David's Son and
David's Lord. In the fullness of time, the promised Messiah was born,
of David's seed, in David's city. He was announced to the nation by
His God-sent herald, John the Baptist, who announced to the people
that the kingdom of heaven was at hand (Matt. 3:2; 4:17, 23). John
called the people to repentance, and exhorted them to prepare their
hearts and lives for the expected establishment of the kingdom.

Jesus began His ministry by first defeating Satan in the wilderness

(Matt. 4:1–11). He then set about preparing the nation of Israel for the setting up of the kingdom. He proclaimed the laws of the kingdom in the famous Sermon on the Mount (Matt. 5:7ff.). He manifested His power in an astonishing and seemingly endless series of miracles (Matt. 8–9, etc.), and manifested His wisdom in revolutionary new teaching. He sent out His heralds (Matt. 10). He issued urgent warnings against unbelief (Matt. 11). And then the religious establishment accused Him of performing His miracles in the power of the Devil (Matt. 12:24). This rejection of Christ and His kingdom could only have one ending—the cross. Moreover, this rejection of their Messiah brought down His curse on their heads. He accused them of blaspheming the Holy Spirit, which He declared to be an unpardonable sin.

A crisis had come. The kingdom of heaven went underground. God's plans and purposes centered in the nation of Israel were postponed. This crisis was every bit as great as the crisis that had ended the monarchy in the days of Nebuchadnezzar.

God had vested two great rights in the nation of Israel. One was political, the other religious. Israel was to be given both secular and spiritual sovereignty over the nations. Because of Israel's failure, however, God terminated its secular sovereignty and handed world dominion over to the Gentiles. With Nebuchadnezzar and the fall of Jerusalem, the "times of the Gentiles" began. The Babylon captivity ended the Old Testament monarchy. Israel became a dependency. The time of Gentile supremacy is to last to the end times. The Antichrist, the last of the Caesars, will be in power when, at the return of Christ, the "times of the Gentiles" will end.

Israel, however, retained its spiritual sovereignty over the nations, even after its secular sovereignty was suspended. But now another crisis had come. The nation of Israel and the Jewish people rejected Christ and handed Him over to the Gentiles for crucifixion. Thus Israel lost her spiritual ascendancy. It was given to the church, which is predominantly Gentile. This period of Gentile spiritual ascendancy began on the Day of Pentecost and will end with the rapture of the church. During this time, a Jew must turn his back on Judaism and turn to Christ if he wishes to be saved. When Israel's spiritual sovereignty was suspended, the nation itself was scattered and dispersed by the Romans. They took Jerusalem in A.D. 70 and ended Jewish national life in A.D. 135 at the time of the Bar Cochba rebellion.

It was with these drastic and far-reaching changes in mind that the Lord Jesus adopted a new method of teaching. God's plan to set up the kingdom of heaven on earth was to be postponed for some indeterminate time, now going on two thousand years. During this age, He would be occupied with a new entity altogether, unknown and undreamed of in Old Testament times—the church. It was for this reason that the Lord began a form of teaching, in the "mystery parables," in which He purposely sought to conceal truth from the world while revealing it to His own disciples.

He clearly states this purpose in Matthew 13, which contains a series of seven parables. In these parables, the Lord teaches that, during this present age, things would be quite different from the way they were in the past. The kingdom of heaven was still going to exist, but it would exist in "mystery" form. Most people would have no comprehension whatsoever of what was really going on. Henceforth there would be three separate entities in the world: the Gentile nations, which would dominate the globe; the exiled nation of Israel, buried among the Gentile nations and blind to spiritual truth; and the church, the mystical body of Christ made up of Jews and Gentiles without racial or religious distinction, but predominately Gentile in composition and character. This truth is developed further by Paul in Romans 9–11.

Of the seven parables, four were spoken to the multitudes, outdoors by the seaside, and three were spoken indoors, secretly, to the disciples. The four parables spoken to the general public all emphasize the seeming outward failure of church and kingdom alike during this present age. The three parables spoken privately to the disciples reveal God's secret plans and emphasize the sure and certain success of those plans despite all the malice, guile, and power of the enemy.

One problem we face in interpreting these parables lies in a failure to distinguish between the kingdom of heaven and the church of Christ. The church has a relationship to the kingdom of God and to the kingdom of heaven. It is, however, quite unique. Believers in the

Lord Jesus, in this age, for instance, are in the kingdom of God, but they are also the "mystical body of Christ," which sets them apart from all other entities in the universe.

Here is an important distinction, however. We are *born again* into the kingdom and we are *baptized* into the church. Jesus said to Nicodemus, "Except a man be born again, he cannot see the kingdom of God" (John 3:3). "Being born again," says Peter, "not of corruptible seed, but of incorruptible, by the Word of God" (1 Peter 1:23). We are born into the kingdom. We are baptized into the church. "For by one Spirit are we all baptized into one body" (1 Cor. 12:12–14).

Insofar as the church has succumbed to Satan's attacks during this age, it has become what we call "Christendom." It is this failure that is emphasized in the first four parables. In this respect, the church is as big a failure in this age as Israel was in the previous age. It is in these first four parables that the history of the kingdom of heaven and of Christendom run together. The essential difference between Israel, the church, and the nations is carefully sorted out for us by the Lord in the last three parables.

Before looking at these "mystery parables," we might do well to finish the story. The "mystery" phase of the kingdom of heaven will end with the rapture of the church. At that time, Israel will have her spiritual sovereignty restored to her, for "the fulness of the Gentiles" will have "come in," as Paul puts it in Romans 11:25.

God will raise up two witnesses, one of whom will be the old Hebrew prophet Elijah. These two witnesses will win 144,000 Jewish converts, who in turn will proclaim the gospel of the kingdom to the unevangelized multitudes still on earth. They will penetrate all nations with the message of a soon-coming King and reap an enormous harvest. Those saved at this time will not be in the church, they will be in the kingdom.

The discredited, apostate, professing church will still be on earth, the true church having been raptured to heaven. The harlot church, will have been, in effect, spewed out of Christ's mouth. The whole corrupt religious system, known as Christendom, will find its headquarters in Rome. It will ally itself with the Antichrist, the papacy thus hoping to get back its lost power. The Vatican will think it can use the Antichrist. Instead he will use the Vatican, and then destroy the apostate church utterly, root and branch (Rev. 17).

The Lord will return at the end of this apocalyptic age, regaining control of the planet at the battle of Armageddon. The Antichrist and his false prophet will be cast into the lake of fire, and the Devil will be chained in the Abyss. The "times of the Gentiles" will have come to an end. The kingdom of heaven will then be restored to Israel. The Lord will sit on the throne of David and usher in the millennial age. The kingdom will have come. It will last for one thousand years (Rev. 20:1–10). It will be terminated by a final rebellion, instigated by Satan when he is released from the Abyss. Satan and his followers will then be overthrown, and Satan will be cast into the lake of fire, and his mischief-making in the universe will be terminated forever.

God's kingdom purposes with relation to the earth will be over. The kingdom of heaven phase of the kingdom of God will be ended. The Lord will surrender the kingdom to His Father (1 Cor. 15:24–28) and the kingdom of heaven will be no more. The kingdom of God will continue on forever and ever. All will be related, then, to a new heaven and a new earth (Rev. 21:1–8).

That is the background of the seven mystery parables. Now let us briefly examine them.

## 1. The parables spoken publicly

*a. The sower: The message of salvation—the dispositional aspect of things*

The first of these parables is the parable of the sower, the seed, and the soil. Over these first four parables we can write the word *failure*, for that is what men see.

The seed is sown. It hardly amounts to anything. The Lord thus reveals *the Devil's method*. He sends his evil spirits to snatch away the seed. Hardly is a gospel service over than a roar of chatter takes over. The solemn atmosphere is gone. The heart-searching words are forgotten. Here and there, a more thoughtful person makes a response. But again there is little to show for it. Sometimes persecution arises and the profession of faith is hastily abandoned. Sometimes prosperity and all that it can buy chokes out the seed. Sometimes poverty and anxious care stifles the initial profession of faith. In any case, much of it comes to nothing. It largely turns out to be a false profession of faith.

Even where the response is genuine, fruitfulness is limited. There is fruit, but precious little of it. Only a small percentage of those who respond go on to full maturity in Christ. The Devil's method is to hinder the work of God.

### b. The tares: The malice of Satan—the diabolical aspect of things

The Lord now sows His men into the world. First it was the apostles and the prophets, now it is the evangelist, the pastor, and the teacher. This time we are introduced to *the Devil's ministers*, who are sown in and among the Lord's workers. They are called "the children of the Wicked One." These are men who propagate heresy. These are those who conceive and cultivate cults. These are the rank unbelievers who become faculty members in seminaries and pastors of liberal churches. Satan thus produces a counterfeit church.

### c. The mustard seed: The myth of supremacy—the dispensational aspect of things

The third parable is the parable of the mustard seed. This parable introduces us to *the Devil's masterpiece*. God introduces His church into this scene. It was intended to be the fruit of the little mustard seed, a humble shrub. Instead it becomes something God never intended for the church to be in the world. It becomes a great tree with far-flung branches, a home for evil spirits. This depicts the full development of Christendom. That which was supposed to be a church becomes, instead, a great worldly kingdom with its own sovereign state, its own head of state, its own armies, and ambassadors. It signs treaties. It persecutes the true church. Its tentacles reach into all parts of the world.

*d. The leaven: The mystery of subversion—the doctrinal aspect of things*

The fourth parable is the parable of the leaven hidden in the meal. This introduces us to *the Devil's message*. Leaven, throughout Scripture, is uniformly and invariably used as a symbol of evil. It is nearly always used as a symbol of doctrinal evil, though Paul uses it also as a symbol of moral evil. The truth is taught, and Satan instantly goes to work to insert into Christian teaching the leaven of false doctrine. Many of the New Testament epistles were written to combat false doctrine.

Such, then, is the outward aspect of things during this age. Everywhere there is failure; the enemy is not only at work, he enjoys great success. He always seems to win. Christendom is the result. When people think of the church, they usually think of that vast system of religion that began to develop around the second or third centuries of the Christian era, and that is today represented by the Roman, Greek, and Orthodox churches, the various Protestant and nonconformist denominations, the state churches, and a host of cults and organizations, all of which claim to be Christian. That is not the church, it is Christendom, and that is what is seen in the first four parables.

## 2. The parables spoken privately

The three parables spoken in private deal with the kingdom of heaven and God's secret and successful plan to bring it to earth in due time.

*a. The treasure: A national postponement—the Hebrew people*

The parable of the hidden treasure is a parable of the nation of Israel. The treasure is hidden in a field, which Jesus has already said is the world. The man in the parable is the Lord Jesus. He knew all about the field and the treasure. He knew about Israel, uprooted and scattered and buried in the Gentile world, a treasure of infinite worth to God. He purchased the field at Calvary. In the book of Ruth, Boaz, the mighty man of wealth, purchased not only Ruth's person but also her property. The story illustrates God's purpose to redeem Israel and to restore her to her rightful position in the world. God has not canceled His kingdom purposes regarding Israel. He has only postponed them.

### b. The pearl: A new possession—the heavenly people

The parable of the pearl of great price is a parable of the true church. In the Bible, the earth is associated with Israel, God's earthly people, and the sea is associated with the Gentile nations. The pearl was to be found in the sea, for the church is largely Gentile in composition.

The pearl was found in the sea, but it was destined for the sky. When we get to the closing chapters of the book of Revelation, we find twelve gates of pearl. All access to the glory land is through those gates. The church has the secret of access to heaven.

### c. The dragnet: A necessary process—the heathen people

The parable of the dragnet in the sea is a parable of the Gentile nations at the end of this age, after the rapture of the church. The net will be lowered again into the Gentile sea. The 144,000 Jewish evangelists will proclaim the gospel of the kingdom to Gentiles far and wide. Millions will be saved. Then, just before the outpouring of the vials of God's wrath, an angel will be sent to preach what is called "the everlasting gospel." Again the net will sweep the wide Gentile sea. It will harvest a mixture of good and bad. The sorting out will be done by the angels at the second coming of Christ.

During the Second World War, we in Britain used to listen to the BBC news. It was always bad. We had been driven out of France, we were being chased out of North Africa, the battle of Britain was raging, and vast armadas of enemy bombers were coming over in successive waves, bombing our cities into rubble and ruin. The BBC, however, always had a pet phrase to cover the situation. It used to assure us that "things were proceeding according to plan." We look at the progress of God's Word and of His kingdom in this world. It seems, mostly, to be bad news. Evil men and seducers are waxing worse and worse. Apostasy is the hallmark of much of the professing church. The stage is being set for the coming of the man of sin. Nevertheless, God is still on the throne. He is unperturbed by it all. Things are proceeding according to plan. God is working to His own agenda; the mystery parables reveal exactly what that agenda is.

## CHAPTER 9

# THE MIRACLES OF JESUS

1. Introduction
2. Transcending natural laws in a supernatural way
   a. Changing water into wine
   b. Feeding the five thousand
   c. Walking on the water
   d. Stilling the storm
3. Transforming needy lives in a supernatural way
   a. Power over disease
   b. Power over demons
   c. Power over death
   d. Power over distance
   e. Power over disability
4. Conclusion

## 1. Introduction

The Lord Jesus performed many miracles. Nobody else performed so many miracles, of such variety, and with such evident proof that he was acting, not just for God but as God. The Gospels record only thirty-five or thirty-six of Christ's miracles. Of these, nineteen are recorded in only one gospel; five are recorded in two gospels; eleven are recorded in three gospels; and one, the miracle of the feeding of the five thousand, is recorded in all four. Of these many and varied miracles, only one was a miracle of judgment—the cursing of the fig tree. All the rest were miracles of government and grace. Most of them simply prove Peter's remarkable summary of the life of the Lord Jesus: He "went about doing good" (Acts 10:38). And so He did. The miracles He performed were ample evidence of His goodness and His greatness. He had come to destroy all the power of the enemy. His miracles were part of the ceaseless battle that raged between the incarnate Son of God and the forces of evil, and of Satan, all the years the Lord Jesus lived on earth.

Although the four evangelists record three dozen of Christ's miracles, they certainly do not record them all. On various occasions in the Gospels, we have whole series of miracles all lumped together in a sweeping statement. For instance, Mark records, "And at even, when the sun did set, they brought unto him all that were diseased, and them that were possessed with devils. And all the city was gathered together at the door. And he healed many that were sick of divers diseases, and cast out many devils" (Mark 1:32–34). Matthew records, "And his fame went throughout all Syria: and they brought unto him all sick people that were taken with divers diseases and torments, and those which were possessed with devils, and those which were lunatik, and those that had the palsy; and he healed them" (Matt. 4:24). Matthew records again, "And great multitudes followed him, and he healed them all" (Matt. 12:15). And again, "And Jesus went forth, and saw a great multitude, and was moved with compassion toward them, and he healed their sick" (Matt. 14:14).

As an old man, thinking back over the astonishing three-and-a-half years he had spent in the company of Jesus, the aged John confessed, just as he put down his pen, "And there are also many other things which Jesus did, the which, if they should be written every one, I suppose that even the world itself could not contain the books that should be written" (John 21:25).

The Lord Jesus performed miracles. They are attested by eyewitnesses, men whose testimony can be made to stand up in court.[1] When the four evangelists tell us about the miracles of Jesus, miracles that defy all the laws of nature, we can rest assured they are telling the truth. These things happened. These men are not spreading cunningly devised fables. They are recording sober facts.

Paul challenged King Agrippa along similar lines. He said to him, when attesting to the person of Christ and above all to His resurrection from the dead, "This thing was not done in a corner" (Acts 26:26).

When God created man, He made him in His own image and after His own likeness. He gave him dominion over the works of his hands and power over the laws of nature. The planet and its potential were put beneath man's feet. Before Adam could enter into the vast potential that was his, however, sin entered, followed by death. The writer of Hebrews, looking upon the wreck and ruin of the world in which we live and at man's limited ability to control his environment, wrote, "Thou madest him a little lower than the angels; thou crownest him with glory and honour, and didst set him over the works of thy hands: Thou hast put all things in subjection under his feet. . . . But now we see not yet all things put under him. But we see Jesus" (Heb. 2:7–9).

The Lord Jesus is called "the second man" and "the last Adam." He came to restore man's lost estates, man's lost dominion. And so He did. We see it in every move He made. *Jesus had mastery over the fish of the sea.* On two occasions, He enabled the disciples to catch a vast multitude of fish when they, themselves, expert fishermen that they were, had toiled all night in the same waters and caught nothing. At a word from their Creator, the fish of the sea, whole schools of fish, came and flung themselves into Simon Peter's nets.

On another occasion, He exhibited the same mastery over a single fish as over a school of fish. When Peter was worried about being able to pay their taxes, Jesus told him to take his fishing line and go down to the lake where he would catch a fish with a coin in its mouth. Sure enough, so he did! Jesus knew all about the one fish in the Sea of Galilee that was swimming around with a coin in its mouth. No sooner had Peter's line hit the water than that fish came in, obedient to the Master's will, to give him the coin he so badly needed. Jesus had mastery over the fish of the sea. They came instantly at His call.

He had mastery over the *beasts of the field.* For forty days the Lord

Jesus wandered far from the haunts of men, in a waste, howling wilderness. He was under constant pressure from the Evil One. But He was not altogether alone. Mark tells us He "was with the wild beasts" (Mark 1:13). The lion, the fox, and the bear, came to keep Him company. They knew Him. They loved Him. They liked to be near Him. He was their Maker and their Master. They felt at home with Him. They nuzzled Him, enjoyed the sheer ecstasy of His presence, looked upon Him as their natural friend, and helped Him pass those long, lonely hours in the wilderness of Judea.

Jesus had equal mastery over *domesticated beasts.* At His bidding, His disciples brought to Him an unbroken colt, an animal upon which no human being had yet sat. The disciples put a makeshift saddle on its back and Jesus took His seat. And what did that unbroken creature do? Did it manifest the wildness of its untamed nature? Did it buck and kick and heave in order to get rid of this unaccustomed weight? Did it shy and stall as it was paraded down the streets of Jerusalem as cheering multitudes pressed in, shouting, cheering, and waving palm branches? Not a bit. It was the happiest colt in the country. It was serving Jesus that day. Jesus had tamed it with a touch of His hand, a single word of His mouth.

Jesus had mastery over *the fowl of the air* (Luke 22:34). Just before the trial, He told Peter that when the disciple had three times denied His Lord, then, and not until then, the cock would crow. And so it did. There in some nearby barnyard a rooster awoke. He beat his wings arrogantly against his body. The first rays of the morning glinted on his brilliant plumage. He held himself erect, powerful, scornful. His glittering eye held a challenge; his lethal spurs ready for war. Every ounce of him, every inch of him, proclaimed his independence. He was about to crow and issue his challenge to the morning when He heard the Master's voice, "Not just yet. Wait." Then came the word, "Now!" And the cock crew. And Peter went out and wept bitterly. The Master was Lord over the fowl of the air as much as over the fish of the sea and the beasts of the field. His was the lordship over all life that Adam had thrown away.

The Lord Jesus, then, as the Last Adam, had complete mastery of all the laws of nature. As the incarnate Creator, indwelt by the Father through the Holy Spirit, he was absolute Master of every law known to science and every law not known to science. He had the power to suspend or supersede all such laws because of who He was, because He was indwelt by the Spirit of God, and because He acted in full cooperation with the Father. So He performed miracles, many miracles, countless miracles. Generally speaking, we can divide the miracles of Jesus into two kinds: those that transcended the natural laws in a supernatural way, and those that transformed needy lives in a supernatural way.

## 2. Transcending natural laws in a supernatural way

His very first miracle was just such a miracle.

### a. Changing water into wine

Every season, in an orderly, systematic process, the laws of nature as they are coded into the nature and character of the vine, operate to change water into wine. It is a biological miracle. The roots of the plant go down into the soil. The sap runs up through the main stem of the vine, and out to the far-flung, clinging arms, to nurture the growing grapes. The juice of the grape contains all the chemical mysteries of wine. What Jesus did in his miracle at Cana was bypass the natural, orderly process whereby wine is produced and telescope them into an instantaneous fiat of creation. He dispensed with the vine, He dispensed with the soil, He dispensed with the sunshine and the rain, He dispensed with the seasons. What He had built into the vine as Creator, He simply set aside. The process was too slow and cumbersome. He performed the transformation instantly, then and there. He willed water into wine. Or, as the poet has phrased it,

> The simple creature,
> Touched by grace Divine,
> Owned its Creator—
> And blushed into wine!

Nobody can explain how Jesus changed the water into wine anymore than anyone can explain how the vine does it. Yet He did it. The first miracle of Moses before Pharaoh was to change water into blood. The first miracle of Jesus was to turn water into wine.

### b. Feeding the five thousand

We have no idea how He did it. The situation was impossible. The disciples wanted Him to send the multitudes away. He challenged the disciples to feed them. It was a question of the law of supply and demand. Philip looked at the demand and said, "Two hundred pennyworth of bread is not sufficient." Andrew looked at the supply. "There is a lad here," he said, "with five barley loaves and two small fishes. What are they among so many?"

Jesus was not disturbed, either by the greatness of the demand or by the smallness of the supply. He took those loaves and fishes into His hands and the miracle happened. Early that morning, or perhaps the night before, a woman had prepared a little lunch for her boy. She had fried some fish in olive oil or grilled them on the coals. She had taken barley flour and baked some small loaves, probably the familiar pocket bread common to this day in eastern lands. Fish from the sea and barley from the field had been transformed into a little lad's lunch. And the boy brought it all to Jesus.

"And do you know what He did, Mother?" he must have told her afterward with shining eyes. "He took my lunch. He gave thanks to God. And he began to break my loaves and fishes into pieces. More and more and more. Soon the disciples were hurrying back and forth to the very last rows with heaping baskets of food. All from my little lunch!"

### c. Walking on the water

We know how to swim in water. We know how to float steel on water. We know about Archimedes' Principle, which states that when a body is immersed in a liquid it displaces an amount of liquid equal in volume to the part of the object immersed in the liquid. We know about the specific gravity of objects: the ratio between the mass of a given volume of any material to the mass of an equal volume of water. We can be sure that Jesus knew all about these things as well. Yet we do not know how to walk on water, but Jesus did.

We know how to water ski, how to be pulled through water at such a speed that we can skim along its surface. Jesus knew how to walk on water, not just calm water, but upon water that had been whipped into treacherous wave-mountains by the storm. Beneath His feet, those wild, unruly waves became a steady pavement on which He could walk as easily as he could walk on the seashore sand. Moreover, He knew how to make Peter walk on that water. Just so long as the disciple kept his eyes firmly fixed on the Master, he too could walk on the waves. The waves were still waves, though, for the moment Peter took His eyes off the Lord, he began to sink. But in some mysterious, miraculous way, the explanation for which is wholly beyond our comprehension, Jesus could change the sea into a sidewalk, both for himself and for Peter.

### d. Stilling the storm

On another occasion, Jesus went to sleep in Simon Peter's boat. (Incidentally, this is the only time in the Gospels we read of Jesus being asleep.) Instantly, a storm was let loose upon the lake. The wind arose, the waves arose, the boat was now full of water, and yet Jesus slept calmly. Miracle number one! When a ship is full of water, it goes to the bottom. Not this one. As the old hymn puts it:

> No water can swallow the ship where lies,
> The Master of ocean and sea and skies.[2]

The frightened disciples woke Him up. "Master," they cried, "carest Thou not that we perish?" What a question! Of course He cared! As if they could perish with Him on board. But He arose and stilled the storm. "Peace!" He said. "Be still." And instantly there was a great calm. So much so that the disciples came and worshipped Him. "What manner of man is this," they said, "that even the wind and the sea obey Him?" Of course they do! He made them. He measures the waters of the seas in the hollow of His hands. He tempers the wind to the shorn lamb. He is their mighty Maker. They know Him. They recognize His voice. They render Him immediate, implicit obedience. How He did it we do not know. We know that He did. So then, we see Him performing miracles by transcending natural laws in a supernatural way.

## 3. Transforming needy lives in a supernatural way

We also see Jesus performing miracles of healing, and He was always doing this. Of the miracles recorded in detail in the Gospels, no less than twenty-three relate to healing. And all these miracles of His were parables in action. We see Him raising the dead, and that reminds us of His power to regenerate dead hearts so that we who are dead in trespasses and sin might live. We see Him restoring sight to the blind to remind us that man is spiritually blind, that he perceives not the things of the Spirit of God. We live and walk in total darkness. But He can make our blind spiritual eyes to see. We see Him make the deaf to hear and we are reminded that, by nature, we are deaf to God's Word; we are unresponsive to His truth. But He can make us hear. We see Him cleanse the leper and we are reminded that sin is leprosy of the soul—foul, deadening, contagious, and deadly. But He can cleanse us of our sin and make us pure and whole and well.

The miracles Jesus performed upon the bodies of men and women and little children illustrate those "greater miracles" He is able to perform on the heart and life and soul and spirit of the lost. He is able to transform needy lives in a supernatural way.

### a. Power over disease

He was forever healing the sick, for He was "the Great Physician." He never lost a case or charged a fee. No case was too hard for Him.

There was, for instance, the woman with the issue of blood. She had been in that condition for twelve long years and, as Mark puts it, "had suffered many things of many physicians." She came to Jesus and touched only the hem of His garment, and at once she was healed (Mark 5:25–34).

There was the woman bent double, who had been in that condition for eighteen years. Jesus healed her in the synagogue on the Sabbath without a moment's hesitation (Luke 13:10–17).

There was the man at the pool of Bethesda. He had been in the grip of some horrible infirmity for half a lifetime—thirty-eight long, weary years. Jesus healed him instantly and did so on the Sabbath, knowing full well that by so doing He was signing His own death warrant (John 5:1–16).

There was the man born blind. Jesus cured this particular blind man in a somewhat different way. He spat upon the ground, made clay, put the clay on the man's eyes, and sent him off to Siloam to wash and to see. Some have suggested that the man had no eyeballs and that Jesus made him a brand new pair from the clay. What a mighty miracle! Yet it was only another paragraph in His death warrant, so far as the leaders of Israel were concerned. Jesus had broken their taboos by performing this miracle on the Sabbath (John 9:1–41).

There were the lepers. On one occasion, Jesus healed ten of them at once (Luke 17:11–19). Think of it. In all the Old Testament era, hardly anyone was cured of leprosy. The first two lepers, Moses and Miriam, were both cleansed. The only other leper cleansed in the Old Testament was Naaman the Syrian. Leprosy was so foul and filthy a disease, so fatal in its consequences, so incurable, that it was regarded by the Jews as "the stroke of God." An elaborate ritual was built into the Old Testament law for the ceremonial cleansing of a cured Hebrew leper (Lev. 13:1–32). The ritual had to be carried out by a priest. There is not one incident in the Old Testament where this ceremony was ever performed. That is why Jesus sent these lepers to the priest "as a testimony unto them." He had power over disease.

### b. Power over demons

There are numerous instances in the Gospels where Jesus casts out demons. He did so with absolute authority and without any of the mumbo jumbo of exorcism common in some ecclesiastical circles. The most famous case of His power over demons was that of the Gadarene demoniac (Luke 8:26–39). The demons in that wretched man recognized Jesus at once, and cried, "What have I to do with thee, Jesus, thou Son of God most high?"

This poor man was known as Legion because a whole legion of demons had taken possession of his tormented soul and tortured body. A legion in the Roman army comprised some six thousand men. The demons pleaded with Christ not to torment them before their time; and begged Him not to send them into "the Deep" (the Abyss—the prison house in the spirit world reserved for the worst offenders against God's laws (Rev. 9:1; 17:8; 20:1, 3). Jesus set the man free, as He did so many others. Moreover, He silenced the demons when they attempted to bear witness to who He was. To this day, no evil spirit can confess that Jesus Christ is come in the flesh (1 John 4:1–3).

### c. Power over death

On three occasions, Jesus raised people from the dead. He raised a little twelve-year-old girl who had been dead for barely an hour. (Mark 5:22–43). He raised a young man who was being carried off for burial (Luke 7:11–17). He raised Lazarus, who had been dead for four days and whose body was already in the process of decomposition (John 11:1–44). The raising of Lazarus was, perhaps, His greatest miracle. Christ's public ministry as recorded in the gospel of John began with a miracle performed at a wedding and ended with a miracle performed at a funeral. People flocked from Jerusalem to Bethany to see Lazarus, raised from the dead and living in the power of resurrection life. Yet, so obdurate is the power of unbelief that the leaders of Israel actually tried to murder Lazarus.

### d. Power over distance

He healed a nobleman's son without ever coming near the house where he lay sick and near death's door (John 4:47–54). When the man arrived home and compared notes with his servants, he discovered that his child had begun to mend "yesterday at the seventh hour," the very moment at which Jesus had said to him, "Thy son liveth."

He healed the centurion's servant (Matt. 8:5–13); a man who had enough faith to believe that Jesus did not even need to come to his home in Capernaum in order to heal. Seasoned Roman veteran that he was, used to command as he was, he told Jesus he was not worthy to have Jesus come under his roof. So, triumphing over distance, Jesus healed the man's servant then and there, without going a step farther; yes, and He used that man's faith as an object lesson to describe the place the Gentiles would soon find in the kingdom of heaven.

### e. Power over disability

One of the most remarkable cures Jesus effected was wrought upon the body of a man who was numbered among His foes. In the Garden of Gethsemane, one of the Lord's disciples drew a sword and smote a man named Malchus, a servant of the high priest, and cut off his right ear (Luke 22:49–51). Jesus simply picked it up and put it back on again!

## 4. Conclusion

The greatest miracle, of course, is Christ himself. He came into this world by means of the Virgin Birth. That was a miracle. He had a human mother but no human father.

He lived an immaculate life. He never sinned in thought or word or deed; as a baby or as a boy; as a teenager or as a workman at the bench; as a traveling preacher; at home, at school, at work, on the highway, in the synagogue, with His friends or confronted by His foes. That was a miracle. Nobody else ever lived a life like that.

He manifested omniscient wisdom. The Jewish leaders brought the cleverest, keenest minds in the country, sharp legal minds, minds trained in the most rigorous of schools. They sought to trap Him in His words, but they never succeeded. They confessed among themselves, "Never man spake like this man" (John 7:46). They said, "Whence hath this man this wisdom, and these mighty works?" (Matt. 13:54).

He died an atoning death. But even as He hung on the cross, He reached up and put out the sun; He reached down and shook creation's rocks; He reached in and tore the veil of the temple; He reached beyond and shook open the tombs and beckoned to the dead; He reached out and saved a centurion and they that were with him.

He triumphed over the tomb. They bound Him with the grave clothes, sealed Him in a cave, and set a guard to patrol the grave. He simply came forth in triumph when the appointed three days and three nights were done. As the hymn puts it:

> Vainly they watch His bed, Jesus, my Savior!
> Vainly they seal the dead, Jesus, my Lord!
>
> Up from the grave He arose;
> With a mighty triumph o'er His foes!
> He arose a Victor from the dark domain,
> And He lives, forever, with His saints to reign.
> He arose! He arose! Alleluia! Christ arose![3]

Then there was his triumphant ascension. Forty days after His resurrection, He gathered His disciples around Him and marched at their head to Bethany. "Ho there! Pilate! Herod! Summon your cohorts! Arrest that man! He has defied the Caesar's seal. He has come forth from the dead. He is walking through your streets!" But no! Out He goes, across the Kidron, past Gethsemane, on up to Olivet's brow. And now He steps boldly and bodily from earth to heaven; out of time and back into eternity.

Ten days later, there came the descending Spirit, just as He had promised. The Spirit came and the disciples were baptized into the mystical body of Christ. The gates of hell were shaken afresh. The church was born and the world was taken by storm. Now, for two thousand years, He has been carrying on those "greater miracles" of His. Not miracles now upon the bodies of men, but miracles of redemption and regeneration; miracles of transformation of life and character.

The old hymn we used to sing in Britain when I was a boy sums it up:

> Jesus! 'tis He who once below
> Man's pathway trod, 'mid pain and woe;
> And burdened ones, where'er He came,
> Brought out their sick, and deaf and lame;
> The blind rejoiced to hear the cry,
> "Jesus of Nazareth passeth by."
>
> Ho! all ye heavy laden, come!
> Here's pardon, comfort, rest and home:
> Ye wand'rers from a Father's face,
> Return, accept His proffered grace;
> Ye tempted ones, there's refuge nigh:
> "Jesus of Nazareth passeth by."[4]

## CHAPTER 10

# WHO DO MEN SAY THAT I AM?

*Matthew 16:13–19*

1. God in His presence
2. God in His person
3. God in His power
4. God in His passion
5. God in His preeminence
6. God in His position
7. God in His permanence

WHO IS HE, THIS PERSON WE CALL JESUS? He is the eternal, uncreated, self-existing Son of God. Nothing less than that will do.

When He lived on earth, our Lord was forever asking questions. It was one of His favorite ways of teaching. Of all the questions He ever asked, this is surely the most revealing, the most soul-searching: "Whom do you say that I am?" The answer to this question will show in a flash where one stands in relation to the great cardinal, fundamental doctrine of the Christian faith—the deity of Christ.

He put the twin questions to His disciples. In the whole range of possible catechism of the souls of humanity there exist no more penetrating questions than these: "Whom do men say that I the Son of man am?" and "Whom say ye that I am?"

The Holy Spirit records the answers of the world: "Some say you are John the Baptist." That is, when these people thought of Him they thought of His *walk*. John the Baptist was unique in His generation. Jesus himself said of John the Baptist that no greater human being was ever born of a woman. In his dress, in his diet, in his deportment, and in his discipline, John stood apart. He was a man sent from God and the people knew it. He performed no miracles, but his message and his martyrdom set him apart as a mighty prophet. When they thought of Christ, they thought of John. "You are John the Baptist," they said. "John the Baptist, risen from the dead."

"Some say you are Elijah." When these people thought of Christ, they thought of His *works*. Elijah was essentially a prophet of action. He was a man, mighty in deeds. His ministry was backed up by the most astonishing miracles. His exodus from earth was all of a piece with his meteoric career—he was caught up in a whirlwind to heaven with the escort of a chariot of fire. "You are Elijah come back again," they said. "That is who you are."

"Some say that you are Jeremiah." Jewish tradition had it that this weeping prophet would come back and would rediscover the sacred ark supposedly hidden on Mount Nebo. "They say you are Jeremiah." That is, when they thought of Jesus, they did so in terms of His *woes*. They thought of Jeremiah and his tears, his sufferings, his lamentations, and his woes. They thought of the prophet who wept over Jerusalem. "You are Jeremiah," they said.

"Some say you are one of the prophets." That is, they thought of Christ in terms of His *words*. They listened to what he had to say. They were impressed, believed Him to be inspired, one of the former prophets returned to speak to the conscience of the age. "You are either a prophet reincarnate, or a prophet risen," they declared.

So gracious, so holy, so miraculous was Jesus that even the careless world ranked Him as one of its greatest and its best. But that will never do. Jesus is not to be compared with other men, even those whom we rank highest of all. To rank Jesus with Confucius, Buddha, Muhammad, or anyone else is to expose a heart of unbelief. To say that Jesus was merely a man is to reveal oneself as blind to the truth of God and dead in trespasses and sins.

So the Lord presses the point. "Whom say ye that I am?" He demands. The question is now made personal. We can no more be saved by another person's belief than we can be damned by another's unbelief. "Whom say ye that I am?" What worlds hung in the balance waiting for the answer to that question from one of His own. "And Simon Peter answered and said, Thou art the Christ, the Son of the living God."

The world's estimate never soars higher than to count Him a prophet. The true believer's estimate never falls below the realm of absolute Deity. "Who is the Son of Man?" Back comes the answer from the enlightened soul, "The Son of God." The whole Bible rises up to endorse that simple reply. From beginning to end, the Bible teaches us that Jesus is the Son of God; God the Son, the second person of the Godhead.

## 1. God in His presence

The Bible reveals to us that God exists in three persons: one God, three persons. The concept is found in embryonic form in the very first reference to God in the Bible. "In the beginning God created the heaven and the earth." The name for God here is *Elohim. Elohim* is plural. The Hebrews had a singular form for expressing the thought of one, a dual form for expressing two, and a plural form for expressing three or more. *Elohim* is a plural noun. It implies that there are three persons in the Godhead. But there are not three Gods. There is one God. Although God is consistently referred to in the plural form throughout the Old Testament, it is a plural form always followed by singular adjectives and singular verbs.

Three persons, one God. The New Testament carries the revelation further. It shows that the three persons of the Godhead exist as a Father, a Son, and a Spirit. There are not three Gods. There is one God, but that God exists as three persons; each separate, each distinct, yet each God in the absolute sense of the Word.

All the attributes of God are ascribed to each person of the Godhead—eternity of being, omnipotence, omniscience, omnipresence, holiness, truth, love. The three primary names for God in the Old Testament are Jehovah, Elohim, and Adonai. They are directly ascribed to each of the three persons of the Godhead. Each one is separately called Elohim, Jehovah, and Adonai. So then, before Jesus ever came into the world at Bethlehem, He existed as God; as Elohim, as Jehovah, and as Adonai. Thus, Hebrews 1:3 tells us that Jesus was the radiance of God's glory, the very image of His substance.

Shortly before Christ went to Calvary, Philip turned to Him and said, "Show us the Father, and it sufficeth us" (John 14:8). It was a tremendous request. What he wanted was the vision glorious; the vision of God that the Seventy saw on Sinai or that Isaiah saw when he saw God high and lifted up. The Lord rebuked Philip. Philip asked for a physical sight of God. Jesus said, "He that hath seen me hath seen the Father" (John 14:9). "I and my Father are one" (John 10:30).

No such utterance ever fell from the lips of even the greatest of the prophets or the boldest of the apostles. Suppose you were to say to someone, "I would like to meet your father," and he replied, "That is not a bit necessary. If you have seen me, you have seen my father. I and my father are one." Surely you would think such a person was a candidate for a lunatic asylum.

Yet Jesus calmly told the disciples that to have seen Him was to have seen the Father. The Father and the Son are two distinct persons, but they are one God. To seek God outside of Jesus or beyond Jesus or not in Jesus is not to know Jesus or the Father at all. Christ was the radiance of God's glory and the very image of His substance.

Had there been two Gods, or if Jesus had not himself been God, then it would have been possible for the Son to have been seen without seeing the Father. In His preexistence, Jesus was God. When He came to earth, He was still God; so much so that once to have seen Him was to have seen the Father.

"I and the Father are one," Jesus said. "I and the Father [two distinct personalities] are [a plural of persons] one [not masculine which would have been implied one person but neuter—one thing, one essence, one substance, one Godhead]."

All that is in God is in Christ. A sharp distinction of persons, but an absolute identity of nature.

## 2. God in His person

The person of Christ is unique. Paul tells us that "in him dwells all the fulness of the Godhead bodily" (Col. 2:9). The Lord Jesus did not surrender His deity when He became a man. There was a change of position but no surrender of His essential Being. God cannot possibly cease to be God.

Jesus was God "manifest in flesh" (1 Tim. 3:16). God was manifest from the beginning of creation. He was manifest in flaming suns and burning stars, in all the vastness of the heavens. He was manifest in the works His hands had made. But He was not manifest in flesh until Jesus came.

The prophet Zechariah aptly described Him. God, speaking though the prophet, said of the Lord Jesus that He is "the man that is my fellow" (Zech. 13:7). The Jews knew what Jesus meant when He spoke of God as His Father. When Jesus healed a man on the Sabbath, He defended His action by saying, "My Father worketh hitherto, and I work" (John 5:17). "Therefore," we read, "the Jews sought the more to kill him, because he not only had broken the sabbath, but said also that God was his Father, making himself equal with God" (John 5:18). That murder was attempted three times (John 5:18; 8:59; and 10:31) and was finally accomplished (Mark 14:61). The Jewish murder of Christ was solely on the grounds that He claimed to be God.

There is a mystery connected with the person of Christ we should never seek to unravel. The great heresies of Christendom have centered around attempts to explain that inscrutable person. There have been those who have sought to emphasize Christ's deity at the expense of

His humanity. There have been those who have sought to emphasize His humanity at the expense of His deity.

Actually, both deity and humanity were perfectly blended and balanced in the person of Christ. The great passage that explains this is Philippians 2:5–8, where Paul tells us that in eternity past the Lord Jesus was clothed in the full panoply of God. He existed, as Paul puts it "in the form of God." "Being [subsisting, existing] in the form of God." The verb is not in the perfect tense, which would imply an estate that once was but that ceased to be. It is in the imperfect tense, which is important. It in no way suggests that Christ's deity came to an end. Paul is not telling us what Jesus *was*, but what His intrinsic nature *is*.

The expression "the form of God" does not merely mean outward appearance. It means that Christ was essentially and naturally God. His deity was not surrendered when He took on humanity. The pre-existent and eternal second person of the Godhead took on humanity. What He gave up was the visible manifestation of the glory that belonged to Him as God, because mankind could not have looked on that glory. What Jesus gave up was the independent exercise of His divine attributes. He still possessed all the essential attributes and properties of deity, but He did not use them except at the pleasure of the Father. This is what is meant when we read that "the Son can do nothing of himself" (John 5:19).

But He took upon himself humanity. He who was "in the form of God" took upon himself "the form of a servant." It is the same word. He appeared among men, not as God in His glory, but as a man, clothed in flesh. He emptied himself, not of deity, but of the form of deity. He who existed in the precise form, or reality that God is, added to himself the precise form of a servant.

It is impossible that His deity could be diminished, or that He could have surrendered any divine attribute, because God is immutable, unchangeable. However, Jesus did condescend to a lowly position, His glory was veiled, and He was despised and rejected of men.

Yet, for all that, Jesus was really and truly God. He was also really and truly man as well. He prayed, wept, slept, ate, drank, asked questions, grew. The two natures were present, and perfectly blended, but He was one person.

## 3. God in His power

Again and again, the Bible tells us that Jesus was the Creator of the universe, a role that called for omnipotent power and omniscient wisdom. During His earthly life, He manifested all the power of God in every realm. He changed water into wine, walked on the waves, stilled the storm, and multiplied loaves and fishes. He healed the sick, cleansed the lepers, raised the dead, and gave sight to the blind. He did so with profusion, with instant and permanent success, and with unfailing authority. He cast out demons with complete authority, silencing them, forbidding them to return, and commanding their instant obedience.

Yet, though coequal with the Father in nature (John 10:30) and in dignity (John 5:23), He chose to be subordinate to the Father. "My Father is greater than I," He said (John 14:28). Greater not in essence or time or dignity or worship or virtue, but greater in position. There is a relationship of order within the Godhead itself. God the Father is the first person, God the Son is the second person, and God the Holy Spirit is the third person. Yet all are equally God.

In His humanity, Jesus always demonstrated this positional relationship between himself as Son and His Father as God. Yet not for one moment did that detract from His deity, as a moment's careful thought will show.[1]

He said, for instance, "What things soever [the Father] doeth, these also doeth the Son likewise. For the Father loveth the Son, and sheweth him all things that he himself doeth" (John 5:19–20). Think what that means. To creation's utmost bound, in the Godhead's most distant and most secret operations and councils, the Son knows what the Godhead is doing; knows it not by communication but by consciousness. The Father shows Him all things, therefore, He must have omniscience to grasp what is being shown. The mind of Jesus was coextensive with the mind of the Father.

He said, "What things soever the Father doeth, these doeth the Son likewise." With the same authority; the same wisdom, the same effect. That is, He fully wields all the processes of God; all creations, all laws, all forces, all powers He handles with irresistible mastery. In other words, He is omnipotent. So stupendous a statement never passed from mortal lips but His.

He said, "[The Father] hath committed all judgment unto the Son: That all [angels, humanity, all creation] should honour the Son, even as they honour the Father" (John 5:22–23). Jesus is the universal judge, which means that He has a personal knowledge of all the untold myriads of mankind multiplied by all the ages of history. He has a minute, infallible acquaintance with the infinite variety of circumstances of each individual, with their opportunities, their character, their secret motives, their hidden passions, their lasting influence for better or for worse. He has a perfect mastery of all the laws of God by which to judge the worlds. He has the absolute right to pass eternal sentence with no court of appeal above Him and no cases reversed.

He said, "As the Father hath life in himself; so hath he given to the Son to have life in himself" (John 5:26). That is life, independent, absolute, and imparted where and when He chooses. "For as the Father raiseth up the dead, and quickeneth them; even so the Son quickeneth whom he will" (John 5:21). Christ has absolute power over the dead. He proved it by raising three people from the dead, one of whom was already decomposing in the tomb. It is this same Christ who will raise all the dead in a coming day, "Verily, verily, I say unto you, The hour is coming, and now is, when the dead shall hear the voice of the Son of God: and they that hear shall live" (John 5:25).

He is God in His power. He says, "All power is given unto me in heaven and in earth" (Matt. 28:18). Only God could make a statement like that.

## 4. God in His passion

Apart from the humanity of Christ, no blood could be shed. The blood that was shed at Calvary is evaluated by God as "precious blood."

It is precious blood because it was the blood that poured through the human veins of a member of the eternal Godhead.

If the life that Jesus laid down on the cross of Calvary was merely a human life, then the Atonement is a farce. The Old Testament law decreed, "A life for a life." If Jesus, on the cross, was merely a human being, however much a perfect, righteous, and holy human being, then His death would avail for only one person. "A life for a life." There is no way that Christ's death could have "taken away the sin of the world" as the Bible assures us it did.

There is only one way that Christ's life could have been a sufficient atoning sacrifice for all the sins of all the millions upon millions of people who have ever lived. The life that He laid down at Calvary was an *eternal* life. The blood that was shed was human blood, but it was the blood of one who was God manifest in flesh. It was precious blood. It was blood of infinite value and worth. Count up all the people who have ever lived on this planet and you still have a finite number. Count up all the sins that those multitudes of people have ever committed. You still have a finite number. It is an enormous number, a number beyond our ability to count, but it is still a finite number; a number that has bounds about it and that can be expressed in mathematical terms. But the life that was laid down for us was not a finite life. It was an infinite life. That is the whole point of Calvary. If Jesus was not God, while hanging on the tree, then our salvation is a delusion.

But we need have no doubts about it. The Bible assures us that Jesus, there on the cross, was no ordinary human being. He said, "Therefore doth my Father love me, because I lay down my life, that I might take it again. No man taketh it from me, but I lay it down of myself. I have power to lay it down, and I have power to take it again. This commandment have I received of my Father" (John 10:17–18). And we know that He did just that. When the work of redemption was completed, Jesus simply dismissed His Spirit. Luke says, "And when Jesus had cried with a loud voice . . . having said thus, he gave up the ghost" (Luke 23:46). Matthew puts it like this: "Jesus, when he had cried again with a loud voice, yielded up the ghost" (Matt. 27:50).

Greek scholars tell us that the force of Matthew's record is this: "He sent forth His Spirit."

The Lord Jesus sovereignly fulfilled all that the Scriptures had to say about His death, and then He calmly dismissed His spirit from His body into the Father's keeping until the resurrection morning.

The one who died on the cross of Calvary was the one described to us as God manifest in flesh. The Holy Spirit assures us that "God was in Christ, reconciling the world unto himself" (2 Cor. 5:19).

## 5. God in His preeminence

The Bible tells us that Jesus was greater than Abraham, greater than Jacob, greater than Solomon, greater than Jonah, and greater than the temple.

To the Jews, there was no greater *person* than Abraham. He was the founding father of the nation. He was the friend of God. He was the progenitor of the race.

To the Jews, there was no greater *patriarch* than Jacob. From Jacob came the twelve tribes. He was one who had wrestled with the Jehovah-angel and had prevailed.

To the Jews, there was no greater *prince* than Solomon. With all his splendor, he was the greatest of Israel's kings, endowed with a gift of wisdom never surpassed. As the Scripture says, "He was wiser than all men. . . . And there came of all people to hear the wisdom of Solomon" (1 Kings 4:31, 34).

To the Jews, there was no greater *prophet* than Jonah. Jonah, who in the power of resurrection life, was able in a single day to bring a heathen nation of a million souls to its knees in utter, total repentance.

To the Jews, there was no greater *place* than the temple. It was built on the spot where Abraham had offered up Isaac, it was sanctified by the Shechinah glory cloud, it was the place where all sacrifice and all service centered.

Jesus was greater than the Jews' greatest person (John 8:53), their greatest patriarch (John 4:12), their greatest prince (Luke 11:31), their greatest prophet (Matt. 12:41), and their greatest place (Matt. 12:6).

The book of Hebrews expands this great theme from the Gospels. The writer of Hebrews tells us that Jesus was greater than the angels, greater than Aaron, greater than Moses, and greater than Joshua. Paul tells us that Jesus has the preeminence "in all things," for "it pleased the Father that in him should all fulness dwell" (Col. 1:18–19).

## 6. God in His position

The Holy Spirit says of Jesus that God "maketh his angels spirits, and his ministers a flame of fire. But unto the Son he saith, Thy throne, O God, is for ever and ever" (Heb. 1:7–8). God addresses the Son as God. He tells us that He sits upon a throne that is God's throne. He sits there by sovereign right, because He himself is God. Who, indeed, but God could sit upon God's throne with its blazing holiness, before which the very seraphim hide their faces in their wings.

When a created being sought to aspire to that throne, even though he was Lucifer, Son of the morning, the loftiest of all God's creatures, he was instantly cast out of heaven. Yet Jesus sits upon the throne of God, and He sits there because He has every right to sit there, even in His human body. He sits there for the simple reason that He was and is and ever will be God the Son in the absolute sense of the word.

## 7. God in His permanence

The writer of Hebrews tells us in a glorious statement of truth that our beloved Lord is "Jesus Christ the same yesterday, and to day, and for ever" (13:8). Ours is no new Christ. He is the Jesus of history (yesterday), the Jesus of experience (today), and the Jesus of eternity (forever).

He was God before He came into the world; before ever the sun and moon and stars began to shine; before ever the rustle of an angel's wing disturbed the silence of eternity. He was God when He took upon himself human flesh and trod these scenes of time. He is God today, gloriously enthroned on high. He is God eternally, forever, as the endless ages roll.

He is Immanuel, God with us (Isa. 7:14; Matt. 1:22–23). He is God over all, blessed for ever (Rom. 9:5). He is God, the living Word (John 1:1–4, 14). He is the Child born, the Son given, the mighty God. He is God, the I Am (John 8:58). He is God to be worshipped (John 9:35–38). He is God our Savior (1 John 5:20). Well might we sing:

> Oh for a thousand tongues to sing
> My great Redeemer's praise,
> The glories of my God and King,
> The triumphs of His grace![2]

## CHAPTER 11

# THE TRANSFIGURATION OF CHRIST

*Matthew 17:1-13*

1. The period
2. The purpose
3. The people
   a. The first group: Peter, James, and John
      (1) James: The church's martyr
      (2) John: The church's mystic
      (3) Peter: The church's messenger
   b. The second group: Moses and Elijah
      (1) Moses: The law—the sacrifices
      (2) Elijah: The prophets—the Scriptures
   c. The third group: The Son and the Father
4. The prospect
   a. His goal
   b. His glory
   c. His grace
5. The postscript
   a. The dispirited church
   b. The demented boy
   c. The drifting crowd
   d. The dead religion

THE EVENING SHADOWS HAD lengthened across the sky. A small group of people could be seen wending their way up the slopes of Hermon, the highest mountain in Palestine. It had been a stiff climb, up and up, until at last some 9,400 feet above sea level, they stood amid the snowfields. For some five thousand feet of elevation, the little band had made their way through the mulberry trees and past vineyards and olive groves. But then the scenery had changed. They had climbed over bare rocks piled in fantastic ridges, heaped above yawning chasms. They had entered the haunt of the eagle, the wolf, and the mountain bear. The shaggy foothills had given no hint of the awesome desolation that lay above. Down below, the tumultuous sources of the Jordan came leaping and bounding out of the roots of Hermon to go singing and swaying into the valleys below. Down below, too, was Caesarea Philippi, a beautiful but almost totally pagan city with stately marble columns and statues to Pan carved in the rocks. Mount Hermon flung its ramparts across the Promised Land. Beyond its snow-white summits lay the great lands of the Gentiles. To the south stood Galilee, Samaria, Decapolis, Perea, and Judah, the country of the Hebrew people groaning beneath Rome's iron heel.

There they stood, four men: Peter, James, John, and Jesus. There they stood on Mount Hermon, the very name of which spoke volumes. *Hermon!* The sacred mountain! Such was the meaning of its name. It was a mountain sacred to the Baal cults of ancient times, with their dreadful altars and horrible fires of sacrifice. *Hermon!* The sacred mountain. From now on sacred for the memory of the Transfiguration of Jesus the Messiah.

As the evening shadows stole across the sky and night drew on apace, Jesus gave himself to supplication while Peter, James, and John gave themselves to sleep. Let us now climb that mountain ourselves and stand amid its snows. Let us use the magic of imagination and go back, carried on wings far swifter than any man-made time machine, carried back in time to the days when Jesus trod the earth.

Let us consider the *period*, the *purpose*, the *people*, the *prospect*, and the *postscript* connected with the Transfiguration of Christ.

## 1. The period

The event is carefully dated by Matthew, Mark, and Luke, all of whom record the incident. It took place a week after the Lord Jesus had declared to His disciples, "Verily I say unto you, There be some standing here, which shall not taste of death, till they see the Son of man coming in his kingdom" (Matt. 16:28).

We need to set the period into perspective. There had been a tragic turning point in the Lord's public ministry. Opposition to Christ's claims had been growing. It began with the Jewish authorities taking a deliberate stand against Him. Matthew records *commencement* of this opposition in chapter 12, the *consequences* of this opposition in chapter 13, and the *culmination* of this opposition in chapter 14. As a result of this growing opposition, the Lord Jesus deliberately changed His method of teaching. He began to conceal His meaning by using parables of a mystical character. The opposition continued.

In chapter 16, Matthew records Peter's tremendous statement of faith in the person of Christ, a statement in which he boldly proclaimed his belief in the deity of the Lord Jesus Christ. "Thou art the Christ, the Son of the Living God!" he declared. It was right after this, right after the growing controversy of the people, and right after the glowing confession of Peter that the Lord began to speak about His sufferings and about the glory that would follow. This, then, is the period at which the Transfiguration took place. For Christ, the cross is now clearly in view.

## 2. The purpose

It is of interest that Matthew, Mark, and Luke all record this incident, but John does not. Yet John was the only one of the four gospel writers who was actually present when the Transfiguration took place. Why is John silent about it in his gospel?

There was a very good reason. John's purpose in his gospel was to demonstrate the absolute deity of the Lord Jesus Christ. Though one might have thought that the revelation of glory that overwhelmed

Peter, James, and John on the mountain would be a perfect demonstration and proof of Christ's claims to be God, that is not the case. The Transfiguration of the Lord Jesus was not intended to be a proof of his deity at all. There are plenty of other proofs of that elsewhere in the Bible as a whole and in the Gospels in particular. If the Transfiguration was not intended to be a demonstration of Christ's deity, what then was it intended to demonstrate? It was a demonstration of the glory of Christ's human life, for Jesus was God manifest in flesh. He was at once the Son of God and the Son of Man.

G. Campbell Morgan points out that the human life of the Lord Jesus went through three stages. The first of these stages was one of *innocence*. The Lord Jesus was immaculately born, born with a sinless nature, born without any taint of sin. He is the only person ever born onto this sin-cursed planet with a nature like that. We are born with sinful natures. Whatever there might be about childhood innocence, it is very quickly dissipated and destroyed by the outworking of the sin nature within. A little baby will manifest a violent temper before it can even walk or talk. A little child will lie and steal and disobey without receiving any lessons in how to do these things.

Mark Twain said, "I do not remember my first lie; it is too far back; but I remember my second one very well. I was nine days old at the time, and had noticed that if a pin was sticking in me and I advertised the fact in the usual fashion, I was lovingly petted and coddled and pitied in a most agreeable way and got a ration between meals besides. It was human nature to want to get these riches, and I fell. I lied about the pin, advertising one when there wasn't any. You would have done it; George Washington did it; anybody would have done it."

But the Lord Jesus didn't. As a child in the crib, He never advertised a pin that was not there. He never had a temper tantrum, never demanded his own way. He grew up. He was never disobedient. He never deceived, never cheated, never answered his mother back, never acted sullen when Joseph told Him there was something he wanted Him to do. He was innocent. He had a mind that was absolutely pure. Never once did He entertain an impure thought. Never once did He contemplate a deceitful action. Never once did He have to apologize for anything He said. He was innocent.

But then came temptation. Human nature is never perfect until it has chosen *right* for itself, and has chosen it against allurement and provocation. So Jesus was tempted of the Devil. As the fierce heat of temptation was turned upon Him, He was exposed to the lust of the eye, the lust of the flesh, and the pride of life. He was found to be totally without sin. A holy man is a man who has looked temptation full in the face and said, "No!" Jesus was tempted in all points as we are, yet without sin. He was victorious over every form of temptation the Enemy could devise. So, there was innocence, then there was holiness!

Then came the Mount of Transfiguration. There we see not innocence or holiness but glory—the glorified humanity of the Lord Jesus Christ. He was metamorphosed before them. The glory that they saw was not the glory of deity but the glory of perfect humanity!

We know nothing of that because there is sin in us. However, the revelation of the glory that blazed through His body and through His very garments on the Mount was a revelation of what He is going to do for us one of these days.

That was the purpose of the Transfiguration. It was intended to show the magnificence of the humanity of the Lord Jesus Christ—which is why John does not pick it up and record it in His gospel. John is primarily concerned with Christ's deity.

## 3. The people

Now we must remove the shoes, as it were, from our feet, for the place whereon we stand is holy ground. Peter, in his epistle, reminds us that this is "the holy mount." We approach with reverence and awe.

We see three groups of people. First, there is Peter, James, and John. Then there is Moses and Elijah. Finally, we see the Son and the Father. Of the seven people present on the mountain, five were creatures of time and two came from out of eternity. Two came from out of the past, three came from the present, and two came from eternity. The Old Testament dispensation was represented by Moses and Elijah;

the New Testament dispensation was represented by Peter, James, and John.

### a. The first group: Peter, James, and John

On three occasions, the Lord Jesus took these men apart from the others to give them a special manifestation of himself. On two of these occasions, they fell asleep, and on both of those occasions there was a prayer meeting.

Jesus took the three disciples aside once to show them His *greatness* at the raising back to life of Jairus's twelve-year-old daughter. He took them aside once again to show them His *grief* in the Garden of Gethsemane. And here He took them aside to show them His *glory*.

As we see them now, they are sound asleep. The shades of night have drawn in. The walk up the mountain has taken its toll on even such hardened troopers as these. Overcome with exhaustion, they've fallen asleep while Jesus quietly prays.

Suddenly their eyes start open! Jesus stands before them bathed in a mysterious light, His face shining like the sun in its strength, His very garments white and glistening. For one brief hour they are permitted to see Him in all the glory of His sinless humanity—man as God intended man to be. Glorious! So far as His humanity was concerned, the Lord Jesus could have stepped right into heaven from the summit of Hermon. His whole being was aglow! It burned and blazed with a majestic splendor unseen on earth since Adam fell. The Bible says of God that He covers himself with light as with a garment (Ps. 104:2). Doubtless that is how Adam and Eve were clothed before the Fall. They were naked and unashamed because they were robed with light. When they fell, the light went out and they stood exposed in all their shame.

Now the second man, the last Adam, stood clothed in light, though not the brightness of innocence or the burning of holiness; this was the blaze of glory. Peter, James, and John rubbed their eyes. They never forgot this experience. Let us pause for a moment to trace the subsequent careers of these three men.

### (1) James: The church's martyr

James was the first of the twelve apostles to die. He died under the sword of Herod, and he died for the faith committed to the saints. He was by no means the only apostle to be martyred. It is probable that all of them eventually met their deaths as martyrs for the faith. Legend has it, for instance, that Andrew traveled to Greece and there was martyred by being crucified on an X-shaped cross, the kind of cross we still call a St. Andrew's cross. Tradition has it that Nathanael was flogged to death and that his body was tied up in a sack and thrown into the sea. Matthew is supposed to have met a martyr's death in Ethiopia. Another tradition says he was condemned to death by the Jewish Sanhedrin. Simon Peter was crucified for Christ. Tradition says he was crucified upside down. Tradition says that John was boiled in oil in the days of Domitian, that the oil had no power to hurt him, and that he eventually died of old age. Thomas is said to have taken the gospel to India and to have been killed by a shower of arrows shot into him while he was praying.

But James was the first. He reminds us that the blood of the martyrs is the seed of the church. There he stood on the holy mount, destined to one day wear a martyr's crown.

### (2) John: The church's mystic

John was a dreamer. John is the apostle who grapples with the more profound aspects of Christianity. John is the apostle who wrote last and who exposed the Gnostics and their phony mysticism. John is the apostle who wrote the Apocalypse, with its symbols and seals, trumpets and triumphs, its mystery of iniquity, and its mystery Babylon, its visions and vials, prophecies and parenthesis. John stood on the holy mount drinking in the mysteries of the kingdom of heaven, catching his first glimpse of a glorified Christ.

### (3) Peter: The church's messenger

It was Peter who preached at Pentecost, charging guilt to the conscience of the Jewish nation for the murder of their Messiah. It was Peter who saw three thousand people at one time swept on a revival tide into the kingdom of God.

Up on Mount Hermon, Peter opened his mouth to speak. He spoke without thinking: "Lord, it is good for us to be here . . . and let us make here three tabernacles; one for thee, and one for Moses, and one for Elias." He was speaking utter nonsense. He wanted to put Christ on a par with Moses and Elijah, yet only a week before, he had risen far, far above such worldly notions. "Thou art the Christ," he had said, "the Son of the living God." On the Day of Pentecost, he would learn to speak under the Holy Spirit's control.

### b. The second group: Moses and Elijah

Why wasn't Abraham, the founder of the Hebrew racial family, there on Mount Hermon? Why wasn't David, the founder of the Hebrew royal family, there? Why wasn't Isaiah, the great writing prophet; or Jeremiah, the great weeping prophet; or Daniel, the great wisdom prophet, there? Why Moses? Why Elijah?

### (1) Moses: The law—the sacrifices

Moses represented the law and the commandments of the Old Testament. It was Moses who had received the law on Mount Sinai, written with the finger of God into the tables of stone. It was Moses who had laid the moral foundations of the nation of Israel. Moses gave the nation its rules and its religion.

Moses stood on Mount Hermon to represent the law, which had much to say about Christ, who himself had declared that He had come not to destroy the law but to fulfill it. Moses was on the mountain to talk about the Old Testament symbols and shadows that formed the warp and woof of the Jewish religion, and which so unerringly pointed to Calvary.

### (2) Elijah: The prophets—the Scriptures

Elijah represented the prophets. God had raised up the prophets because the people had turned their backs on the law and the commandments. The prophets' task was to call the people back to God. When Elijah first arrived on the scene, a new day had dawned in Israel. He represented the conscience of the Old Testament. The prophets had a great deal to say about Christ. They foretold when and where He would be born, how and why He would die. The prophets had sought to quicken the conscience of the people. Elijah was there, on Mount Hermon, to represent them.

So Moses and Elijah were on the Mount of Transfiguration to talk to Jesus about Calvary, about "his decease which he should accomplish at Jerusalem" (Luke 9:31). The word for "decease" is an interesting one. It is an unusual word for death. It really means "exodus." Moses and Elijah were there to talk to the Son of God about His coming exodus. Moses had made his exodus from life through the dark port of death, dying alone in the arms of God on the bleak reaches of Mount Nebo. Elijah had made his exodus in a chariot of fire, and had been caught up alive into heaven. Moses was on Mount Hermon to represent those who believe and who die. Elijah was there to represent those who believe and are raptured.

These two men from the past had come to talk to the Lord about his exodus, about the death that would fulfill all the types and shadows and direct prophecies of the Old Testament. Moses was there to talk to the Lord about the sacrifices demanded under the law. Elijah was there to talk to the Lord about the many Old Testament prophecies of His death—to talk to Him, for instance, about what Isaiah had said, "He is led as a lamb to the slaughter . . . and the Lord hath laid upon him the iniquity of us all" (Isa. 53:6, 7). He was there to talk to

Him about what Daniel had said, and what Zechariah had said, and what all the others had said. What a conversation it must have been. We are told nothing of what the perfect man said to those two men from out of the past. But there they were, talking of His forthcoming decease.

### c. The third group: The Son and the Father

The Son had just been unveiled as glorious in His perfect humanity. The Father now proclaimed Him perfect in His deity: "This is my beloved Son, in whom I am well pleased; hear ye him" (Matt. 17:5).

There, upon the sacred mountain, amid the splendors of its snows, with saints of bygone ages summoned out of the past, with Peter, James, and John, the companions of His earthly sojourn, standing shivering in their fear, the Lord is proclaimed as the Son of God.

The voice came out of the cloud. This was no ordinary cloud. It was a bright cloud. The brightness of the cloud and the paralyzing fear it begot suggests that this was nothing less than the Shechinah cloud, the cloud that throughout the Old Testament period spoke of the visible presence of God among His people. This was the cloud that marched before Israel in the wilderness. This was the cloud that sat enthroned upon the mercy seat between the cherubim, on the sacred ark, beyond the veil in the most holy place. This was the fiery pillar that had long since been picked up and removed from Israel to glory. Now it was back to signal the presence of the living God there on the mountain.

## 4. The prospect

The central person of the whole dramatic incident was, of course, God's beloved Son. The great purpose of the vision was to focus attention on Him. In this incident, three things were underlined in prospect: His goal, His glory, and His grace.

## a. His goal

His death "which he should accomplish at Jerusalem" (Luke 9:31). That was Christ's goal. That was why He came down from the heights of heaven to be born as a man among men. That is why He came down from the mountain to resume His journey to the cross. He needed no urging from Moses on the basis of law. He needed no urging from Elijah on the basis of prophecy. It was for this purpose He had come into the world. All other men are born to live; He alone was born to die. His death would not be an accident or a cruel twist of fate. It would be an accomplishment! He was going to destroy Satan and deliver mankind.

## b. His glory

If the underlining of Christ's goal focuses our attention on his first coming, then the underlining of His glory focuses our attention on His second coming. For Jesus is coming again. As the old hymn puts it:

> Our Lord is now rejected,
> And by the world disowned,
> By the many still neglected,
> And by the few enthroned,
> But soon He'll come in glory,
> The hour is drawing nigh,
> For the crowning day is coming by and by.[1]

When that day dawns, the glory of His humanity and the glory of His deity, the glory that blazed forth on the holy mountain and the glory He had with the Father before the world began, will combine to give men a glimpse of glory beyond the brightness of the noonday sun.

## c. His grace

"They saw no man save Jesus only." Up on the holy mountain, Peter, James, and John saw the man, Christ Jesus. He came, He touched them and said, "Arise and be not afraid." Then walking between them He came down with them from the mountain. That was His grace. He had acted as the mediator between God and mankind. The disciples had been able to visit the holy mountain because Jesus had been there. They were able to come down alive because He was there. The Lord, perfect man and perfect God, mediated there between God and man. Because He did, Moses and Elijah (representatives of the dead and raptured saints) were able to go back to heaven. Because He did, Peter, James, and John, representatives of the saints on earth, were able to come back down from that holy place and resume life down here.

## 5. The postscript

Down in the valley, the other nine disciples were surrounded by a great multitude and were hemmed in by the scribes. There was a distracted father and a demon-possessed boy. There they were, powerless to cast out the demon, under scrutiny of the crowd, and goaded by the Jewish religious leaders. It was a perfect cameo of the world. In that one scene, we see the dispirited church, the demented boy, the drifting crowd, and the dead religion.

### a. The dispirited church

Christ was absent. He had gone on high. The believers were powerless in the face of crisis. They had no thought of the fasting and prayer by which, so often, the real power comes. "Why could not we cast him out?" the disciples asked Christ upon his return from the mountain (Mark 9:28). It was because they had not availed themselves of the spiritual weapons of power. It was because of their unbelief. They mirror the church of our day and age in all these ways.

### b. The demented boy

Luke tells us it was the father's only son. The only son of a human father and the only Son of the heavenly Father are now to come face-to-face. The wretched boy was demon-possessed, held in the fierce grip of the Evil One. What a picture of lost men in a world that doesn't know Christ! How sad that the church was powerless in the face of such desperate need, just as it is largely powerless today.

### c. The drifting crowd

Also on the scene was a great mass of mankind, tossed and pulled, this way and that—the crowd, with its lack of concern, its lack of conviction, its lack of conscience, and its lack of everything. The crowd was there, gaping at the powerless disciples, and perhaps enjoying their dilemma, and listening to the sarcasms of the scribes.

### d. The dead religion

The religious leaders were there; the scribes, who claimed to be specialists in the Scriptures. There they were, set in their opposition to Christ and gloating over the wretched failure of His people. Into that scene comes the returning Christ. He brings with Him those of His people who have been with Him during His absence; those who have already seen His glory. Instantly all is changed! So it will be in a coming day. Even so, come Lord Jesus!

## CHAPTER 12

# MY BELOVED
*Song of Solomon 5:10-16*

1. The purity of the beloved
2. The position of the beloved
3. The person of the beloved
   a. His sovereignty
   b. His strength
   c. His sight
   d. His sweetness
   e. His sayings
   f. His skill
   g. His substance
   h. His stand
   i. His splendor
   j. His smile

I WAS DRIVING SOME TIME AGO with Stan Ford, an English preacher friend of mine, through some particularly magnificent scenery. All of a sudden, Stan could stand it no longer. He simply lifted up his hands in a gesture of awe and admiration and he cried out, "Well done, Lord!"

We have all probably felt like that. We have felt our hearts well up within us over some glorious piece of scenery, over some fresh and overpowering glimpse of Calvary, or over some sudden and unexpected answer to prayer. We simply cry out loud, "Thank you, Lord!" or "I love you, Lord!" These heartfelt, spontaneous expressions are treasured by our Lord. These are the things that make Calvary well worthwhile to Him. He sees of the travail of His soul and is satisfied.

The Shulamite portrayed in the Song of Solomon experienced such emotion when she thought of her beloved, a shepherd from whom she had been separated by circumstances beyond her control. At the time of our story, she was virtually a prisoner in Solomon's magnificent palace. He was doing everything in his power to dazzle and seduce her. Her frightened, lonely heart cried out, however, for her beloved. She remained unmoved by all the pomp and circumstance of the world around her. The constant pressure of its king to yield to his advances left her cold and fearful. Her lonely heart cried out for her beloved, her dear but absent shepherd.

Let us borrow the Shulamite's language for a little while and lift the whole story to a higher realm. This eloquent, lovely woman, whose heart was indicting a good matter, and whose tongue was the pen of a ready writer, will teach us how to talk about our Beloved, our absent Shepherd. Sometimes, He seems so far away. We battle the allurements and temptations of this present evil world seemingly on our own. The Shulamite will show us what to do and say under such circumstances.

We first note that she deliberately occupies her heart and mind with thoughts of her shepherd. With such thoughts flowing like molten lava from her lips, with such warm emotion erupting from the hot heart that beat within, the subtleties and sophistries of Solomon could only fall upon deaf ears. Not for all his wealth, flatteries, and offers would she be false to the one who had won her heart.

Her passionate words revolve around three great facts—the *purity* of her beloved, the *position* of her beloved, and the *person* of her beloved.

## 1. The purity of the beloved

"My beloved is white and ruddy" (Song 5:10). White is the symbol of purity; ruddy is the symbol of glowing health. That was what David looked like when Jonathan first set eyes on him. "He was ruddy, and withal of a beautiful countenance, and goodly to look to" (1 Sam. 16:12).

White and ruddy! The Lord, in His wisdom, has left us no physical portrait of himself. Contemporary depictions that show Jesus with long hair and an anemic expression on His face are, after all, only the reflection of an artist's imagination. When Jesus trod the earth, he was a full-blooded man. His muscles had been hardened at the carpenter's bench and by ceaseless hikes up and down the hills and valleys of His native land. He was not effeminate, pale-faced, round-shouldered, and weak-kneed. He was robust and healthy and strong. Life flowed in the fullness of its tide through His veins. He was a perfect man. He was all that Adam was before the Fall. He was the most magnificent man who ever lived. White and ruddy! Purity and passion in perfect balance! A dynamic, glowing, glorious figure of a man.

White and ruddy! The first thing we think of when we think of our Beloved is His purity. It was a purity before which all sin, all suggestiveness, all temptation, withered and died as a snowball does before the fire.

It was not that He was never tempted, but temptation never had a chance with Him. Satan's sordid suggestions were doomed to abysmal failure from the very start. Satan did not stand a ghost of a chance of seducing our Beloved from His purity. It was a white-hot purity, such as that before which the shining seraphim hid their faces in their wings. It was a white-hot purity, burning and blazing within a wondrous, perfect vehicle of human clay. It was a holiness that shone out of His eyes and burned on His tongue, and which tinctured all He said or thought or did.

Satan came to Jesus in the wilderness when the Lord had been without food for more than a month. In a prolonged fast, the sense of hunger is said to leave after three days, but when the limits of endurance are reached, it comes back with all its force. That was the moment when Satan struck. He struck along the line of *appetite:* "Command that these stones be made bread" (Matt. 4:3). There was no doubt in Satan's mind about the deity of Christ. He knew perfectly well that Jesus *could* change stones into bread, just as He later changed water into wine. In His hands, a little lad's lunch could multiply into an ample feast for a multitude. "Command that these stones be made bread." It was an attempt to kill Jesus. A forty-day fast cannot be broken with bread; it must be broken gradually, with fruit juice first and then weak soups. A loaf of bread would have killed Him. But He was hungry. All His human flesh cried out for food. But bread made to the Devil's recipe was no bread for Him. His holiness blazed out. "Man shall not live by bread alone" He said, "but by every word that proceedeth out of the mouth of God" (Matt. 4:4).

Satan tried again. He took Jesus to the pinnacle of the temple, the high point of the temple enclosure, which looked down over the Kidron Valley. "Cast thyself down!" he said. This time Satan struck along the line of *assertiveness.* "You trust God? Then put Him to the test. Do something daring, something spectacular." Again the Lord's blazing purity killed the thought. "Thou shalt not tempt the Lord thy God," He said.

Persistently, Satan came back with yet another idea. He struck now along the line of *ambition.* "Worship me," he said, "and I will give you the kingdoms of this world and all their power and glory." This time Jesus simply told Satan to go away. He would not have the crown without the cross. "Worship me," said Satan, "And I'll abdicate my throne to you." Jesus could have laughed in his face; the lie was so obvious, so transparent. It was ambition out of the will of God that had transformed Lucifer, the anointed cherub, the leader of the choirs of heaven and the most illustrious and beautiful and brilliant of all God's creatures, into Satan, the incarnation of evil, vice, wickedness, and sin.

The temptations with which Satan tempted Jesus are real enough that millions have fallen for them down through the ages. But the tempter would vie with our Beloved in vain. Jesus could not sin. He could not sin for the simple reason that His burning holiness made sin impossible.

"My beloved is white and ruddy," said the Shulamite. And so is ours. Let us consider not only His purity, but also his position.

## 2. The position of the beloved

"My beloved is white and ruddy, the chiefest among ten thousand" (Song 5:10). Again our thoughts go back to David, the great shepherd of Israel, who went down into the valley to fight Goliath of Gath. Everyone else thought that Goliath was too big to fight; David thought he was too big to miss! Once Goliath was dead, the soldiers of King Saul routed the terrified Philistines. When the troops returned from their pursuit, they sang a new song: "Saul hath slain his thousands, and David his ten thousands" (1 Sam. 18:7). David was the chiefest among ten thousand, and for many in Israel he remained just that. He reigned in their affections despite the fact that it was Saul who continued to sit on the throne.

"My beloved is the chiefest among *ten thousand.*" But He is more than that! We take our stand with John on eternity's shore. There, high and lifted up, we see the throne of God and Him who sits upon it like a jasper and a sardine stone. We see the rainbow, the river, the tree of life, the wondrous city (Rev. 4:3; 22:2). We see one step into the spotlight of it all—the Lion of the tribe of Judah, the root of David, the Lamb of God with seven eyes and seven horns. He takes the scroll, the title deeds of earth into His hands and instantly all heaven bursts into song (v. 8). John could not count them. He simply says they were numbered by the myriads—ten thousand times ten thousand and thousands of thousands.

Our Beloved is the chiefest of them all. John proves it. From then on, the Lamb fills the book. He is mentioned four times in that same chapter and again and again throughout the book of Revelation. Indeed, when we come to the last two chapters, which describe for us the wonders of the glory land, we find that it is the *Lamb,* the *Lamb,* the *Lamb* all the way through. He is the chiefest among "ten thousand times ten thousand, and thousands of thousands (Rev. 5:11). That is His position.

### 3. The person of the beloved

The Shulamite lingers long and lovingly over the person of her beloved. She talks about his head, his locks, his eyes, his cheeks, his lips, his hands, his belly, his legs, his countenance, his mouth. She describes ten things about the person of her beloved. Everything about him fills her heart with joy. Now, with her, we think of our Beloved's sovereignty, strength, sight, sweetness, sayings, skill, substance, stand, splendor, and smile:

#### a. His sovereignty

"His head is as the most fine gold" (Song 5:11). Gold, in Scripture, is a symbol of sovereignty. When the wise men brought Jesus a gift of *gold,* they simply acknowledged Him as a king. Nebuchadnezzar, in his dream, saw an image with a head of gold. "Thou art this head of gold," Daniel told him, acknowledging that Nebuchadnezzar was a God-appointed king (2:38).

That is the first thing about the person of our Beloved. He carried himself with the royalty, the mien and majesty, the carriage and dignity, of a king. He is every inch a king. When He came to earth, He laid aside His royal robes and clothed himself in human flesh. His robed His humanity with ordinary working man's clothes. Just the same, He carried himself with an air of authority and sovereignty. The demon world acknowledged it instantly. Peter saw it on the Mount of Transfiguration: "Thou art the Christ," he said. "Thou art the anointed one. Thou art the Son of God."

#### b. His strength

"His locks are bushy, and black as a raven" (Song 5:11). Bushy black hair is the very symbol of virility and vital force. It suggests a person in the vigorous prime of life, a young man in all the force and power of his strength. Such is our Beloved.

He is strong. Our thoughts go back to Samson with his long,

unshorn locks. His hair was the secret that Delilah sought, the secret wherein his great strength lay. Samson, shorn of his locks, was as weak as a kitten. But Samson with his hair tumbling down his shoulders was able to rend a lion. He was strong enough to hoist the gates of Gaza on his shoulders and carry them, bolts and bars and all, way up the hill.

Thus, too, our Lord. They could nail Him to the tree—because He allowed them to, but they could not kill Him. He could say, "No man taketh [my life] from me, but I lay it down of myself" (John 10:18). They could lock Him in the tomb, but no power on earth or in hell could keep Him there. On the resurrection morning, He simply hoisted the gates of hell onto the self-same shoulders that had carried the cross to Calvary and bore them away in triumph. As we sometimes sing:

> Death cannot keeps its prey,
> Jesus, my Savior;
> He tore the bars away,
> Jesus, my Lord![1]

That is our Beloved!

### c. His sight

"His eyes are as the eyes of doves by the rivers of waters, washed with milk, and fitly set" (Song 5:12). Rotherham puts it like this: "His eyes like doves by the channels of water, bathed in milk, set as gems in a ring."

What eyes He has, this Beloved of ours. They gazed out over nothingness before the worlds began and watched as an expanding universe threw its tangle of stars over the limitless bounds of infinite space. His eyes picked out our planet and watched as the darkness rolled back before the dawn of day, as the mountains heaved themselves up from the depths of the sea and rolled back the angry waves of the mighty deep, as the atmosphere moved in to keep apart the vast oceans suspended in space from the waters of the seven seas. His eyes saw verdure spread its blanket of green like a mantle of life across the hills and vales. Then, as life in countless forms swarmed through the seas, filled the skies, and took possession of the land, those blessed eyes still watched. He watched, too, as the dust of the earth took the form of a living man. The first sight that Adam ever beheld was the wondrous eyes of our Beloved.

Those eyes of His saw seven demons in Mary Magdalene's heart. Those eyes scared the demons out of their devilish wits and they fled in terror, leaving Mary as the devoted servant of our Beloved for evermore. Those eyes saw the body of Lazarus in his tomb and saw Lazarus himself yonder in glory, tuning up his harp. As those wondrous eyes caught his, Lazarus put down his harp and hastened back to earth. Those eyes looked into the eyes of Judas in the upper room. They told him, as plain as print, that Christ could see the blood money in the traitor's purse. Those eyes looked upon the rooster on that fateful crucifixion morning. At once, the cock crowed in warm response. Those eyes then turned and looked at Peter, bringing a Gethsemane of grief into the disciple's soul. Those eyes gazed at the naked sun as Christ hung on the tree. At once, the sun hid its blushing face in blackest darkness rather than gaze a moment longer on what men were doing to our Beloved. At last, those eyes closed in death and remained thus closed while this wretched world revolved three times in agony, carrying the dead form of heaven's Beloved. What eyes they are!

Those eyes of His danced with good fellowship in the upper room over a piece of broiled fish and honeycomb. Those eyes of His gaze even now from the Father's throne in glory. They see us as we gather in His name, and they beam with satisfaction. Those eyes will gaze into ours at the moment of death. Death will dissolve into life. The sight of His eyes will be our first experience of paradise.

### d. His sweetness

"His cheeks are as a bed of spices, as sweet flowers" (Song 5:13). To be near Him is to breathe the fragrance of ointment poured forth and to be wrapped in the perfume of spices and flowers. To be near Him is to be bathed in sweetness. It is impossible to be near Him and not bring some subtle sense of His presence to others we meet. This is our Beloved! Oh, to be so near to Him, so close to Him that our cheeks might be put alongside His in our daily quiet time! Oh, to enjoy His sweetness and love.

Shall we ever forget His cheeks? When He grew into manhood, Christ wore a manly beard upon those cheeks. And there, either in the house of Caiaphas or else in Pilate's judgment hall, some great brute took that beard in his callused hands and wrenched it from the Lord's cheeks. And He let him do it! And, wonder of wonders, He loved that man with an everlasting love. No wonder D. L. Moody used to picture Jesus after His resurrection, sending Peter or James or John to find that fellow to tell him that he was forgiven of his coward's deed of shame.

*e. His sayings*

"His lips like lilies, dropping sweet smelling myrrh" (Song 5:13). The most wonderful words ever uttered in mortal tongue fell from Christ's lips. Even His enemies testified, "Never man spake like this man" (John 7:46). They marveled, indeed, at the gracious words that proceeded forth from His mouth.

The Jews used sweet-smelling myrrh at their funerals and weddings so that it might add its perfume to soothe their sorrows in life's saddest hour and to express their joy in life's gladdest hour. Think of the sweet-smelling myrrh that fell from Jesus' lips when He attended a wedding! "Fill the waterpots with water," He said. Then, as the poet puts it:

> The simple creature,
> Touched by grace Divine,
> Owned its Creator—
> And blushed into wine!

Think of the sweet-smelling myrrh that fell from Jesus' lips when He attended a funeral. "Thy brother shall rise again!" He declared. Then He added, "I am the resurrection, and the life: he that believeth in me, though he were dead, yet shall he live: And whosoever liveth and believeth in me shall never die" (John 11:25–26). Resurrection life! Spiritual life! Eternal life! All in a single sentence, and all proved wonderfully true a moment or two later when Lazarus came marching out of the tomb.

Nor could the world itself contain the books that could be written about those wonderful words of life that fell each and every day from those lovely lips of His.

### f. His skill

"His hands are as gold rings set with the beryl" (Song 5:14). Those hands were placed on the heads of little children. They touched the casket in which a dead man lay, and instantly the dead man leaped to life! Those loving hands touched the leper. He could have cleansed the leper with a word, from a distance, calling across the great gulf that separated the leper from the rest of mankind. But no! He *touched* him.

Think of it! That poor, unclean, leprous-ridden man was one of this world's untouchables. Yet he dared to draw near to Jesus. People warned him off. They shouted at him to stay back, to stand back, as Moses in the law decreed. But still he came, daring the danger of being stoned along the way. The people backed up before him. If he would not keep his distance, they would; for their very lives. On he came, until at last, a miserable, unhappy soul, he stood face-to-face with Jesus. And Jesus *touched* him. It was the first touch he had received since that horrible disease had fastened on his flesh.

His hands! His royal hands! His hands decked with gold rings and beryl. Think what men did to those hands. But those same hands hold the scepter now. The fate of the universe, the planet, and each individual person, is in those hands.

### g. His substance

"His belly [or, more literally, his *body*] is as bright [or polished] ivory overlaid with sapphires" (Song 5:14). Before He came into this world at Bethlehem, the Lord Jesus lived as an eternal, uncreated, self-existing spirit. He was God the Son, the second person of the Godhead. He never ceased to be God, but when He became man, He took upon himself *substance*. He took a human body.

The singer of the Song describes it as "bright ivory overlaid with sapphires." The ivory tells us that the body Jesus assumed was a true, solid, material, real body. Ivory is something hard and substantial. You can pick it up and handle it. The body of Jesus was a real body. It was not some form of make-believe body. It was a body as real and as solid and as substantial as yours and mine. It performed all the normal functions of a body. Jesus ate and drank and slept and grew in stature. He had a real body.

The ivory, moreover was bright ivory. That is, it was polished. Polished ivory suggests something brought to a beautiful finish. All its innate, inherent beauties of substance are enhanced. Its perfections are obvious to the eye. The Lord Jesus kept His body in perfect condition. He never allowed it to rule Him. It was always the perfect vehicle through which He could express the glorious life of God in physical terms. In Him dwelt "all the fulness of the Godhead *bodily*" (Col. 2:9, emphasis added).

Then, too, the ivory was overlaid with sapphires. The sapphire is a blue gem, a precious stone that displays in its very nature, in its deepest depths, the color and glory of heaven. The body of Jesus was *of* heaven—it was conceived of the Holy Spirit. The body of Jesus is now *in* heaven. After the resurrection, He took that body back to glory with Him, and there, in that glorified human body of His, He now sits on the throne of God. Even the wounds, the marks of Calvary, are there. One of these days, we shall see our Beloved in His body.

### h. His stand

"His legs are as pillars of marble, set upon sockets of fine gold" (Song 5:15). Pillars of marble: what a picture of magnificent stability and strength. Set in sockets of gold. Again, Christ's eternal and essential sovereignty is seen. Think how He took His stand for God in all that He said and did. He took His stand for God at the age of twelve. His first recorded words were these, "Wist ye not that I must be about my Father's business?" (Luke 2:49). He took His stand for God in the river Jordan. He took His stand for God when Satan came to tempt Him. He took His stand for God when He cleansed the temple. He took His stand for God when He attacked Satan's hold upon the hearts and minds and souls of men. He took His stand for God in everything He said and did. He took His stand for God before Caiaphas, Herod, and Pilate. His legs were pillars of marble.

On the cross, they broke the legs of the thieves, but His legs they could not break. Those legs were pillars of marble. Even the tough, callous soldiers of Rome did not dare to raise their hammer to them.

### i. His splendor

"His countenance is as Lebanon, excellent as the cedars" (Song 5:15). The cedars of Lebanon were renowned across the ancient world for their beauty, majesty, and stateliness. Stamped on the face of Jesus was an expression of sublime royalty and dignity. No one ever saw His face register doubt or perplexity. That face of His was always radiant with the splendor of the life He lived.

That face will one day banish both heaven and earth. That face will one day beam on us as He welcomes us home. We shall never be able to take our eyes off His face. One old hymn says: "Oh, the soul-thrilling rapture when I view His blessed face, and the luster of His kindly beaming eye!"[2] Another exclaims: "One glimpse of His dear face all sorrows will erase."[3] And yet another says: "Just to be there and to look on His face; will through the ages be glory for me!"[4] The face of Jesus will be heaven for every child of God. No tongue can tell its glories. It is like Lebanon, excellent as the cedars. Everything of manliness and majesty and magnificence shines in that face. We shall be thrilled through and through at the sight of it.

### j. His smile

"His mouth is most sweet" (Song 5:16). Our wonderful Lord, with a countenance like Lebanon, excellent as the cedars, is no remote, unapproachable, cold, impassive, distant Lord. Oh no! He loves us. His countenance will break into a smile of welcome at the sight of us. "His mouth is most sweet."

Do you remember how the Song of Solomon begins? Recall the very first word after the title: "Let him kiss me with the kisses of his mouth: for thy love is better than wine" (Song 1:2). Oh yes! His mouth is most sweet. "Yea, he is altogether lovely. This is my beloved, and this is my friend" (Song 5:16).

## CHAPTER 13

# THE BETHANY HOME
*John 12*

1. The worker: Martha (v. 2)
2. The worshipper: Mary (vv. 3–8)
   a. How her worship was expressed (v. 3)
   b. How her worship was examined (vv. 4–6)
   c. How her worship was extolled (vv. 7–8)
3. The witness: Lazarus (vv. 9–11)

IT WAS THE SABBATH DAY, THE Lord's very last Sabbath on earth; the last Sabbath, indeed, of the old dispensation. The last Sabbath, that is, except one, and that one Jesus would spend in the tomb. It would be His last day in the tomb. On the morrow, He would rise from the dead and Judaism as a religion would have no more meaning. It would be as dead as its last Sabbath. So then, it was the Sabbath. The Lord spent His last Sabbath at Bethany, just over the brow of Olivet, at the home of His dear friends Martha, Mary, and Lazarus.

The Jews enjoyed their Sabbath despite every effort of the Pharisees and rabbis to rob them of its joys and turn its delights into drudgery. Each house was adorned on Friday evening so as to meet the Sabbath; adorned as for a bride. The Sabbath lamp was lighted. Festive garments were donned. The choicest food was put on the table, though a man must work all week to provide it or public charity supply it. On the

Sabbath, there must be no mourning. The Sabbath stood alone among the other days of the week. Each other day had its pair, but the Sabbath stood all by itself. The Jews said that when the Sabbath complained to the Creator that it stood aloof and alone, the Creator married it to Israel. According to the rabbis, even the tortures of Gehenna ceased for the day of Sabbath. And when the Sabbath morning broke, the Jews hurried to the synagogue, and on the way home they lingered.

The Sabbath had been ordained by God as a day of rest. And the Lord rested this final Sabbath day and hallowed it. His work on earth was almost done. The countdown to Calvary had now begun. So, with that greatest and most arduous and most awesome of all works before Him, Jesus sought out the one home on earth where He felt at home, the home of His three Bethany friends.

We would do well to get the timetable in our minds. This Sabbath was the fifth day before the Passover. On the morrow, the Lord would ride triumphantly into Jerusalem. The next day, the third day before the Passover, He would curse the fig tree and withdraw God's blessing from Israel. The day after that would be the second day before the Passover. He would deliver His Olivet discourse. The following day, the day before the Passover, was what the Jews called the Preparation Day, the day they killed the Passover lamb, the day they killed Christ. Even as the Jews were slaying their lambs, Christ, the Passover Lamb, would be slain and would bow His head and die.

So then, we creep into that Bethany home on this momentous Sabbath. Within the week, the Lord would be dead. He would be in His tomb. He would rise from the dead as soon as the week was over, early in the morning at the end of the next Sabbath, "as it began to dawn toward the first day of the week" (Matt. 28:1). It is this that gives such significance to all that happened in that Bethany home on this particular Sabbath day.

There were three people living in that Bethany home—*Martha* (the worker), *Mary* (the worshipper), and *Lazarus* (the witness). They are the three kinds of people every local church needs.

## 1. The worker: Martha (v. 2)

"There they made him a supper," we read in John 12:2, "and Martha served." John adds the note, "But Lazarus was one of them that sat at the table with him." Lazarus was still front-page news. The story of the raising of Lazarus was still being told all over Jerusalem and all around the country. It was public knowledge. Nowadays, some church group or special interest group would put Lazarus on a TV talk show. At least his story would be authentic. They would promote him and interview him and get him to give his testimony. They would use him to raise money. Then some publishing house would send around a ghost writer and they would publish a sensational experience-oriented best-seller—*Lazarus, Raised from the Dead: The astonishing story of a man who died and lived to tell about it!* Then Lazarus would be sent on the road to promote his book and make someone's fortune.

The real Lazarus had more sense. We see him maintaining as low a profile as possible, taking his seat at his own table in his Bethany home and installing Jesus in the seat of honor at the head.

Martha was a worker. "Martha served," John says. She had done that before. Luke tells us about it (10:38–42). That time she had complained bitterly because Mary was not pulling her weight in the kitchen. She had now learned the joy of serving without any thought of self, reward, recognition, or what other people were doing. She served!

All she wanted to do now was what she did best, wait on tables, minister to the Lord's people. Every church needs its quota of Marthas. These are the people who run the nursery and give the little ones their first and most important impressions of church. These are the people who make sure that things are kept clean and polished, who attend to the hundred and one things that are so necessary for the comfort and well-being of all. Where would we be without the Marthas? This is a Godlike work, for Jesus "came not to be ministered unto, but to minister, and to give his life a ransom for many" (Mark 10:45). Giving His life in service was as important as giving His life in sacrifice.

So Martha was in her place. Martha served. And everyone was much better able to enjoy the festive occasion because she did. It was

Martha's way of saying her personal thank you to Jesus for raising
Lazarus from the dead.

## 2. The worshipper: Mary (vv. 3–8)

We always find Mary of Bethany at Jesus' feet. Every local church
needs its quota of Marys, people who know how to get to the feet of
Jesus, people who know how to worship and adore.

Thinking back over the years, John recalled three things about
Mary's worship on this last Sabbath. The whole scene gives us a perfect
cameo of a local church. The worker was there, the worshipper was
there, and the witness was there. The rank and file of the disciples were
there—Peter, with his spurts and starts and ups and downs; John with
his deep devotion to Jesus; James the son of thunder, martyr material
in the raw; Thomas with his stolidity, stubbornness, and skepticism;
Andrew with his gift for making friends and bringing people to Jesus;
Philip with his questions; Nathanael with his lofty ideals; and Judas
with his treacherous heart and black, unregenerate soul. And Jesus in
the midst, and the crowds not far away. The first thing John remembers
about Mary's worship was how it was expressed.

### a. How her worship was expressed (v. 3)

"Then took Mary a pound of ointment of spikenard, very costly,
and anointed the feet of Jesus, and wiped his feet with her hair: and
the house was filled with the odour of the ointment."

Nard was a liquid perfume of great value, very expensive. It was the
very best that money could buy. In one lavish gesture, Mary poured it
all out over the feet of Jesus. Then, with a gesture that scorned what
other people might think, she flung herself at those perfumed feet
and mopped up the excess spikenard with her hair. It was an act as
extravagant as the first.

What John remembered after some sixty or seventy years was the
fragrance. The whole house was filled with it. Such is worship. Worship gives its best, it does not scrimp, it spends. Worship does not

stop to consider what people will say. Worship is the overflow of a heart in love with Jesus. Worship is not intimidated by the sneers of the worldly minded. Moreover, everyone present, when true worship is offered, carries away something of the fragrance of it all.

### b. How her worship was examined (vv. 4–6)

Judas Iscariot voiced his opinion. "Then saith one of his disciples, Judas Iscariot, Simon's son, which should betray him, 'Why was not this ointment sold for three hundred pence, and given to the poor?'" (John 12:4–5). That was Judas's estimate of both Mary and Jesus. So far as he was concerned, this kind of worship was sheer waste. Judas has plenty of company. There are multitudes of people who think that money given to the Lord's work is a waste. Why not spend that money on social services? Why not give the money to the poor? Why waste money trying to win savage tribes to Christ when there are thousands of poor people right here at home who need handouts?

Nor did Judas, with his carnal, materialistic mind, hesitate to put a price tag on Mary's worship. It was about the equivalent of a working man's annual wage. Judas waxed hysterical with hypocritical wrath at the thought of it. All that money poured out in one wasteful act! All that good money! For Jesus! Waste! That is what he thought it was.

John had nearly seventy years to think about Judas. "He was a thief," he says bluntly. "He kept the bag," he added. That was the real reason for his agitation. The word for "thief" is the word from which we get our English word *kleptomaniac*. That explained a lot of things. It explained why the accounts were always coming up short. The unsuspecting disciples, for years, had accepted the explanation that Judas was so concerned about the poor that whenever they had a surplus in the bag he would give it to the poor. Now, John knew the truth. Whatever surplus they had went out of the bag and into Judas's bank. He was salting it away. He was buying property with it, lining his nest. He was a thief.

"Why was not this ointment sold and given to the poor?" Well, of course, it was given to the poor. It was given to Jesus—the one who, "though he was rich, yet for your sakes he became poor" (2 Cor. 8:9).

The one who could say, "Foxes have holes, and birds of the air have nests; but the Son of man hath not where to lay his head" (Luke 9:58). The one who, when He died, left behind in material possessions just the clothes He had on His back. It was given to the poor.

### c. How her worship was extolled (vv. 7–8)

Judas's cutting, rude, and sneering remarks must have cut Mary's sensitive soul like a lash. She stood speechless. Jesus came at once to her rescue. "Let her alone," He said. "Against the day of my burying hath she kept this. For the poor always ye have with you: but me ye have not always."

"Against the day of my burying hath she kept this." That is the key. And to understand the full significance of it, we must go back and put ourselves in Mary's place. For this spontaneous act was not nearly so spontaneous as it seems. It was the result of some very deep thinking and some very careful planning. Mary was acting with great deliberation. She had carefully thought through what she did that day. The thought had occurred to her some time before. It had been nurtured and nourished, and it had matured.

Mary had often listened to Jesus. She had sat at His feet and had learned from Him. She had heard Him talk about His forthcoming death and burial. Alone, among all the disciples of Jesus, she believed what He said: He was going to die. She said to herself, "He is going to die. He is going to be buried. He will need spices for His burial. I will take care of that. I have my life savings, so I will buy spikenard, plenty of spikenard. I will have it all ready for his burial."

She did just that. At some point, she accosted a merchant, negotiated the transaction, and concealed the costly ointment among her few treasures. Nobody knew about it but her and Jesus, who knew everything and needed not to be told.

Then the unexpected happened. Lazarus died. Spices were needed for his burial. We can be sure that Mary, who loved her brother almost as much as she loved Jesus, had been sorely tempted to lavish her hidden spikenard on her dear brother's mortal remains.

However, she said to herself, "No! I did not buy this spikenard for Lazarus. I bought it for Jesus. It is not for Lazarus's burial. It is for Jesus' burial." So Jesus said, "Against the day of my burying hath she kept this." He knew! He had known all along. He knew she had it, where she kept it, and how much she paid for it. He knew the name of the merchant and knew why she had withheld it from Lazarus. "Against the day of *my* burial hath she kept this," He said. Mary must have looked at Him in astonishment. Why, He knew her every secret thought. He knows ours, too.

Then one day something happened. There was a resurrection! It took place in their own backyard, down at the bottom of the garden, at the tomb where Lazarus lay. Jesus had come along, and Lazarus, dead, buried, and decomposing in his grave, had been brought back to life. Raised from the dead! For days afterward, Mary pondered this mystery in her great, loving heart. She would say to Martha, "Tell me again, sister, what was it Jesus said to you that day?" And Martha would repeat the words she had learned by heart. "He said, 'I am the resurrection and the life.'" Mary, with her spikenard still intact against the day of Jesus' burial, added that to her secret store of information. She thought long and earnestly about it. She would lie awake at night thinking it through.

Then one day the light dawned. Of course! How could she have been so dull? He was going to die. He was going to be crucified. He had said so. He was going to be buried. He had said that too. But He was going *to rise again.* He had said so! On the third day, He would rise!

She thought about what the Scriptures had said. She thought of the prophetic, messianic sixteenth Psalm, "Thou wilt not . . . suffer thine Holy One to see corruption." He was to be buried. But He would not need spikenard to offset the stench of the tomb, for He would not see corruption at all.

So Mary said to herself, "The very next time Jesus is here, I will give it to Him then. Why wait until He is dead? I will give it to Him while He is yet alive." And so she did. It was a marvelous statement of her faith.

She gave it to Him a week before His death and burial, because she now believed in His resurrection. No wonder the house was filled with the fragrance of worship such as that! Mary seems to have been the only one who understood the significance of the Cross.

Mary of Bethany stayed away from the crucifixion. You find the other Marys there: Mary Magdalene, Mary the mother of Jesus, and Mary the mother of James and Joses, but not Mary of Bethany. She was already standing on resurrection ground.

### 3. The witness: Lazarus (vv. 9–11)

Every local church needs people like Lazarus in its midst, people who witness effectively to the unsaved about Jesus. We read, "Much people of the Jews therefore knew that [Jesus] was there: and they came not for Jesus' sake only, but that they might see Lazarus also, whom he had raised from the dead."

We have no idea how long Lazarus lived at Bethany. He had always been a decent, moral, law-abiding, synagogue-attending, Bible-believing Jew. More! He had become a believer in Christ. His home at Bethany had become a gathering place. People who knew and loved Jesus met there. Jesus was welcome there. His people were made to feel at home there. Lazarus was a believer. But nobody had ever made the two-mile trip from Jerusalem to Bethany to see him just because he was a believer in Christ. Nobody!

Now they came in droves. What made the difference? A man living a resurrection life. A man living day-by-day, situation-by-situation, moment-by-moment in the power of resurrection. Up until then, Lazarus had been a *believer*, a genuine, committed believer, but he had not been a *witness*.

After his experience of death, burial, and resurrection, Lazarus could not help himself. Just by virtue of the new life he was now living, he was a witness. He did not say, "Today I am going to knock on doors and witness for Jesus." He did not take a course in soul-winning, or memorize key texts. He could not help himself. He was a witness. He simply lived a resurrection life. And people came from all over to see the miracle of a man living a new life in Christ.

Suppose we could have asked him, "How do you do it, Lazarus? What is the secret of this dynamic new life of yours?" He would have said something like this, "I was not always this way. For years I was just a nominal believer in Christ. I loved the Lord and I wanted to please Him. He was the most important person in my life. I loved Him and I loved His people. I did all the right things, said all the right things, and was quite sincere. Then, one day I died. I died to everything. I died to my house, I died to my business, I died to my sisters, I died to my efforts to be a witness. I died and I was buried. The old Lazarus was very dead indeed. And everybody knew it.

"Now, you don't expect much from a dead man, do you? You just bury him. He is full of corruption. He is offensive. There is nothing more useless than a corpse. This condition lasted for four days. I cannot remember a thing about it. A dead man cannot talk, he cannot respond, he does not have any opinions, he cannot conduct business, he cannot witness—except to his rottenness.

"So, you see, I died and was buried. I came to an end of myself. Then Jesus came. He gave me a new life. His life! I came to my senses one day, and there I was on resurrection ground. So, you see, I am not the same old Lazarus you used to know. The life that I now live is the life that Jesus gave me."

People came from near and far to see the new Lazarus. There is something wonderfully attractive about the life of a person who has been identified with Christ in death, burial, and resurrection. And people believed. Not all of them. Some found this new life in Christ hateful. But many found the compelling attractiveness of the new Lazarus irresistible, and went away believing in Jesus, too.

## CHAPTER 14

# THE LORD'S ENEMIES
*John 8:48*

1. They should have gone down deeper
2. They should have gone up higher
3. They should have gone back further
4. They should have gone in sooner
5. They should have gone on longer

IT IS AN ASTONISHING AND TERRIBLE revelation that the Lord Jesus had enemies. And that He still does. It is a pejorative commentary on the nature of sin. Occasionally we meet people who nurse a special hatred of the Lord Jesus. Some do so through ignorance, as the young Saul of Tarsus did. But some revile Him and blaspheme Him and slander Him out of sheer malice.

One might have thought that Jesus would have had nothing but friends. After all, what was there not to like about Him? He was the most friendly, personable, and approachable man who ever lived. He had an attractive personality. Though we know nothing specific about His personal appearance, surely we may be permitted to infer, from the fact that He was a perfect man, that He was at least as "goodly to look to" as His forebearer David.

He was loving, cheerful, helpful, and kind, and wholly without prejudice, partiality, or bias. Peter, summing up the three-and-a-half remarkable years he had spent in the Lord's company declared, "[He] went about doing good" (Acts 10:38). And He was always the same. He never had to apologize for anything He said or for anything He did. He was as much a friend to publicans and sinners as He was to the aristocratic Nicodemus or the ruler of the Capernaum synagogue. He was known as "a friend of publicans and sinners" (Matt. 11:19). His enemies sneered at Him for that. But it tells us volumes about His compassion for the downtrodden, the despised and rejected of men. No one ever appealed to Him in vain. He had a well-earned reputation, among His closest friends, for His generosity to the poor. He was no respecter of persons. He loved Pilate as much as He loved Peter. He was as cordial to the woman at the well as He was to the rich young ruler. He loved Judas as much as He loved John. He displayed a sublime love to all people that was as unwavering as it was unwearying.

He attracted rich and poor, bond and free, great and small, wise and foolish, young and old, men and women. Strong men would leave their businesses to follow Him, and women instinctively fell in love with Him. Indeed, in all the Gospel record, we never read of a woman who was not attracted to Him and who did not sense in Him the perfect gentleman and friend.

He was as tireless in His ministry to individuals as to the multitudes. He made the blind to see, the deaf to hear, the lame to walk. He healed all manner of sickness, sometimes on a lavish scale. No case was too hard for Him. He went to the pool of Bethesda just to find the most difficult case, a man who had lain there helpless for half a lifetime. And He healed him. He cast out evil spirits with absolute authority. He cleansed lepers. He raised the dead.

Surely He should have had known nothing but the devoted friendship of all mankind. He never told a lie. He never cheated anyone. He never traded in rumor or gossip. He was never spiteful, vengeful, resentful, or mean.

He came from a land where He was worshipped by a countless angelic throng. In His own country, His slightest wish was law. Ten thousand times ten thousand angels hung upon His every word and rushed to do His bidding. He was loved and praised and obeyed and applauded. So it is all the more surprising that when he came to earth, He ran into bitter, implacable, merciless, unreasoning, malicious, and impenitent foes.

There is only one explanation for this. He was *good.* He was devastatingly honest. He looked at people with eyes that saw through all of life's little disguises. He was of impeccable character, absolutely incorruptible, and of stainless, dazzling purity. He was a man of flawless integrity. His enemies have been trying in vain for two thousand years to find one flaw in His character. He was perfect.

So we are brought face-to-face with this extraordinary fact. Someone came to this planet who was absolutely perfect, was accomplished and attractive and kindness itself. Yet there were those who hated Him. The great question is *why?* The only possible answer lies in the fact that He was so good and they were so bad. And badness hates goodness as darkness hates light.

In the first place, Christ rejected their various *political platforms.* The Zealots, for instance, were all for war with Rome, for one great confrontation in which they would take on the Roman Goliath and overthrow him. All they wanted was another David. What they wanted was a militant Messiah, one who would smash the power of Rome and set up the great kingdom foretold by the prophets. They wanted Jerusalem to be the capital of a new world empire. Jesus rejected their agenda.

The Herodians , by contrast, wanted some kind of an accommodation and cooperation with Rome and were willing to settle for some kind of home rule, and a partnership-alliance with the empire. They wanted something that would preserve the establishment. Jesus ignored their agenda as well.

There were those, like the Sadducees, as represented by the corrupt Annas and Caiaphas, who wanted, at all costs, to avoid anything that would upset the status quo. The present arrangement, however unsatisfactory, enabled them to hang on to some semblance of power. Jesus saw right through those hollow men and wanted no part in any agenda of theirs.

So, there was a nucleus of men who felt they had cause to fear this man and to hate Him. He threatened their position, their prosperity, and their power.

But, then, too, He rejected their *religious persuasions.* Over the previous four hundred years, a new system of Bible interpretation had come into vogue among the Jews. It consisted of allegories, homilies, and somewhat unsophisticated commentaries. The example had been set by Ezra the scribe.

Then had come the *Mishna.* A new hermeneutical scheme had been added. Greek reasoning was used as the main tool for interpreting the inspired Word of God, which had been given, not by reasoning, but by revelation to the patriarchs and prophets of old. This system was brought to full flower by Rabbi Hillel about thirty years before the birth of Christ, and it played havoc with the Scriptures. There were two schools of thought. One was developed by Hillel (whose pupil Gamaliel became the teacher of Saul of Tarsus). Hillel was somewhat of a liberal, and in his own day had a good following, but his rival, Shammai, had a far greater following.

Behind all these new religious speculations was the notion that God had given *two* legal codes to Moses—the *written* law and the *oral* law. The written law was contained in the Torah, the five books of Moses; the oral law had supposedly been given directly to Moses and had been passed on orally down through the centuries. By the time of Christ, this so-called oral law already carried more weight than the Bible. Jesus referred to it bluntly as "your traditions." He rejected the entire rabbinical system of interpretation and refused to go along with their pontificated rules. He rejected, for instance, their teachings about the Sabbath. They had already added countless petty rules and regulations to the Sabbath observance and had virtually destroyed its significance as a day of *rest.* They made its observation a heavy burden, more than anyone could bear.

So here was another group of enemies. The Lord refused to endorse the schools of Shammai or Hillel. This was very evident, for instance, when they tried to trap Him into taking sides on the issue of divorce. He took them back, not to some notable rabbi, but to the Torah, to the Scripture itself. Indeed He "taught them as one having authority, and not as the scribes" (Matt. 7:29) and "the common people heard him gladly" (Mark 12:37). This only added to the malice with which He was eyed by the religious establishment of the day.

Moreover, He rejected their *social practices*. There could be no greater feather in the cap of a Jew than to make a proselyte. Jesus scorned the practice. All they did was produce a prodigy of self-righteousness a thousand times more objectionable than themselves. The Pharisees and their proselytes were zealous beyond measure in the matter of their tithes, even tithing the mint in the garden. But they quite forgot mercy and righteousness. They were walking whitened sepulchers, all clean and showy on the outside, but full of extortion and uncleanness within. They had evolved all kinds of frivolous grounds for divorce; a man could divorce his wife, for instance, if she burned his supper. They despised the Gentiles as "dogs" and entertained a profound contempt for all Gentile ways. It was not safe, the rabbis taught, to leave cattle in their charge or to allow their physicians to attend the sick. Their houses were unclean and no Jew must cross their thresholds.

The Lord Jesus had no use for such social practices. He loved all men regardless of their country and customs, and intended to sweep the Gentiles by the countless millions into His church.

So, given what they were and what He was, it is not so surprising after all that He had enemies. There were many, especially in the ruling and religious establishments, who saw themselves threatened by this unconventional Messiah, who began His public ministry in the nation's capital by driving out the money changers and merchants who had lucrative concessions there. One thing is sure. His enemies were powerful, vocal, and organized, and their enmity was of such a diabolical nature that it would not rest until they had Him nailed to a cross and buried in a tomb. And even then it would not rest. It continued throughout the entire period covered by the book of Acts, and it has persisted down to the present day. It was an enmity, however, that was self-defeating, and which has come back, like a boomerang, to smite them time and time again.

For their enmity is a terrible thing. They constituted themselves as the enemies of the living God and His well-beloved Son. They were like the people in the Lord's parable; like the man who started to build a house and yet failed to count the cost, and the king who went to war and yet failed to assess the power of the foe. Before declaring war on the Son of God and on his Father in heaven, they should have made sure they could win.

## 1. They should have gone down deeper

They rubbed their hands at Calvary, gloating over the anguish of the hated Nazarene. They gathered around, rabble and rabbis alike, to poke fun at Him. They even urged Pilate to break His legs, as if the Scriptures, too, could be broken—the Scriptures that declared that no bone of His would be broken. They would have liked to have dumped His body into the fires of the Valley of Hinnom, had they dared, and had not two of their Supreme Council interfered. As it was, they persuaded Pilate to seal the tomb and to set a watch.

They should have gone down deeper. Beneath the tomb, creation's rocks reached down, deeper and deeper into the very core of the planet. They should have gone down to the Cretaceous rocks, and deeper still to the famous Jurassic rocks, and down below those to the Permian rocks, even deeper than that to the Cambrian rocks, and down below those to the Laurentian rocks.

They should have gone down to the deepest foundations of the earth and put their wicked hands on the rocks. For, at His command, the rocks cried out. They rent and tore and shivered and shook. Matthew tells us about that. He tells us that on the day Christ died, creation's rocks rent. He tells us, furthermore, that on the day He arose from the dead, the earth rent and shook once again. These enemies of Christ should have rearranged the fault lines of the earth. For those earthquakes were God's answer to His foes.

Those earthquakes showed God's ineffable contempt for puny man's attempts to do away with His Son and lock Him in a man-made tomb. Why, He had the power in His hand to rend and tear to pieces not only that rock-hewn tomb, with its stone and seal and sentries, but to tear to pieces Jerusalem itself and the whole of the Promised

Land and the whole world and every star and galaxy in space. If they wanted to be rid of His Son, they should have gone down deeper. They should have gone down, indeed, to hell itself and stopped His mouth. For that is where His soul went. He went there to proclaim to the dead that the seed of the woman has conquered the seed of the serpent, that salvation had been accomplished, and that life and death and immortality had been brought to light.

## 2. They should have gone up higher

On the morning of the Resurrection, two angels came down from heaven. We are not told which two they were, but likely enough that they were Gabriel, the *messenger* angel, and Michael, the *martial* angel. For fear of them, the keepers became as dead men, and when they recovered their wits, they fled with a howl of terror for their very lives.

Yes indeed, the Lord's enemies should have gone up higher. Later on, they arrested the disciples, pursuing the same senseless course they had begun in arresting Jesus. They clapped their hands when Herod murdered James, and cheered him on when he would have murdered Peter.

But they should have gone up higher! They should have arrested Gabriel and Michael and all the heavenly host. There were twelve legions of angels, more than seventy thousand of them, with drawn swords, waiting on the battlements of heaven for a chance to usher in Armageddon then and there and make an end of it. They should have arrested them.

What did God care for the sophistries of Caiaphas the high priest, or for the plots and plans of Annas, the former high priest and Caiaphas's father-in-law? What did God care for Pilate's robes of state, and for his signet ring, or for his high connections, through his wife, to the seat of power in Rome? What did God care for Tiberias Caesar, a disgusting man held in contempt by the Romans themselves? What did God care for the Roman army, for all its boasted fame as the most efficient fighting machine on earth?

If it was war they wanted, then He had armies greater and mightier than theirs. One angel in one night could smite all the great host of Sennacherib. Maybe Caesar and Pilate did not know that, but Caiaphas and Annas certainly did—except that these sophisticated Sadducees professed not to believe in miracles.

They should have gone up higher. If they wanted to vent their hatred, spite, and wickedness on the Son of God and seal Him in His tomb, then what about the angels? The priests and scribes should have gone up to heaven and arrested them. That is, if they wanted to have any hope of succeeding in their wickedness.

### 3. They should have gone back further

It was all very well for them to scheme and suggest plans for getting rid of the Son of God. It was all very well for them to buy off Judas Iscariot. He went cheaply enough, selling the Lord of glory for the price of a female slave.

It was all very well for them to bully Pilate. He had so many crimes on his conscience that the mere threat of reporting him to Caesar made him like putty in their hands. It was all very well for them to force Pilate's hand so that Christ was given a criminal's death; and to force his hand again with half-believed rumors of a promised resurrection so that he was willing to set the seal of Caesar on the sepulcher. The enemies of Christ should have gone back further.

These mighty men of the Sanhedrin should have gone back a thousand years in time and stopped David from writing: "Thou wilt not . . . suffer thine Holy One to see corruption" (Ps. 16:10). More, they should have stopped the Holy Spirit of God from inspiring David to write it, and prevented the third person of the Godhead from revealing that astonishing truth. David, doubtless, had no idea of the ultimate meaning of what he wrote, but he wrote it just the same, a truth revealed to him by the Holy Spirit and recorded with an inspired pen. "Thou wilt not . . . suffer thine Holy One to see corruption."

They could lock Christ in that tomb and they could hope that, like Lazarus, He would soon be rotting and corrupting in His grave. But

He was not like Lazarus or anyone else. He was God's Holy One. There was no trace or taint of sin in Him. His body could have lain there, incorruptible, for a billion years. His incorruption had been declared by divine decree and no decree of the Sanhedrin could change it. That body was held, incorruptible, pending the third day, when He would rise from the dead.

They should have gone back and stopped the very words from being uttered, for once uttered they were powerless to change them. "For ever, O Lord, thy word is settled in heaven" (Ps. 119:89). What could they do about that? "Heaven and earth shall pass away," Jesus said, "but my words shall not pass away" (Matt. 24:35). What could they do about that? They could doubt it, deny it, and distort it, but they could not alter it. Their decree came too late, far too late.

## 4. They should have gone in sooner

It is a strange fact that the disciples did not believe what Jesus told them about His coming death and resurrection. The only one who entered into the truth of His resurrection was Mary of Bethany. But His *enemies* were haunted by His words. "We remember that that deceiver said, while he was yet alive, After three days I will rise again" (Matt. 27:63).

They were terrified lest He prove the saying true. Much as they hated to admit it, Jesus had demonstrated extraordinary power. It had climaxed only recently with the astounding resurrection of Lazarus, an amazing miracle that it was impossible for them to doubt or deny. So, faced with His promise to rise again, what should they have done?

They should have gone into Joseph of Arimathea's sepulcher. They should have rolled away the stone from the door themselves and wrapped those binding grave clothes even tighter about that dormant form to make sure He was still their prisoner. They should have pulled that napkin down over His head to suffocate any stirring breath. They should have held that body firm and fast on its rocky bed. They should have made that body resurrection-proof. They should have been there, in the chill of the early morning light, to stop His spirit from returning to its house of clay. They should have gone in sooner. By the time the soldiers came with their electrifying news, it was too late.

## 5. They should have gone on longer

Faced with the accomplished fact of a resurrected Christ, they should have summoned the soldiers from the fortress and stormed the upper room where the disciples had gathered. They should have come in through the door as Christ was coming in through the wall, and they should have arrested Him then and there. They should have gone on longer.

Or, failing that, faced with one who could appear and disappear at will, they should have kept a strict watch on the Mount of Olives and arrested Him before He had a chance to step into the sky and ascend into glory.

But they did not do any of these things. They were born losers. They chose to be His enemies. They failed to count the cost. They failed to reckon on His almighty power.

And now they are dead. They know for certain now just who He is. They are in a lost eternity now, awaiting the summons to the great white throne. They already acknowledge his lordship! It is His absolute lordship over all created realms that keeps them where they could not keep Him. Already they are saying, "Jesus Christ is Lord!" And to think they might have known Him as *Savior* and Lord! Such is the abysmal folly of becoming an enemy of Christ by choice.

## CHAPTER 15

# THE BOOK! THE BODY! THE BLOOD!

*Hebrews 10:7, 10, 19*

1. The book (v. 7)
   a. Startling prophecies
   b. Startling pictures
2. The body (v. 10)
3. The blood (v. 19)

IF WE WERE TO COMPILE A LIST OF the great chapters of the Bible, the list would have to include such chapters as Genesis 22; Psalm 23; Isaiah 53; and Hebrews 10. We could add many more chapters to the list, but these would surely be at the heart.

In the great tenth chapter of Hebrews, numerous texts and topics clamor for exposition. There is the expression, "shadow of good things to come" (v. 1), which excites our imagination. There is the expression, "every priest standeth. . . . But this man . . . sat down" (v. 11–12). There are the expressions, "one sacrifice for sins for ever" (v. 12), and "this man . . . sat down . . . henceforth expecting" (vv. 12–13). There is the expression, "perfected for ever" (v. 14). There is the threefold repetition of the words, "Let us" (vv. 22–24). There is the expression, "this man," which begs to be pursued throughout the New Testament. There is the warning against doing "despite unto to the Spirit of grace" (v. 29). There is the great statement that arrested Martin Luther and launched the Reformation: "The just shall live by faith" (v. 38). The list could be extended even further. What a chapter this is! But here are three great expressions that most assuredly draw us to Calvary and to a contemplation of the person and work of Christ: "the book . . . the body . . . the blood" (vv. 7, 10, 19).

## 1. The book (v. 7)

When Jesus stepped out of eternity into time, He declared, "Lo, I come (in the volume of the book it is written of me,) to do thy will, O God." It all begins, so far as we are concerned, with a book. However, the story really begins long ages before the first page of that book was ever penned. It began in a dateless, timeless past, when God the Father, God the Son, and God the Holy Spirit decided that they would act in creation. They knew that if ever they acted in creation, the day would come when they would have to act in redemption. The reason for that must be sought in their own character. Perfect love and perfect justice combined to make it inevitable that fallen sons of Adam's ruined race, born in sin and shapely in iniquity, should be offered what the writer of this epistle elsewhere calls "so great salvation" (Heb. 2:3).

No member of the Godhead was taken by surprise by human sin. It was all foreseen and taken into account before ever the first angel was brought into being. It was decided by the Godhead that God the Son would be responsible for the great transaction, and that God the Spirit should be responsible for the glad tidings. The Son would inhabit the body; the Spirit would inspire the book. The book would tell people verbally about God's so great salvation. The body would enable them to see it visually.

We begin with the book. It was the Holy Spirit who went to work in history to produce that book. It took something like fifteen hundred years of our time for Him to write it. Though He used a variety of instruments, He followed two simple principles: Divine revelation would impart truths otherwise unknowable, and divine inspiration would make sure that the various people He employed to get things written down would write only what He himself had in mind.

The people He employed came from places as far apart as Rome in the west and Babylon in the east. For instance, there was Moses, schooled in all the wisdom of the Egyptians; David, a shepherd boy from the Judean hills; Daniel, a royal prince in Babylon; Amos, a Jewish cowboy; Nehemiah, a Persian politician; and Ezra, a scribe. Later, the Holy Spirit used Paul, writing from Rome; Peter, writing from Babylon; James, writing from Jerusalem; and John, writing from Patmos. Yet for all this diversity there was an astonishing unanimity. Gradually, the book took shape. The English poet John Dryden has well penned the words:

> Whence but from heaven
> Could men unskilled in arts,
> In different ages born, from different parts,
> Weave such agreeing truths?
> Or how, or why, should all conspire to cheat us with a lie?
> Untold their pains, unwanted their advice,
> Starving their gains, and martyrdom their price!

Yet, when it was all put together, it all pointed in one direction—to the coming into this world of a Savior, a Messiah. One who was the Son of Man, the Son of Abraham, the Son of David, the Son of God. Thus, we consider the book, beginning with its startling prophecies.

### a. Startling prophecies

What other man, save Jesus alone, in all of this world's history has had his coming, his character, and his career all mapped out ahead of time? Did anyone detail for us the coming and career of Julius Caesar, of Napoleon, or of Winston Churchill?

The Bible, however, sets forth, in broad brushstrokes, the story of a man called Jesus, centuries before His birth. He was to be born in Bethlehem, an insignificant town in a tiny province of a great world power. He was to be born of the Jewish people, of a particular tribe, the tribe of Judah, and of a particular family, the family of David. At the time of His birth, there would be a massacre of babies in Bethlehem. He was to come "out of Egypt"—truly a puzzling prophecy, until it was so simply and naturally fulfilled! He was to be heralded by an Elijah-like prophet. His ministry would be concentrated in Galilee. He would perform miracles and would speak with singular authority. He would be betrayed by a friend, and the exact amount of the transaction was foretold. He would be executed, not by the Jewish method of stoning but by an alien method of crucifixion. His executioners would gamble for His clothes. They would offer Him vinegar to drink. He would be buried in a rich man's tomb. His lifeless body would be preserved from decay. He would rise again the third day. He would ascend on high.

This startling collection of prophecies were made in an almost offhand, matter-of-fact manner. And they all came true. The book, however, was not only filled with startling prophecies, it was also filled with startling pictures.

### b. Startling pictures

These are pictures, illustrations, and object lessons of a highly specialized nature. We sometimes call them "types." In effect, they are picture prophecies. The Holy Spirit used people, events, rituals, customs, buildings, and common things to symbolically convey important truths regarding the person and work of Christ.

Look at just one example out of scores scattered throughout the Old Testament. Think of what happened on the annual Jewish feast of Passover. By the time Christ was crucified, in fulfillment of the type, the Jews had been religiously keeping this divinely appointed feast for some fifteen hundred years. It was a feast instituted by God to commemorate the birth of the nation after the children of Israel had faced near extermination in Egypt.

On the tenth day of the first month, they were required to take a lamb, one lamb for each family. The lamb had to be tethered the day

it was purchased and kept under constant observation to make sure
it was unblemished. The lamb was to be killed on the fourteenth
day of the same month. That day was called "the preparation of the
Passover."

The lamb was to be killed at a specific time, "between the two
evenings," which according to the ancient historian Josephus refers
to the time between the sixth and ninth hours. The lamb was spitted
on two pieces of wood, one running through it horizontally, the other
at right angles so that it was actually impaled on a cross. It was then
roasted in the fire and afterward eaten. In all this, the Jews were to
be careful to break no bone of the Passover lamb.[1]

All this ritual was a picture prophecy. To the month and to the day,
Jesus arrived in Jerusalem to fulfill what had been ritually enacted
for centuries. He arrived on the tenth day of Nissan, the first month
of the Jewish religious calendar. The Sanhedrin "bought" Jesus from
Judas Iscariot for thirty pieces of silver, and from then on, the Lord
"tethered" himself in Jerusalem, going only so far as nearby Bethany
at night but returning each day. He was now kept under constant
surveillance both by Judas, who sought a convenient time to betray
Him, and by the priests who sought a convenient time to kill Him.
They had ample time to see that He was without spot or blemish.

On the exact day, at the exact time, when Jews all across the country
were killing their lambs, God's true Passover Lamb was expiring on
the cross of Calvary. A supernatural darkness reigned supreme from
"the sixth hour to the ninth hour," during which time Jesus became
the actual sin-bearer. Once the light was turned back on, Jesus bowed
His head and died.

So, to the month and to the day and to the hour, the Lamb of God
was slain for the sins of the world. Moreover, no bone of His body was
broken. He was miraculously preserved from that, even though the
legs of the two thieves crucified with him were broken.

Such was the startling picture set before the Jews annually, century after century. And thus, to the letter, the picture came to life at
Calvary.

The book, then, is not only a book of startling prophecies, it is a book of equally startling pictures. Both the prophecies and the pictures pointed down through the centuries to Jesus. "In the volume of the book it is written of me," He said. Sometimes in crowded narrative, sometimes in pithy proverbs, sometimes in long chronologies, sometimes in direct prophetic utterance, sometimes in homespun parables, sometimes in carefully selected histories, one way and another, the book is all about Him.

## 2. The body (v. 10)

"Sacrifice and offering thou wouldest not, but a body hast thou prepared me" (Heb. 10:5). "We are sanctified [by] the body of Jesus Christ once for all" (v. 10). The offering of the body of the Lord Jesus as a sacrifice for sin was the great goal toward which all the animal sacrifices of the Old Testament led.

When God made man in His own image and after His own likeness, He gave him a body and a soul. That is to say, He gave him a physical frame and five senses, along with intellect, emotions, and will. Then He gave Adam something He had given to none of the animals; He gave him a spirit. All animals are locked into specific patterns consistent with their species. God did not lock man into a behavior pattern. He did not want merely a superior animal. He wanted human beings—people, not puppets. The divine plan was that man's human spirit should be inhabited by the Holy Spirit, that man should be inhabited by God. Thus the human spirit, cooperating with the Holy Spirit, would rule the faculties of the soul and the senses of the body and would always act in cooperation with God.

Sin altered all that. When sin came in, the Holy Spirit vacated the human spirit. Man in sin has a body; he has the various senses of the body; he has intellect, emotions, and will; and since the Fall, he has a conscience—the vice-regent of God in his soul—but he is spiritually dead. The spiritual part of him is like a lamp without oil. Man in sin has no governing principle. Sometimes he is governed by his senses, sometimes by his intellect, sometimes by his emotions, sometimes by his will, sometimes by his conscience, sometimes by a combination of these things, but he is not only spiritually dead, he is lost. He tries to fill the empty space in his spirit by resorting to religion, or pleasure, or business, or intellectual pursuits, or something else. But he is lost and needs to be born again, as Jesus bluntly told Nicodemus, that respectable, religious, self-righteous ruler of the Jews.

When Jesus came, He was man as God intended man to be. He was man inhabited by God. His body was indwelt and controlled by the Spirit of God. Thus, He did always those things that pleased the Father.

The key to the recovery of the human race in Christ lies in the fact that in Him dwelt all the fullness of the Godhead *bodily*. In Christ, God, was manifest in flesh. The Lord Jesus, so to speak, was "God in focus." Basic to all this, was the body that was prepared for Him.

It was a body just like ours, except that it was free from all taint and stain of sin. It was free from any physical blemish or imperfection, free from sickness, free from any inherited tendency toward wrongdoing.

The word for "prepared" here is *katartizo*. It is rendered various ways in the English New Testament. In Hebrews 11:3, it is translated "framed." In 1 Corinthians 1:10, it is rendered "perfectly joined together." In Matthew 4:21, it is used to describe the fishermen who were "mending" (*katartizo*) their nets.

The human body of every other individual has been damaged. Sin has invaded it in all its parts. It can be deformed at birth, it is subject to disease, it can fall prey to disaster, and it is overtaken at last by death and dissolution. The human body had to be "mended" for Jesus. He had to appear on earth in a body similar to the one that God had prepared for Adam, a body wholly free from the ravages of the Fall.

The word *katartizo* can be rendered "to make perfect." That, perhaps, is the best rendering here in Hebrews 10. "A body hast thou *perfected* for me." Thus the Lord Jesus had a perfect human body. We can be sure that he was well-proportioned, handsome, in perfect health, aglow with physical vitality. He must have been a striking individual, even on the level of the purely physical. He was an absolutely magnificent physical specimen. There had been no one like Him since

Adam's fall. That body was created for Him by the Holy Spirit with the cooperation of the Virgin Mary. Thus, He is called "the seed of the woman." He had a human mother but He had no human father.

We do not know by what mysterious process His body was fashioned in the Virgin's womb. We do know that He was "conceived of the Holy Spirit."

The genetic code for creating that body was supplied directly by the Holy Spirit. The human body has some six trillion cells, each of them a wonder of creation. Those cells are fashioned and function according to the dictates of what we now call a genetic code. With Jesus, there were no broken chromosomes, no faulty cells, no built-in deficiencies. All was perfect.

In due time, He was born and, wonder of wonders, the angels came streaming down the stairways of the sky to gaze in awe at God, manifest in flesh. The wise men and the shepherds came. They fell at His feet and worshipped Him. Nothing like it had ever happened before. Nothing like it will ever happen again.

He lived in that body for thirty-three-and-a-half years. He went through all the normal process of growing up. He was a baby, then a boy, then a brother, then a businessman, and always a believer.

Until at last, after thirty years, that body of His, toughened and hardened at the carpenter's bench, kept in perfect trim by a vigorous outdoor life, was in every way the perfect vehicle for the burning soul and the blazing spirit within. He was ready to take to the road. For three-and-a-half years, He traveled here and there, teaching, comforting, healing, showing men what God was really like. He touched and cleansed the lepers, multiplied the loaves and fishes, turned water into wine, raised the dead, and stilled the storm. He hungered, He wept, He went about doing good.

Indeed, the complete record of His amazing life would provide books enough to fill the whole world full, should it all be written. All we have are a few memos and memories. One day we will have it all.

The time came for His body to be offered in sacrifice. We see that body bowed and bent in dark Gethsemane. We see it lashed and ploughed by a Roman scourge. We see it bent beneath the weight of the cross. Yet so strong was He that, despite a scourging under which many a man died, He was still able to carry that heavy cross part of the way to Calvary. We see that body spiked to the cross. We see them give Him vinegar and gall to drink. We see Him bearing our sins in His own body on the tree. We see all the Old Testament sacrifices, mere "shadows," the writer of Hebrews calls them, fulfilled in the offering of that body of His. Until, at last it hung limp and lifeless, the spirit departed to His Father's care and His soul down to hell to proclaim His triumph.

He was pronounced dead by Rome. We see that body taken down from the cross. We see it washed and anointed and wrapped and placed in a borrowed tomb. We see it miraculously preserved from corruption. Three days later, we see that body rise in triumph as foretold. We see Christ appear and disappear at will in that same body, now forever scarred. We see Him rise in that body from Olivet's brow. Finally, we see Him seated in that body at the right hand of the Majesty on high. The book! The body!

## 3. The blood (v. 19)

"Having, therefore, brethren, boldness to enter into the holiest by the blood of Jesus." We sometimes sing:

> Not all the blood of beasts
> On Jewish altars slain,
> Could give the guilty conscience peace,
> Nor wash away the stain.[2]

That was most certainly true. Rivers of blood flowed from Israel's crimson altars down long centuries. Those rivers flowed ever toward Calvary. Now we can sing:

> But richer blood has flowed
> From nobler veins,

To purge the soul from guilt,
And cleanse the reddest stains.[3]

The blood that Jesus shed on Calvary was no ordinary blood. God, who alone knows the proper, relative value of things, calls it "precious blood." He warns solemnly against trampling on it.

When the Passover feast was originally instituted in Egypt, the children of Israel were instructed as to what they must do with the blood of the Passover lamb. That blood was to be caught in a basin. It was to be applied to the doorposts and lintels of each house. What was left was not applied to the doorstep. Instead, the bowl of blood was placed on the doorstep. There was to be no trampling on that blood.

The blood of man is corruptible, the blood of Christ is incorruptible. It is the blood of an absolutely unique human being. There was no drop of Joseph's blood in Jesus' veins. More than that—there was no drop of His mother's blood either.

Every doctor knows that the blood that flows through the veins and arteries of a baby in the womb is not its mother's blood. It is only after the embryo has been impregnated that the baby's blood begins to form. Blood cells develop just like all the other cells of the body. Not one drop of the mother's blood ever passes to the child. On the contrary, the developing infant has to be protected from its mother's blood. If the mother has blood of a different type than that of the baby, it could be lethal.

The blood type of the Lord Jesus was like no other blood type on earth. It was the blood of an absolutely unique human being. It was the blood of a person who had a human mother but no human father. His blood is therefore rare beyond all things. It is indeed precious blood.

We are entitled to ask what happened to that blood. The types of the Old Testament are as accurate as mathematics and that becomes evident when they are properly understood. It is from the symbolism and typology of the Old Testament that we learn what happened to the blood of Jesus. That symbolism and typology is interpreted in Hebrews 9 by the Holy Spirit.

First, He draws our attention to the tabernacle. He reminds us how the high priest, once a year, passed through the veil into the Holy of Holies. "Not without blood," the Holy Spirit reminds us, *"not without blood"* (v. 7). The high priest had to take with him the blood of the goat that had been slain as part of the ritual of the Day of Atonement. "Which," adds the Holy Spirit, "was a figure" (v. 9), or a parable.

Let us get the picture clearly in our minds. The high priest entered into the Holy of Holies amid clouds of incense. The incense blotted out his person and filled the place with fragrance. He also carried a basin of blood in his hands. That blood he had to sprinkle on and before the mercy seat. It was sprinkled between the cherubim, where God dwelt in the Shechinah glory cloud.

"But," adds the Holy Spirit—and we would do well to mark these significant *buts* in the Bible—*"but* Christ being come an high priest of good things to come, by [means of] a greater and more perfect tabernacle, not made with hands, that is to say, not of this building" (v. 11). The Holy Spirit is now going to show us the antitype. He shows us Christ doing in the real New Testament world what the Old Testament high priest did in the picture-book Old Testament world. He shows us Christ entering into the true Holy of Holies in heaven, where God sits on the mercy seat, in a glory no man can approach.

"But Christ being come an high priest of good things to come, by [means of] a greater and more perfect tabernacle, not made with hands, that is to say, not of this building [the earthly tabernacle and temple]; neither by [means of] the blood of goats and calves [which was how the Old Testament high priest went in], but by [means of] his own blood he entered in once into the holy place, having obtained eternal redemption for us" (vv. 11–12). The parallel is deliberate, exact, and perfect. Christ has now gone into the Holy of Holies in heaven, taking with Him His own blood.

The deliberate use throughout of the preposition *by* draws for us the exact parallel. Three times the Holy Spirit uses it in the passage. The preposition itself signifies an action passing on to its accomplishment. It denotes the passing through of whatever it is that is interposed between the beginning and ending of the action. In this case, it was the veil that acted as a barrier between God and man—its great function was to keep people out of the presence of a thrice-holy God.

Our great High Priest has now passed through this obstacle. More than that, He has torn it down. He has passed through the veil. He has purified the real mercy seat in heaven by means of His own precious blood.

That blood, on the mercy seat in heaven, is the eternal witness to God and to the universe that our sins have been put away once and for all by the shedding of that blood at Calvary.

"The heavenly things themselves [are purified] with better sacrifices" (v. 23). There is a figure of speech used here, called *heterosis*, that can render the phrase "one greater and better sacrifice."

That is what happened to the precious blood of Christ. It is now in heaven on the mercy seat. By virtue of that blood, our sins are cleansed and our way is cleared into the Holy of Holies itself.

The book! The body! The blood! Surely, when we think of the one of whom the whole book speaks, when we think of whose body it was that was shattered on Calvary's tree, when we think of just whose blood it is that now speaks better things than that of Abel's, what is there left to say but "Hallelujah! What a Savior."

## CHAPTER 16

# THE SEVEN SAYINGS OF CALVARY

1. A word of testimony (Luke 23:34)
2. A word of transformation (Luke 23:43)
3. A word of tenderness (John 19:27)
4. A word of terror (Matt. 27:46; Mark 15:34)
5. A word of torment (John 19:28)
6. A word of truth (John 19:30)
7. A word of triumph (Luke 23:46)

MOST PEOPLE ARE INTERESTED IN a person's last words. We tend to invest them with more than usual significance. Winston Churchill, after a full and exciting life, professed to find death tiresome. "I am bored with it all," he said.

The French novelist Honore de Balzac looked up at his doctor and cried, "Send for Bianchon! He will save me!" He was delirious. Bianchon was one of his fictional characters.

Johann Wolfgang von Goethe, the illustrious German poet, novelist, and playwright, felt himself going out into the dark. He cried out on his deathbed for "more light!"

Mark Twain was contemptuous to the end. He said, "Whoever has lived long enough to find out what life is, knows how deep a debt of gratitude we owe to Adam, the first great benefactor of our race. He brought death into the world."

Jan Hus, the Bohemian reformer and martyr burned at the stake in Germany on July 16, 1415, sang a hymn so loudly he could be heard through the crackling flames. Just before he died, he made a prophetic statement. He said, "You may cook the goose today, but God will raise up a gander and him you will never roast." In the Bohemian language, the name Hus means "goose." In German, the name Luther means "gander." At the time of Hus's death, Martin Luther had not yet been born.

And, of course, everyone knows of D. L. Moody's triumphant utterances as death entered his bedroom. He took a considerable time in dying. He went right through the portals of death. He saw his two beloved grandchildren, Dwight and Irene, who had died young. He announced, "This is my coronation day! This is glorious."

All such notable sayings—and there are hundreds of them on record, good, bad, and indifferent—pale into insignificance when compared with the last sayings of Jesus as He hung on Calvary's cross.

He spoke seven times. His sayings can be divided into three types: sayings that reveal His *tenderness,* His *travail,* and His *triumph.*

There were sayings that reveal His *tenderness.* He spoke a word connected with His enemies. For them, He offered a prayer. He spoke to the dying thief. For him, He had a promise. He spoke to His mother. For her, He had a provision.

Then there were sayings that reveal *His travail.* One of these cries revealed His mental anguish. He cried, "My God, my God, why hast thou forsaken me?" One of these cries revealed His mortal agony: "I thirst!"

Then there were sayings that reveal *His triumph.* One was concerned with the past: "It is finished!" One was concerning the future: "Father, into thy hands I commend my spirit."

Each one of these statements by our Lord could be expanded into a sermon unto itself. Taken together they reveal the terrible sufferings of Christ and His infinite grace and fortitude, beyond anything ever recorded of any other man who ever lived on earth.

## 1. A word of testimony (Luke 23:34)

"Father, forgive them; for they know not what they do." This word of testimony reveals to us that Jesus practiced what He preached. Most people consider the high and holy standards of the Sermon on the Mount to be too idealistic to be practical. Therefore, they either ignore them altogether or relegate them to the millennial age. They are laws that call for absolute perfection. Jesus *lived* them. For instance, He taught us to forgive our enemies. On the cross, He showed us how it should be done.

Even as the hammer was poised above the open palm of His hand, even as the soldier positioned the nail, there were twelve legions of angels, with drawn swords, straining over the battlements of heaven, waiting for a word that never came. Instead, quite a different word was heard on high, one that disarmed those avenging hosts. "Father, forgive them; for they know not what they do."

The angels sheathed their swords and said, "Isn't that just like Jesus." Forgiveness. That great amnesty has lasted now for nearly two thousand years.

"Father, forgive them." He forgave the man with the hammer in his hand. He forgave those men already proposing to gamble for the clothes still warm from His body. He forgave the man who crowned Him with thorns. He forgave the man who hit Him in the face and the man who plucked the beard from His cheeks. He forgave those men who bore false witness against Him. He forgave Caiaphas and Annas, those poor, deluded men who plotted and planned it all. He forgave those men who bought off poor Judas. He forgave the fox, Herod, and his men who mocked and maligned His majesty. He forgave unhappy Pilate, who signed the infamous warrant for His death. He forgave those men who jeered and triumphed in His agony and pain.

What a testimony! Surely, nobler words were never uttered. It was a stay of execution for a sin-cursed race now crowning all its other infamies by murdering the Son of the living God.

"Father!" He said. Not "Elohim" because they had outraged God as the God of Creation. Not "Jehovah" because they had outraged God as the God of Covenant. But "Father." He deliberately avoided the high courts of heaven. He went directly to His Father. "Father," He said, "forgive them; for they know not what they do." In all courts, ignorance of the law is never accepted as an excuse. But that was the only excuse that could be made here. It could not be made in court so He bypassed the court and took it to the supreme Judge himself, who was also His own, dear Father in heaven.

Christ's cry of forgiveness set the tone of the great age of grace in which we now live. It is an age during which God sovereignly holds back His avenging hand and maintains a great silence, awesome, mysterious, and often challenged by foolish men. Little do those who challenge God to break that silence realize that, once that silence is broken, the great amnesty will be over. It will mean the end of the day of grace and mercy and the beginning of the day of wrath.

How different from the normal language of men is this great "Father forgive them" of the Savior. One of England's more famous monarchs, Elizabeth I, had a favorite at court, the Earl of Essex. One day she gave him a special ring, as a token of her affection, and told him that if he were ever accused of a crime, no matter what, he had only to send her that ring and she would grant him the opportunity to appear before her in person and plead his case.

The day came when the earl was accused of high treason. He was found guilty and eventually executed. The queen waited for him to send her that ring, but she waited in vain. Because the ring never came, she allowed the sentence of death to stand, though it pained her heart.

Years later, the Countess of Nottingham lay dying. She was a relative but no friend of the long-since-dead Earl of Essex. The countess sent a messenger to the queen. "Would her Majesty come? She had a confession to make. She could not die in peace until it was made." The queen came and stood by the deathbed of the anxious countess. The countess produced the fateful ring. It appeared that the Earl of Essex had given it to her with the urgent request that she take it straight to the queen. She had failed to do so. Now she begged the queen's forgiveness.

She had appealed to the wrong woman. Queen Elizabeth was livid with rage. She seized the dying countess and shook her until her teeth rattled. "God may forgive you, Madam," she screamed, "but I never shall." And with that she stormed out of the room. We can be thankful that the Lord Jesus is not like that.

## 2. A word of transformation (Luke 23:43)

"Verily I say unto thee, To day shalt thou be with me in paradise." There were three crosses raised against the skyline of Golgotha. The Lord of glory had company in His death—two malefactors. It seems likely, moreover, that the very cross on which He hung had been prepared for yet another thief, a robber named Barabbas.

As the two thieves writhed in torment on their trees, they joined the howling mob in cursing and reviling the Son of God. Low as they had come themselves, they still found some kind of twisted satisfaction in finding someone they could mock and curse. There is no more terrible exposure of the dark wickedness of the human heart than that. They did not commiserate with their fellow sufferer. They cursed Him as if He, the Lord of glory, were the author of their evil deeds and present pains.

Presently, however, one of the thieves fell silent. He grew thoughtful. The scales fell from his eyes. It suddenly dawned on him just exactly who this man, Jesus of Nazareth, really was. We do not know by what mysterious thought process He came to faith in Christ, against all the seeming, outward evidence, but come he did.

He read the title on Christ's cross: "This is Jesus of Nazareth, the King of the Jews." He would have remembered, perhaps, what he had learned as a boy about the coming Messiah, the Son of David. He heard the gospel from Christ's enemies, who said, "He saved others, himself He cannot save." He heard the mocking priests, "If thou be the Son of God, come down from the cross." The Holy Spirit opened his eyes to the truth.

He put the various pieces together. Jesus! King! Savior! Son of God! He did not know how or when, but this man who had done nothing amiss was all of these things. Perhaps he remembered the stories about Jesus that were such common knowledge in the land in those days. Perhaps he had heard Him preach. Perhaps he had seen Him perform a miracle. He arrived at the certain knowledge that this man who could forgive His enemies was a king. He was going to inherit a kingdom, somewhere, sometime, somehow. Faith leaped up fullgrown, triumphant, and Spirit-begotten in his soul.

The repentant thief rebuked his still cursing companion. He turned to Jesus, saying, "Lord, remember me when thou comest into thy kingdom" (Luke 23:42). Surely never, in all the annals of history, has greater faith been confessed. Nor did he have to wait long for a response. Nor was the response, when it came, obscure. The blessed assurance was loud, glad, and clear, "This day shalt thou be with me in paradise."

The word the Lord Jesus used for "paradise" is the word the Greeks used to describe a pleasure garden. It is the word the translators of the Septuagint used to describe the Garden of Eden. Old Testament expressions such as "the garden of the Lord" bring the same thought into focus.

The Jewish expositors viewed hades, the abode of the dead, as divided into two areas separated by a vast and impassible gulf. Jesus confirmed this idea in His teaching on the rich man and Lazarus. The rich man was in hades, in the place of torment, remembrance, consciousness, anguish, and despair. The transported Lazarus was in a place of bliss and rest. The description of flame and quenchless thirst shows us the terrors of the place where the rich man was. The description of Lazarus as being "in Abraham's bosom" shows us that conscientious fellowship and well-being were the features of the place where Lazarus was. Jesus told the dying thief he would be *there*, in the "paradise" section of hades, with Him, that day. He took the prospect far beyond the mere hope of rest and repose with the founding father of the Hebrew nation. Whatever the place was like, it would most surely be a garden of endless delights the moment Christ's foot touched its shores.

Thus, the dying thief, a few hours later, watched the Lord Jesus, as

He bowed His head and died. "He is gone," he whispered to himself, "but He will be waiting for me." Sure enough, shortly afterward the soldiers came to conclude the brutal work of that day by smashing the poor fellow's legs, throwing the weight of his body on his heart, causing an almost immediate death that was the end of his sufferings. He closed his eyes on earth and opened them to look straight into the smiling face of Jesus. And there before them rolled the wonders and the beauties of such a paradise as the thief had never ever dreamed could be.

We can be sure that nail-scarred hand clasped nail-scarred hand and the Lord Jesus took that ransomed soul with Him into that wondrous paradise as the firstfruits of Calvary.

### 3. A word of tenderness (John 19:27)

Jesus said to His mother, "Woman, behold thy son!" Then he said to the disciple John, "Behold thy mother!" Though the Lord's thoughts were filled with thoughts of His Father, He still had room enough and to spare in His mind for thoughts of His mother.

That sword, of which the aged Simeon had spoken, was piercing her breast now. She, of all that throng that milled around the cross, knew the truth about Him. She knew just who He was and from whence He had come. There she stood, watching the brutal and the ribald scene, helpless to do anything but let Him know that she was there. But she must not be there. The day would come when a large segment of the professing church would exalt her above all women, claim immaculate conception for her, deem her the queen of heaven, and bestow upon her the attributes of deity. They would even go so far as to call her "co-redemptrix"—just as much our redeemer as Christ.

No! She did not belong there. But to whom could he commend her? She had her family, of course—James and Jude and Joses and the sisters. But they would never do, especially James. Then He saw John, the beloved disciple, and at once the great transaction was done. He gave her a new son. He gave John a new mother. And, from that moment, John treated her as if she were his mother indeed. John's own mother, Salome, was there (Matt. 27:56). Some think she was

Mary's sister. From that moment, John had two mothers, his own and that of Jesus.

We cannot help but wonder what happened to Mary in later years. Seven or eight weeks later, she was in the upper room on the day of Pentecost. Very likely, she had been in that same upper room when Jesus had appeared to His disciples on the day of resurrection. Likely, too, she was on Olivet with John when Jesus ascended into heaven. Probably, too, she was with John at Ephesus.

One person I know thinks it possible that "the elect lady" to whom John addressed his second epistle, was the Lord's own mother. Whatever the case, we can be sure that her presence in John's home was a benediction. Her presence in any church where John ministered would be a source of blessing to one and all. Often Jesus would smile down from heaven upon his beloved disciple and think of the reward He had prepared for him in glory for his faithful sonship to that Galilean peasant, of David's line and lineage, who was his bequeathed mother.

This divine solicitude of the Lord Jesus for His mother is full of instruction for us today. It is generally thought that Joseph, Jesus' foster father, was dead, and that he had been dead for many years. The Lord did not cast His mother out on the dreary waters of this world to make the best life she could for herself in her advancing years. Nor did he leave her to the care of her own natural children, none of whom it appears, at this stage, had any sympathy with His claims. Doubtless His arrest and trials, His condemnation and crucifixion, appalled them. They would want to put as much distance as they possibly could between themselves and Him, lest the authorities decide to make a clean sweep of the whole royal family—they all had the blood of David in their veins through both Mary and Joseph.

Nowadays, it is increasingly fashionable and acceptable to put one's elderly parents into a home of some sort, sometimes of necessity. Sometimes, however, it is simply a convenient way to solve a problem. But this is a cold and callous age. The Lord's dying care and concern for the physical, emotional, financial, and spiritual well-being of His mother should speak volumes to us all.

## 4. A word of terror (Matt. 27:46; Mark 15:34)

Jesus knew it was coming. He had known it was coming from eternity past when He and His Father and the Holy Spirit devised redemption's plan. That greatest of all the pagan philosophers, Socrates, cried out to Plato, "O Plato, Plato, it may be that the gods can forgive sin, but alas I do not see how." Socrates did not have the answer.

Nor did guilt-ridden Macbeth. When advised by Lady Macbeth to get some water to wash away the stain of murder from his hands. Macbeth replied:

> Will all great Neptune's ocean wash this blood
> Clean from my hand? No! this my hand will rather
> The multitudinous seas incarnadine,
> Making the green one red![1]

But Jesus knew how and why God could forgive sin. The answer lay in the provision of a sinless substitute. He was that substitute. The terror of it wrung from His soul that most terrible of all cries, "My God, my God, why hast thou forsaken me?" It is the central cry of the seven and it is the only one recorded by two of the evangelists.

It was His anticipation of this dread hour that drove Him to Gethsemane. There He poured out His heart. There He stormed the battlements of heaven with His anguished cry, "Father, if it be possible, let this cup pass from me: nevertheless, not as I will, but as thou wilt" (Matt. 26:39). It was the anticipation of this, the greatest of all horrors, that caused Him to sweat "as it were great drops of blood falling down to the ground" (Luke 22:44).

In Gethsemane, it was still "Father! Father!" As He was being nailed to the tree, it was still "Father, forgive them." But not now. Now it was "Eli, Eli, lama sabacthani." It was not even "Jehovah!" It was Elohim. The waters had now come into His soul. He who knew no sin had been made sin for us.

That is the deepest mystery of redemption's plan. The Lord Jesus not only died for me, He died as me. He died not only for each and every sinner ever born of Adam's sin-cursed race, but *as* each and every sinner. Think of it! He died *for* and *as* every vile and wicked man and woman on this terrestrial ball. The hymn writer has caught the truth of it:

> All thy sins were laid upon Him,
> Jesus bore them on the tree;
> God, who knew them, laid them on Him,
> And, believing, thou art free.[2]

When that terrible moment approached, God put out the sun. The work of creation was done in light; the greater work of redemption was done in the dark. God drew the veil of a midday midnight over the brow of Golgotha, before He entered into reckoning with the great substitute. The inconceivably vast sum total of this world's sin was now heaped upon Him—as if He himself, in His own person and in His own body, had committed each and every act, and uttered each and every word, and conceived each and every thought and imagination.

No wonder the darkness was rent by this terrible cry. It has been called "Immanuel's orphan cry." "My God, my God, why hast thou forsaken me?" Between Christ and God there was now a great gulf fixed. A fellowship and companionship that had been perfect and complete for countless eternities was now broken. In utter, incredible isolation and loneliness, the cry was wrung from the broken, desolate heart of Jesus. In those dread hours, He tasted what every Christ-rejecting soul must taste, the ultimate horror of being abandoned by God. The only answer to this terrible cry, which must have wrung the very Father's heart, was silence.

In His extremity, as at all other times in His life, the Lord Jesus turned to His Bible. And, as so often before, He turned instinctively to the book of Psalms. He turned to Psalm 22. Doubtless, He quoted the whole psalm, and a wonderful psalm it is. But all the answer He received was silence.

I was a boy in Britain. I well remember there was no boyhood punishment dreaded more than that of being "sent to Coventry by one's peers." The expression dates from England's civil war when Oliver Cromwell's Roundheads battled the King's Cavaliers. The city of Coventry was a strongly pro-Roundhead town. The phrase, "Being sent to Coventry" was a Cavalier phrase. No Cavalier would want to be sent to live in a Roundhead town. The phrase spoke of being banished from the king, of being excluded from society, of being completely ostracized. Eventually, the phrase found its way into English school life and had a special awfulness in the great English boarding schools. For if a boy transgressed the schoolboy code, he was "sent to Coventry" by his peers. That meant nobody would speak to him. He was treated as if he had leprosy or the plague. Anyone who spoke to him was banished with him to a world of loneliness, isolation, and exclusion. Being "sent to Coventry" meant that one had become a pariah, an outcast, an untouchable.

We can only imagine the feelings of a boy thus banished by his peers and cut dead by his fellows. He had the mark of Cain on him. But being "sent to Coventry" was nothing at all compared with the utter abandonment of the Lord Jesus by God and man. There He hung, on that center cross, alone, in the dark, and separated from God, because on Him now rested the sin of the world.

## 5. A word of torment (John 19:28)

For three hours the terrible silence and darkness reigned. Then the storm clouds rolled away and the sun broke through. The darkness fled. Three hours! Just three hours of our time, but a whole eternity of His, a whole eternity of suffering had been telescoped into those three long hours.

Then Jesus spoke again. He said, "I thirst!" He had begun His ministry by being hungry in the wilderness; now He ended it by being thirsty on the cross. There is no torment that can compare with the terrible agony of thirst. The rich man in hell cried out for just one drop of water. Jesus cried, "I thirst!" Our history books and storybooks tell many tales of the horrors of extreme thirst. We think, for instance, of Samuel Taylor Coleridge's famous poem, "The Rime of the Ancient Mariner." The mariner had shot the albatross that had brought good luck to the voyage and a fair, following wind. At first his companions applauded him, for all seemed well. The fog and mist that had been bothering them were gone.

> The fair breeze blew, the white foam flew,
> The furrow followed free;
> We were the first that ever burst
> Into that silent sea.

The ship had rounded the cape and was in the Pacific. Before long, however, it was totally becalmed.

> Down dropt the breeze, the sails dropped down
> 'Twas sad as sad could be;
> And we did speak only to break
> The silence of the sea!

The sky turned to the color of copper. The heat was oppressive. The sun blazed down. Not a breath of wind stirred.

> Day after day, day after day,
> We stuck, nor breath nor motion;
> As idle as a painted ship
> Upon a painted ocean.

> Water, water every where,
> And all the boards did shrink;
> Water, water, every where
> Nor any drop to drink.

The sailors began to die of thirst. They died cursing the ancient mariner, though "every tongue, through utter drought, was withered at the root." The last sailor died, leaving the ancient mariner alone.

> Alone, alone, all, all alone,
> Alone on a wide wide sea!
> And never a saint took pity on
> My soul in agony.[3]

Alone! Alone with his sin and a raging thirst. Well Jesus had come through the sin-bearing and through the loneliness of hell. Now the raging thirst came back. Think of it! He, of all men, was thirsty! Every river and lake in the world belonged to Him. Many a time I have stood at Niagara Falls and watched the water pour, in an endless cataract, over the brink of the gorge into the great chasm below, just as it has been doing for millions upon millions of years.

The Niagara River winds its way for about thirty-eight miles from Lake Erie to Lake Ontario. Every year some fourteen million people come to view the spectacle of the three falls: the massive Horseshoe Falls, the American Falls, and the smaller Bridal Falls. The Indians called the spot, "The Place of Thundering Waters." Every minute, thirty-three-and-a-half million gallons of water fall 180 feet to the boiling maelstrom below and throw back up into the air large, billowing clouds of white spray. The one who hung thirsting on Golgotha's hill that day was the one who made those falls.

One word from Him and the mighty Nile would have gathered up the waters of Lake Victoria, flung them across the desert, hauled them up the passes in the Judean hills, swirled about His nail-pierced feet, climbed up the cross, and bathed His parched lips.

One word from Him and ten thousand angels would have descended the sky with vials filled and spilling over with water from the crystal stream that flows by the throne of God.

When He cried, "I thirst!" someone more sensitive than the rest dipped a sponge in vinegar, stuck it on a reed, or perhaps a soldier's spear, and gave Him *that* to drink.

He had now been on the cross for six long hours. Every bone in His body was out of joint and a stabbing point of pain. His back was torn and rent from the scourging He had received. His brow was still stabbed by the crown of thorns. His muscles were cramped and screaming out their torment. His strength was about gone. His tongue was cleaving to His jaws. He cried, "I thirst!"

## 6. A word of truth (John 19:30)

"It is finished!" He cried. The Lord Jesus ran His mind's eye down all the Old Testament Scriptures. He searched the books of the Law and of the Prophets and the Writings from Genesis to Malachi. From Genesis to Malachi, in our King James Version, there are 1,089 chapters made up of 23,214 verses. These, in turn, are made up of 593,439 words. He scanned them all. He reviewed the types and the shadows, the direct prophecies and the more subtle prophecies. He sorted out all the Scriptures that had to be fulfilled at His first coming from all the Scriptures that relate to His coming again. He reviewed Isaiah 53; Psalm 22; and Psalm 69. He surveyed the significance of each and every one of the more than half a million words of the Old Testament. He looked back over the thirty-three-and-a-half years of His life, every one of the some twelve thousand plus days of His life. Then He made a pronouncement. He said, "It is finished."

That is a tribute to His prodigious memory, to His power of total recall, to the sovereignty of a mind unsullied by sin and therefore able to employ the full one hundred percent capacity of His mind. Man in sin cannot use more than two percent of his brain. Christ checked off the long list in His mind. He waited until the last prophecy was fulfilled, when they gave Him vinegar to drink. Then He announced, "It is finished."

That was it! There was no more to be done. He had finished the work His Father had given Him to do. As He had pronounced the word *finished* over the work of creation (Gen. 2:1), so now He pronounced it over the work of redemption. The resurrection and the ascension were still to come, but they were a foregone, inevitable result of His finished work.

Finished! The word is *tetelestai,* the passive tense of the word *teleo.* The Greek word means far more than the completion of something. It means that whatever it is that is finished has been rounded out to perfection. No more can be added to it. The entire purpose of God in redemption, for which the Father had sent Him into the world to accomplish, was now perfectly done.

F. W. Boreham tells us that *tetelestai* is a farmer's word. When into the flock was born a little lamb so beautiful, so shapely, so free from spot and blemish as to be perfect, the farmer would say, *"Tetelestai!"*

It is an artist's word, when the painter has put the last, finishing touches to a magnificent landscape, or the sculptor has chiseled the last fine line to a marble statue. When the work is finished, perfect, he would say to himself, *"Tetelestai!"*

It is also a priestly word. A grateful worshipper wishing to bring an offering that would tell God how much he loved Him, how grateful he was for all His benefits, would go through the herd until he found a mighty bull, strong, handsome, all grace and muscle and power. He would bring it to the altar and the priest would examine it minutely. He would then stand back and admire it. *"Tetelestai!"* he would say.

The Lord, as He hung on the cross, with only a few moments of life now left to Him, surveyed the whole field of inspired Scripture and the entire span of His earthly sojourn. There was not one jot or tittle of the Word of God that had been overlooked. The plan was perfect in its conception in eternity past and perfect in its execution on the cross of Calvary. He said the only thing He could say. He said, *"Tetelestai!"* Thus it is that today we rest, as God rests, in a finished work.

## 7. A word of triumph (Luke 23:46)

"Father," He said, "into thy hands I commend my spirit." Father! The relationship was restored, proof that the work had been accomplished to God's entire satisfaction.

The thing that astonished the soldiers when they came to hasten the end of the sufferers on Golgotha's hill was that Christ was already dead. The two thieves were still alive, and the soldiers accordingly broke their legs in one last act of brutality to push them on out into eternity on a crescendo of pain. But Jesus was already dead. Death by crucifixion was not a swift death. It was a fiendishly slow death. A strong man could linger on a Roman cross for days, finally dying, not from loss of blood, but from sheer exhaustion. Jesus, however, was already dead by the time the soldiers came.

He had already declared that this would be so. "No man taketh [my life] from me," He said, "But I lay it down of myself. I have power to lay it down, and I have power to take it again. This commandment have I received of my Father" (John 10:18). How could anyone take His life from Him? He was the Creator of the universe and the Author and Sustainer of life. "I am the resurrection, and the life," He told Martha on the way to the tomb of Lazarus (John 11:25). Then He proved it by raising Lazarus from the dead.

No indeed! When it was all over, Jesus deliberately and sovereignly dismissed His Spirit into the care and keeping of His Father. Nor did He do so with one last feeble gasp. Oh no! He gave a mighty shout! And having shouted with a voice that shook the earth beneath His feet and rent the temple veil and split wide ten thousand tombs across the length and breadth of the land, He departed this life of His own violation and will.

Such, indeed, was the death of Christ. Three days later, He was back from the dead with the keys of death and hell in His hands.

## CHAPTER 17

# THE RESURRECTION
*1 Corinthians 15:3-8*

1. The fact is stated (vv. 3–4)
   a. The cross (v. 3)
   b. The cemetery (v. 4a)
   c. The calendar (v. 4b)
2. The fact is substantiated (vv. 5–8a)
   a. Seen by His friends (v. 5)
      (1) Seen by the man who denied Him (v. 5a)
      (2) Seen by the men He discipled (v. 5b)
   b. Seen by His flock (v. 6)
   c. Seen by His family (v. 7a)
   d. Seen by His followers (v. 7b)
   e. Seen by His foe (v. 8)

TO MY MIND, THERE IS NO GREATER chapter in the New Testament than 1 Corinthians 15. Of course, there are other great chapters in the Bible. We would have to list Psalm 22; Isaiah 53; Romans 8; and Revelation 4–5 as vast mountain peaks, towering above all others in the Himalayas of divine revelation. But, in my opinion, 1 Corinthians 15 is Mount Everest itself.

The chapter divides into two main parts: regarding the *resurrection of Christ* (vv. 1–19), and the *resurrection of Christians* (vv. 20–58). In our study here, we are going to consider the resurrection of Christ. It, too, is seen in two parts: as *an indisputable fact of history* (vv. 1–11), and as *an indispensable fact of theology* (vv. 12–19). Thus we survey the general scope of this amazing chapter. To begin with, then, the resurrection of Christ is seen as an indisputable fact of history.

## 1. The fact is stated (vv. 3–4)

First of all, Paul takes us to the cross and the cemetery, and points us to the calendar.

### a. The cross (v. 3)

"For I delivered unto you first of all that which I also received, how that Christ died for our sins according to the scriptures."

"He died" could be written over the lives of millions upon millions of people. Every graveyard in the world testifies to the universal nature of death. All the great men of history share this epitaph, "He died." Some died bravely, others died in terror. D. L. Moody died as he lived, bursting with eagerness to experience more of Christ. Voltaire died in stark fear. His atheist friends barred the way to his room lest the dreadful death of a champion scoffer might become generally known. His nurse was so appalled at the nature of his torments that she vowed never again to attend the deathbed of an atheist, not for all the money in the world.

There is nothing unusual about the statement, "He died." Adam and Eve died. Cain and Abel died. Methuselah, who lived for 969 years died. Noah died. Abraham, Isaac, and Jacob died. Joseph died. David and Daniel died. Moses died. He was given a state funeral "on Nebo's lonely mountain on this side of Jordan's wave," but he died.

The Pharaoh who planned the first Jewish holocaust died. Alexander the Great died, weeping because there were no more worlds to conquer, he who could not conquer himself. Julius Caesar died. Filthy old Tiberius, during whose reign Jesus was murdered, also died. Annas and Caiaphas, men who led the Jewish rejection of Christ, and Pilate, who signed His death warrant, all died. There is nothing remarkable about the fact that millions of people have died.

What is remarkable about the death of Christ is that He died *according to the Scriptures* (Isa. 53). His death was prophesied in all its various details. It was prophesied that He would be betrayed by a friend (Ps. 41:9). It was foretold that He would be crucified, long before death by crucifixion was in vogue (Ps. 22:16). It was prophesied that no bone of His body would be broken (Ps. 34:20). It was foretold that He would be given vinegar and gall to drink (Ps. 69:21). It was foretold that He would be "with the rich in his death" (Isa. 53:9). What is so extraordinary about the death of Christ is that He died according to the Scriptures.

There were many witnesses to His death. Jerusalem was teeming with pilgrims. Josephus tells us there were probably more than a million people in Jerusalem at the time of the Passover feast. We can be sure that there was a large crowd of them on Calvary's hill that day to see Him die.

It is amazing to what lengths people will go to avoid the truth about Christ. One so-called liberal theory that is supposed to account for the story of a resurrected Christ, is that Christ did not die at all. A somewhat desperate theory, indeed. The theory is called the swoon theory. According to this notion, Christ did not really die on the cross, He simply swooned. Later, in the cool interior of the tomb He revived, managed to escape and three days later showed himself alive, thus promulgating the resurrection story.

In order for this theory to be true, we would have to believe that a Roman soldier would not know death when he saw it; that the centurion in charge of the execution mistook a fainting man for a dead man, and that he reported to the governor that Christ was dead when He was not dead. The eyewitness account is that "he was dead already" when the soldiers came to make a swift end to His sufferings. To make sure He was dead, and hadn't just swooned, they ran a spear through His side into His heart.

In order for the swoon theory to be true, we would have to believe that the representatives of the Sanhedrin, who had moved heaven and earth to get rid of Jesus, left the scene of the execution without making sure that the man they hated was really dead.

Moreover, we would have to believe that the friends of Jesus who embalmed His body were also deceived, and that they wrapped the body of a living man in restricting bandages and sticky spices, knowing full well that those bandages would congeal and harden into a case-like sheath within a few hours.

But that is not all. According to this theory, Jesus had to escape from the tomb. That would mean that in his weakened state He had to get out of those bandages, which would now be set into a solid cast. Then, having somehow done a Houdini escape trick, He put the bandages back the way they were—intact, as if they still contained a body. Then, with every bone out of joint from the crucifixion, He rolled back the stone covering the mouth of the grave—a stone so heavy that the women who came to anoint the body that Sunday morning debated all the way to the tomb how they, with all their united strength, could so much as budge it (Mark 16:1–3).

We're also to believe that Jesus was able to elude the guards whose very lives depended on their properly discharging their duty. Then, three days later, according to this theory, Jesus perpetrated a deliberate fraud, pretending to be alive from the dead, when in fact He had not died at all. We are asked to believe all this, in the face of all the facts that Jesus was the most honorable and truthful man who ever lived.

Clearly, this rationalistic theory simply does not hold water. The fact of the matter is that Jesus died. Moreover, He died according to the Scriptures. Nobody in those days had any doubt at all that Jesus had died. So Paul takes us to the cross.

### b. The cemetery (v. 4a)

"He was buried," Paul says. Nobody has ever doubted that. He was buried in a brand-new tomb. It was a tomb that belonged to one of the richest men of His day, Joseph of Arimathea. Joseph was a dissenting member of the Sanhedrin, totally opposed to the cynical plans of that governing body to arrange for the murder of Christ. He provided the tomb. His friend Nicodemus, another dissenting member of the Sanhedrin, provided the spices. No less than one hundred pounds of spices—worth a king's ransom.

The body was wound round and round with the linen strips, dipped in a sticky, fragrant mixture of spices. As mentioned, these bandages and spices would eventually dry like concrete, leaving the body completely encased in a tight-fitting, tailor-made coffin. The body was put into the tomb and the tomb was closed with a massive stone. The stone was shaped like a wheel and ran on a groove. Once the tomb was closed, it was sealed with the imperial seal of the Roman governor, to make sure nobody tampered with the sepulchre or its contents. A guard was detailed to keep a twenty-four-hour watch on the tomb for the next three days.

### c. The calendar (v. 4b)

"And that he rose again the third day according to the scriptures." What a day that was! God had circled it on His calendar in glory before time ever began. Before the mystery of iniquity raised its head in the universe, God decided then that all three members of the Godhead would be involved in man's redemption. All the details and all the dates were settled in heaven. The Lord Jesus would enter into human life, and in cooperation with the Father and the Spirit, would put the plan of redemption into effect. The date was circled on God's calendar for the Lord's birth. The date was circled for His baptism. The date was circled for His death. The date was circled for His burial. Above all, the date was circled for His resurrection.

The Lord Jesus never took His eye off that date. All through His earthly sojourn, He read His Bible and remembered that date. He could see it in His mind's eye. He could remember the time when He and His Father and the Holy Spirit settled on that date. He remembered it when, in the work of creation, on the third day, the continents, long submerged and buried in their watery grave, burst forth from their tomb and reached toward the sky. He remembered it when Jonah emerged from "the belly of hell" on the third day.

He talked about it more and more as He saw the day approaching. It was that date on the calendar in glory that enabled Him to go through with it all. "Never mind, fellows," He would say to his disciples, "I'm going to be crucified and buried. But cheer up, there is a date circled on God's calendar in glory. On the third day, I'm going to rise again." And, sure enough, He arose.

What a morning that was in the history of this poor, old, sin-cursed world.

Come back, for a moment, to a date in British history, a Sunday morning in 1815. The battle of Waterloo had been fought and won, but the people of England still anxiously awaited news of the battle. There was no electricity, of course, no radio, no telegraph. News was relayed by a semaphore. The battle had been fought and the signal was sent. But it was interrupted by fog. The message that came through was simply, "Wellington—Defeated." It was the worst of news. The country went into mourning. Napoleon would again be master of Europe. The Napoleonic wars would have to be fought all over again. It was a very dark day. But, the next day, the skies cleared and the full message was received. It said, "Wellington—Defeated Napoleon."

On the day that Christ died, the disciples went into mourning. The message that was received was terrible: "Christ—Defeated!" That was the word. After all He had said and done, His foes had nailed Him to a cross of wood and buried Him in a Jerusalem cave. It was the worst of news. Jesus was dead. In heaven, the flags flew at half-mast. The word was circulated, man had murdered his Maker. Death reigned. For three days and three nights, that was the word. Satan had triumphed. But then, on the first day of the week, the true message was received. "Christ—Defeated Satan."

When the Lord raised Lazarus from the dead, it was by means of a call from the outside. Lazarus came forth, sure enough, but still wrapped in his grave clothes, a reminder that he would die again. They had to loose him and set him free. Christ, by contrast, rose right through His grave clothes. He marched out through that sealed and guarded door, and shortly afterward, showed up in the upper room. No wonder the word of the angel was, "The Lord is risen indeed!"

Nor has the good news altered with the passage of time. He says, "I am he that liveth, and was dead; and, behold, I am alive for evermore, Amen; and have the keys of death and hell" (Rev. 1:18).

Yet so stubborn is man's evil heart of unbelief that the Sanhedrin concocted a tale to explain the empty tomb. What a silly lie they told. Their theory was even more far-fetched than the so-called swoon theory. When the intellectual Greeks heard the news, they laughed. When the religious Jews heard it, they lied. And what was the lie? "The disciples came and stole the body," they said. Then they bribed the guards to say that while they slept the disciples had plundered the tomb. While they slept, indeed! In the Roman army, the penalty for sleeping on guard duty was death, especially if what was being guarded was stolen. Had they really been asleep, the guards would have been the first to deny it. But think for a moment about what they were saying: "While we slept, the disciples came and stole the body." What would a judge and jury think of a witness who took the oath, seated himself in the witness box, and announced, "Your Honor, ladies and gentlemen of the jury, I consider myself a competent witness to what occurred because I was sound asleep when it happened."

No, Jesus did not swoon. No, the disciples did not steal the body. Jesus arose! That day had been circled on God's calendar since before time began. It was a red-letter day. It will be a red-letter day for all eternity. So, then, the fact is stated. Christ arose.

## 2. The fact is substantiated (vv. 5–8a)

"He rose again the third day," says Paul (v. 4). And Paul ought to know. No one else has had even a tenth of Paul's knowledge of the facts. Within a short while of the event, Paul had mastered all the evidence for and against the fact of the resurrection. For a while, he chose not to believe in it, because it was an awkward fact that did not fit in with his religious beliefs. However, he eventually became the most zealous ambassador of the risen Christ the world has ever known. Something must have happened to change his mind. Something did! He met the risen Christ.

We have a saying, "Seeing is believing." Of all the "many infallible proofs" by which the risen Lord proved himself to be alive after His resurrection, perhaps the most convincing is that "He was seen." Paul parades before us an impressive array of perfectly credible witnesses.

### a. Seen by His friends (v. 5)

#### (1) Seen by the man who denied Him (v. 5a)

"He was seen of Cephas"—another name for Simon Peter. It is not at all unlikely that this timely appearance saved Peter from following Judas to a suicide's grave. Peter must have been desperate.

We can picture Peter giving Paul his own private tour of Jerusalem on the occasion of Paul's first visit to the city after his conversion. Peter would have shown him the upper room. He would have pointed out where Jesus sat and where he himself had sat. He would tell him how the Lord gave the best morsel to Judas, how they had all trusted Judas, and how they had thought, when he left the room suddenly, that he had gone to give money to the poor.

He would have taken him to Gethsemane. "Here is where He prayed," he would have said. He would have told Paul how the Lord had warned him that he would betray Him, and how he had argued about it. He would tell of the coming of Judas, and how he had cut off the ear of the high priest's servant, and how Christ had put it back on again. He would show him just where Jesus stood when, finally, the arrest was made.

He would have taken him to where the high priest lived, conscious, perhaps, that Paul knew the house much better than he did. "And here is where it happened," he would have said, "here it was that I denied Him three times, Paul, and once with a few round fisherman's oaths."

After denying his Lord, Peter had slunk away. Perhaps he had gone to Gethsemane. Perhaps it was the thought that Jesus had prayed for him, foreknowing this dark hour, that stayed his hand from suicide.

"He was seen of Cephas," said Paul. Peter himself would never stop talking about it until his dying day. He had outrun John to the tomb, he had seen the evidence, but he had still doubted. But then he met Him, and that settled it. "He was seen of Cephas."

### (2) Seen by the men He discipled (v. 5b)

"He was seen . . . of the twelve," Paul says. He had talked to them all, except Judas. There could be no doubting their united testimony.

They would take him back to the upper room. They would show him how they had barred and bolted the door and windows. They would tell him how they had cowered there in fear, dreading a knock on the door. They would tell him where they had been sitting when Christ had suddenly appeared in their midst and showed them His hands and His side.

These were not giddy schoolgirls. These were not hysterical enthusiasts who half-hoped for a resurrection and were ready to interpret any eerie feeling or ghostly shadow as the real thing. They were all thoroughly skeptical. They were all convinced that the great movement was over. Indeed, two of them had already headed for home at Emmaus, only to come back with a marvelous story to tell. Thomas would confirm to Paul his own determined unbelief.

The witness of these men would be accepted at face value as gospel truth in any court of law in our land to this very day.

### b. Seen by His flock (v. 6)

"After that," Paul says, "he was seen of above five hundred brethren at once; of whom the greater part remain unto this present, but some are fallen asleep" (v. 6). We can be sure that Paul and Luke had personally talked to many of these eyewitnesses, if not all. If, as seems likely, Paul wrote 1 Corinthians in A.D. 55, it was only a little more than twenty years since all this had happened. If you could parade five hundred witnesses, drawn from all walks of life, of average intelligence and good integrity, who all had the same thing to say, surely it would be taken as proved.

*c. Seen by His family (v. 7a)*

"After that, he was seen of James" (v. 7). The Lord had four half-brothers: James, Joses, Simon, and Judas, and at least three sisters. None of them believed on Him until after His resurrection. It was the conversion of James that convinced them.

We know a few things about James from references to him in the book of Acts and from his epistle. We get the picture of a somewhat narrow-minded man. His ideas of religion were largely based on asceticism and good works. He was strong willed and had a dominating personality. He was inclined to be as rigid as a Pharisee.

We can well imagine he was hard to get along with in that Nazareth home, especially after Joseph died. He would always consider himself to be right. He would want his own way. His opinions must not be questioned. He had no patience at all with the way Jesus was going about the business of being a national Messiah. He thought He was mad. On the cross, Jesus did not leave His mother to the care and keeping of James. He knew better than that. He commended her to the care of His disciple John.

The conversion of James resulted from a private interview with the risen Christ. Soon afterward, James convinced the other members of the family and they all joined the growing remnant in the upper room to await the coming of the Holy Spirit.

Paul was impressed by the conversion of James. He and James had nothing much in common, apart from their faith in Christ and their absolute conviction that He had risen from the dead, but Paul was thoroughly convinced of James's sincerity.

*d. Seen by His followers (v. 7b)*

"He was seen . . . of all the apostles" (v. 7). That is, He was seen by an extended group of key believers, men who later became leaders of the church. No doubt Matthias, who was later added to the Twelve, was one of them. Probably James was one as well. Perhaps Barnabas was there.

*e. Seen by His foe (v. 8)*

"Last of all he was seen of me also," says Paul (v. 8).

"The tenth of March," says John Newton, "is a day much to be remembered by me. For on that day, the Lord came from on high and delivered me out of deep waters."

He lost his mother when he was just seven years old. Soon afterward, his life's anchor began to drift. When he was eleven, he went to Africa, "That I might be free to sin to my heart's content," to use his own words. He paid a high price for his sin. He fell into the pitiless hands of the press gang. As a deserter from the navy, he was flogged until his back was in ribbons. He was lucky not to be hanged. He became involved in the barbarities and atrocities of the slave trade. Sinking lower than the low, he became a slave himself, the slave of a slave. He was sold to a black woman who made him depend for his food on crusts she tossed under the table.

He was saved in a storm at sea. It was a terrible storm. The ship was filling fast with water when John Newton cried out to God for mercy—his first prayer for many a long year. He sought mercy and found it on March 10, 1748. He was then twenty-three. It seemed to him that the Savior looked into the very depths of his soul. He wrote:

> Sure, never to my latest breath,
> Can I forget that look;
> It seemed to charge me with His death,
> Though not a word He spoke.[1]

He became one of the greatest forces for good in the history of the Church of England. His influence affected a veritable galaxy of great men—men who in turn helped change the world.

Thus it was with Saul of Tarsus. "Last of all he was seen of me!" he exclaims. "As of one born out of due time," he adds. He was born again from the most savage and bitter hatred to become the greatest apostle, the greatest missionary, and the greatest theologian in the entire history of the Christian church.

It happened on the Damascus road. He was posting northward from Jerusalem, toward the Syrian capital, armed with warrants for the arrest of all the Christians he could lay his hands on. So far as he was concerned, Jesus of Nazareth was an imposter and a blasphemer, and Christianity was a heretical cult that needed to be stamped out before it spread too far. Saul had already made many a widow, many an orphan. He had already terrified many a weak Christian into blasphemy. He was the Sanhedrin's golden-haired boy. He was the Torquemada of his day, merciless in his hate, tireless in his zeal, ruthless in his task, rabid in his unbelief.

But the iron had already entered his soul. The face of Stephen haunted him. He had listened to Stephen's brilliant, Holy Spirit-anointed defense before the Sanhedrin. He had heard him pray for his persecutors. He had seen his face glow with the light of another world. He had heard him claim, even as the stones were battering in his face, that he could see Jesus standing at the right hand of God. He was haunted by the face of Stephen, the first recorded martyr of the church.

Then he met Jesus. "Who art thou, Lord?" he said. The answer to that question, "I am Jesus whom thou persecutest," settled the question of his salvation, once and for all. "What wilt thou have me to do?" he said. The answer to that question settled the question of his future service once and for all (Acts 9:5–6).

He saw Him. He saw Him as the Lord from heaven. He saw Him in all His glory, a risen, ascended, glorified man in a battered human body, ablaze with the light of another world. From then on, Paul was no longer haunted by the face of Stephen. He was haunted by the face of Jesus. "He was seen of me also," he said.

So then, this is what sets our message apart from all others. We do not preach religion, we preach resurrection. Our invitation to men and women, boys and girls, is not to subscribe to a creed, however noble. We simply want to introduce them to a man who is alive from the dead. What could be more thrilling than that?

## CHAPTER 18

# BUT WE SEE JESUS

*Hebrews 2:9*

1. The turmoil
2. The types
3. The tragedy
4. The tomb

MARK WELL THE "BUTS" OF THE BIBLE. They are the hinges on which great events turn. We read of all the glories of Solomon, of his wisdom, his wealth, and his works. Then comes the "but" in his life. "But king Solomon loved many strange [foreign] women" (1 Kings 11:1).

We read of all the might and magnificence of King Uzziah and how he was marvelously helped until he was strong. Then comes the "but" in his life. "But, when he was strong, his heart was lifted up to his destruction" (2 Chron. 26:16).

We read of ourselves that we were dead in trespasses and sins, enslaved to the world and led prisoners by the prince of this world. We read that we were children of wrath, even as others. Then comes the "but" in our lives. "But God, who is rich in mercy, for his great love wherewith he loved us, Even when we were dead in sins, hath quickened us together with Christ" (Eph. 2:4–5).

Here, the apostle paints a picture of Adam's ruined race. Man was made a little lower than the angels and crowned with glory and honor.

He was set over the works of God's hands, a monarch of all he surveyed, God's vice-regent to govern the garden, the globe, and no doubt, eventually the galaxy. All things were put in subjection under his feet. The apostle almost seems to have been carried away in transports of delight at the dignity and destiny of man. Then he remembered that, today, in actual fact, all things are not in subjection to man. Man is a fallen being, heir to a lost estate. All his great expectations have come to nothing. They lie in ruins and rubble at his feet. The world is filled with war and famine and pestilence. Nature is red in tooth and claw. Everywhere there is disease, disaster, and death. Satan has become the prince of this world. Millions are heading down the broad road to destruction. It is all so sinister and so sad. Then comes the apostle's "but": "But we see Jesus" (Heb. 2:9).

That is the expression that grips and holds our hearts. Come what may, we see Jesus. That changes the whole picture. Let us consider some ways in which that is gloriously true.

## 1. The turmoil

We can only guess at the high destiny for which God created and ordained the human race. We gather some inkling of it, however, from the fact that, consequent upon the Fall, God sent His own Son into the world as a human being, in order to reinstate the human race to its original election and call. For man was created to be inhabited by God. Indeed, so great was the dignity and destiny bestowed by God on Adam and his race, it evoked the envy and malice of Lucifer, the fallen cherub. He invaded our planet from outer space to tempt Adam and Eve into sin.

The temptation was clever, convincing, and complete. First Eve, then Adam, fell for Satan's lies. The moment they did, the light went out and the guilty pair were left standing naked and ashamed, the inner throne of their spirit vacated by the Holy Spirit. They were empty, lost, and undone. The light that had clothed their nakedness, and which had illuminated their innermost beings, had gone out. They were lost and in the dark. Every human being since has been conceived in sin and "shapen in iniquity" (Ps. 51:5). The governing, guiding principle of the indwelling Holy Spirit of God is missing. There are people who are intellectually brilliant, but they are lost. There are those who can feel deeply about things, but they are lost. There are others who can summon up the resources of willpower, and bring resolute determination to bear upon the course of their lives, but they are lost. There are people who can think brilliantly and feel deeply and resolve adamantly, but they are lost. There are people who are devoutly religious, but they are lost. Man in sin is not what God had in mind.

Man has lost control of the world he was intended to rule. In our own day, "evil men and seducers . . . wax worse and worse" (2 Tim. 3:13). We have more knowledge today than man has ever had, but we have less wisdom. Economic and ecological disasters threaten us. Apocalyptic weapons abound and will soon be in the hands of international terrorists. Millions of people on this planet never have enough to eat, desert lands are spreading, horrendous new diseases lurk in the human bloodstream. There are terrible inequities and horrible injustices in this world. Vice and violence are epidemic in society. Millions are enslaved to drink and drugs and sex.

All this turmoil is the result of the temptation and the Fall. Satan gloats over it all with fiendish glee. Countless millions of his unseen servants (evil spirits, fallen angels, principalities, powers, the rulers of this world's darkness), invisible, but potent and real, hold the race in bondage and thrall.

But we see Jesus. He came, man as God intended man to be, man inhabited by God. Satan tried his collection of temptations on Him, but they did not work. Jesus could say, "I do always those things that please the Father." That was the driving force behind His magnificent and sinless life. Satan stirred up the world to do its worst. Men spat in Jesus' face, beat Him, battered Him, scourged Him, and crucified Him. Then they buried Him. But He tore away the iron bars of death and rose in mighty triumph from the tomb. He lives now forever in the power of an endless life. Man, as God intended man to be, triumphant over all.

We see Jesus. And He is coming back. In the Old Testament, redemption was set before God's people in two books and in two ways. There is redemption by *power*, and redemption by *purchase*. The book of Exodus exemplifies redemption by power, and the book of Ruth exemplifies redemption by purchase. Jesus came the first time to effect the redemption of the human race by purchase; He is coming back, soon, to effect the redemption of the human race by power. *But we see Jesus!*

## 2. The types

The Old Testament religion was largely one of types, pictures, shadows, and illustrations. They were very vivid, very accurate, very real. But they were only types.

The story of Abraham at Moriah is a type. Here we have the first mention of love: *the love of the Father for the Son.* "Take now thy son, thine only son Isaac, whom thou lovest, and get thee into the land of Moriah; and offer him there for a burnt offering upon one of the mountains which I will tell thee of " (Gen. 22:2).

First, there was the place. How it must have haunted Abraham's dreams. It is mentioned again and again. Now he pictured it as a smiling, sunny glen, carpeted in green, bathed in the same light of the setting sun. Now he saw it as a dark canyon between towering crags where dark shadows plunged the place into eternal gloom. Now he envisions it as one of those dread high places where the Canaanites sacrificed their screaming little ones on the red hot lap of Moloch. Now he pictured a haunted spot that cried aloud to high heaven for a visitation of wrath. There was *the place.*

Then there was the plan. He was to take his only begotten, his well-beloved son to a place of death. He was to march resolutely forward, turning neither to the right hand nor to the left. One hand would hold the knife, the other hand the fire. The knife spoke of death, and the fire of that which comes after death. In his heart there was a searing agony of pain. All he could think of was Isaac, his Isaac, the one who filled his heart with laughter and love.

Then there was the plea. "My father!" Isaac said. "Here am I, my son," replied Abraham. "Behold the fire and the wood," said Isaac, "but where is the lamb?" Ah! Where indeed? The best Abraham could do was blurt out, "My son, God will provide himself a lamb" (Gen. 22:7–8).

So they went, "both of them together," all the dark and dreadful way. They were together to the bitter end. That was the Old Testament story. But now we see Jesus. Centuries later, the great apostle summed it all up for the Hebrew people: "By faith Abraham . . . offered up [*his only begotten son*] . . . Accounting that God was able to raise him up, even from the dead" (Heb. 11:17–19, emphasis added).

In Genesis 24, we have the second mention of love: *the love of the son for his bride*. Truly the types are as accurate as mathematics.

When the Jews read the Bible, they met people like Abel, Isaac, Joseph, Moses, Joshua, David, and Solomon. They read the stories and drew moral lessons from them. They read the Bible and were confronted with history and rituals, all of which held lessons they barely understood. They read about the tabernacle, the sacrifices, and the feasts; they read about the journey from Egypt to Canaan, and the history of David's times. They saw a rich history of people and places, promises and principles. *But we see Jesus*. In Him we have a key to the types that the most learned rabbis never had.

## 3. The tragedy

It comes surging into our lives, unbidden and unwanted. We pray for the healing of this one, the deliverance of that one, and often we pray seemingly in vain. Daily we read of war and famine, earthquake and tornado, sickness and death. They come and leave people prostrated with grief, anger, dismay, and fear. We pray, but the heavens seem as brass. The blandishments and banalities of the "name it, claim it" school of thought only play cruel games with people. The common ills of mankind overtake the righteous as well as the unrighteous.

The Lord's disciples on one occasion felt themselves abandoned to their fate. There they go. We can see them as they push off from shore, a dozen men in a decent-sized boat. They have had a day of it, indeed. They had seen Jesus feed five thousand men, plus women and children, with a little lad's lunch. Andrew was still full of it, no doubt. "What about that, Peter? I never saw anything like it. That little kid tugged my sleeve and offered to give his lunch to Jesus. He would not take no for an answer." They had been kept busy hurrying here, there, and everywhere with armfuls of food for the hungry multitudes. Then, when it was all over, there had been twelve full baskets left over. The solid evidence of it lay there, at their feet, in the bottom of the boat. The crowd had wanted to crown Him both Lord and Christ then and there. And now the disciples were rowing for the other shore, secure in the knowledge that they were in the very center of the Master's will.

Then it happened. The storm came, howling down from the hills around the lake, whipping the water into giant waves, threatening at any moment to capsize the boat and send them to a watery grave. Several of them knew the depth of their peril. They had fished that lake all their lives and knew its treacherous ways. Still, they did their best, rowing with all their might, but the harder they tried, the worse it became. The future of the church, and the future of the world was in that boat. How the Devil would have liked to have sunk it. Then Jesus came. He came walking on those threatening waves as if he were walking across a furrowed field. The awestruck disciples learned the lesson of their lives. Those same waves that threatened any moment to be over their heads were already under His feet.

So it should be with us when the storms of life burst in all their fierce fury on our frail vessels. Disaster strikes. Death comes in the door. The boss tells us we've been fired. Sickness seizes on us and the bills pile up. There is a costly fire. One of the children is picked by the police. One of the partners in the marriage demands a divorce. The storms can come from a hundred directions. *But we see Jesus.* Not for one moment has He ceased to love us. His power still energizes the universe. Ten thousand times ten thousand angels still wait to do His will.

Think, for example, of Stephen. He had been appointed a deacon of the church because of his character and convictions, and because he was evidently filled with the Spirit. His power in the gospel infuriated the Sanhedrin. He was arrested and put to the question. Before the day is over, he will be taken out to execution by a maddened mob, led by a furious young Pharisee named Saul. But Stephen *saw Jesus*. He saw heaven opened. He saw glory and joy unspeakable. He saw the Son of the living God standing to welcome him home. The very sight of it caused his face to shine like that of Moses on the mountain. Jesus changed tragedy into triumph.

When tragedy comes surging into the lives of those who are strangers to Christ, where can they turn? They turn to their friends, who they hope will tell them, "Everything is going to be all right." They often become bitter and say harsh things about God. But when such things come surging into our lives, *we see Jesus*.

A friend of mine who has been involved in missions for many years tells of a Jewish businessman who took him out for lunch one day and told him a harrowing story of personal horror in a Nazi concentration camp. He saw his own son brutally put to death. He had become bitter against God, especially against the Christians, whom he accused of doing nothing to stop the terror. He wound up his blistering and withering attack by saying, "Where was your God when my son was killed?" My friend looked at him and said, "He was just where He was when His own Son was killed."

## 4. The tomb

Death is inescapable. It dogs our footsteps everywhere we go in life. It has our name and address on its list of prospects. We are ever only a heartbeat away from it. The moment we began to live, we began to die, for every breath we breathe is one breath more but also one breath less. We never know when death will burst in on us with its pitiless syllable, "Now!"

Death is no respecter of persons. It stops at the king's palace as readily as at the peasant's shack. It is not deterred by color, class, or creed. It is the fly in the ointment of life.

Those who have the means will spend a fortune on physicians to hold death at bay for just another year or two. The latest fad is to have one's mortal remains deep-frozen in the vain hope that, one hundred years from now, science will be able to effect a resurrection.

Everything about death is horrifying to us. Often death's portals are made terrible with physical pain. We will sometimes wake up in the night in a cold sweat, terrified by nightmares in which our legs were paralyzed and some dark monster or dread pursuer is hot on our trail. We face reality. One day or night, as sure as we lie between the sheets, we are going to die. The body will be taken to the mortuary and then on to the cemetery. As surely as we live and breathe, we will one day die. For the unsaved, the horror and dread of the tomb is something to fear. Neither science nor religion nor philosophy has anything worthwhile to say in the face of death.

Christian Scientists pretend that "death is an error of mortal mind." But the woman who taught that doctrine has been dead and buried herself these many years, and her tomb can be seen in Mt. Auburn Cemetery in Cambridge, Massachusetts. She has been in her tomb now since December 3, 1910. She had plenty of warning, because she buried three husbands before her own turn came to die. She buried George Washington Glover six months after she married him in June 1844. She buried Dr. Daniel Patterson in 1896, having first divorced him. She buried Asa Gilbert Eddy on June 3, 1882, after he died of heart disease. Mary Baker Eddy said he died from "mental arsenic," but that was a self-deluding lie. For death is not an error of mortal mind. Death is very real indeed.

To deny the reality of death does not alter the fact of death. The Bible says, "It is appointed unto men once to die, but after this the judgment" (Heb. 9:27). For the unsaved, death is something to be feared, for beyond death lies "the second death," a great eternity of woe, "the blackness of darkness for ever," an eternity shut out from God and His Son and from all that is good and pure and holy and blessed. But we do not see death, *for we see Jesus.*

Jesus confronted death for us at Calvary. There He destroyed "him that had the power of death" (Heb. 2:14). He went marching out of life with a mighty shout as a glorious Conqueror. He took the tomb by storm. "I lay down my life, that I might take it again. No man taketh it from me," He announced, "I lay it down of myself. I have power to lay it down, and I have power to take it again. This commandment have I received of my Father" (John 10:17–18). He died to the accompaniment of rending rocks and bursting tombs and the tearing of the temple veil.

Down He went to the regions below. In hell He told of His triumph. To those in Abraham's bosom, it was news of new life; to those across that vast and yawning gulf, it was confirmation of a second death. He remained there three days and nights while the earth spun round and round on its axis, following the path He himself had ordained. Then, up from the grave He arose. "I am he that liveth, and was dead," He cried, "and have the keys of hell and of death" (Rev. 1:18).

On His way back from the dark domain, He stopped by the tomb for His body and vanished into the night. He summoned an angel from on high to roll back the stone from the door. The angel was summoned to put the fear of the living God into the souls of the soldiers watching over Christ's tomb. They fled for their very lives to tell their lords and masters what had happened.

For the next forty days, Jesus remained in the environs of this planet. He had some things to do before going home. The disciples needed to be convinced "by many infallible proofs," that He was indeed alive from the dead. That the tomb had been conquered, once and for all. Once, for all time. Once for all sins. Once for all who put their trust in Him.

After completing the task of convincing the disciples of the reality of His resurrection, Jesus took them out to Bethany. What a procession it must have been. There they go, the disciples of Jesus, the nucleus of the church, walking with a resurrected man. Out through the city gate, they make their way, down across the Kidron, on past the garden of Gethsemane, on up to the brow of Olivet. Then came the last good-bye, and suddenly, as they stood and stared, His feet left the ground. They watched with bated breath as He arose and as the cloud came and received Him out of their sight.

Oh yes! *We see Jesus.* We see Him now seated at the right hand of the Majesty on high, "from henceforth expecting till his enemies be made his footstool" (Heb. 10:13). We see Him waiting for the time when every blood-bought child of God will share in His triumph over the tomb.

He is coming back one of these days; coming with a mighty shout to awaken the dead. The dead in Christ will rise first, then we who are alive and remain will be caught up with them to meet the Lord in the air.

We shall be changed. In a moment. In the twinkling of an eye. We shall receive a body like unto His glorious body, able to virtually annihilate time and space, a body engineered for the vastness of space and for the ages of eternity. We shall be saved to sin no more. There will be no more sickness, no more death, no more parting.

*We see Jesus.* Now we see Him through a glass darkly; then we shall see Him face-to-face and we shall say like the Queen of Sheba, "Behold, the half was never told me." Everything will be suddenly brighter and bigger and better and bolder. Everything will be more beautiful, more boundless, more brilliant than we ever imagined.

When I was a little boy in school, I was told by an observant teacher that I needed glasses. I could not see what was written on the board. When I looked at a tree, the leaves were all fuzzy. When I looked at the board, I could not make out the words. So my mother had my eyes tested and I put on my first pair of glasses. Suddenly, I could see. It was like being in a new world. In that day, we shall see! It will indeed be a new world.

## CHAPTER 19

# THE ROAD TO EMMAUS
*Luke 24:13–32*

1. The two disciples and their misery
   a. Their direction
   b. Their discussion
2. The two disciples and their mystery
   a. The stranger
   b. The Scriptures
3. The two disciples and their ministry
   a. A new vision
   b. A new volition
   c. A new vocation

IT WAS RESURRECTION DAY! It was the greatest single day in all the history of the world. There has never been another like it. Jesus, having conquered sin and Satan, had now conquered the sepulchre as well. Angels from the realms of glory were bursting with the news. They keep showing themselves to men to try to get the message through those clouded human minds and cloddish human hearts: *"The Lord is risen indeed!"*

It was now afternoon as two of the Lord's disciples, who had been around the city all morning, and who had heard the news of the empty tomb from various sources, are heading for home.

## 1. The two disciples and their misery

Their grief stemmed from unbelief. They did not believe a word of the marvelous stories circulating around the city. Because they did not believe, their future seemed as black as the grave. Of course it was! Unbelievers do not have a bright future, only a dark one, a very dark one indeed.

### a. Their direction

They were moving in the direction of unbelief, having turned their backs on the whole thing by leaving Jerusalem. The other disciples back in the city were in a poor state of soul as well, but at least they were still in Jerusalem, where the Lord was said to have appeared. At least they were gathered in fellowship, though a sad and uninspiring fellowship it was. Nothing was happening in their meetings. They were coming together more out of habit than anything else, and with the vague hope that things might pick up, but they were not expecting much. They were certainly not expecting the supernatural. They gathered together to talk about the Lord's death. They talked about Him, about His character, His teaching, His miracles, His marvelous personality. And they talked about His cross. That was better than nothing.

But these two on the road out of town had had enough. They were heading for home; they were through. We can understand that. Some of us have about had enough of dead formal meetings where nothing happens, where there is not the slightest touch of the supernatural. It does not take long for people to get fed up with coming and going to meetings where all they have is a sterile discussion of truth without any hope or expectation of anything going to happen.

So these two disciples were heading for home. They were through with going to meetings; they had other things to do. They were wrong, of course. Walking out was no solution. They were as coldly unbelieving as the others. At least the others were waiting where things *could* happen, but these had left the fellowship, the first of the disillusioned apostolic band to scatter.

We do not know much about them. One of them is called Cleopas. His name means "my father is renowned." Maybe so, but his renown died with him. As to the other, we are not even told his name. Some have thought that it was Luke. It is an attractive thought, but pure speculation. Others have thought that the unnamed disciple was the wife of Cleopas. That seems to make more sense. Here they are, husband and wife, heading for home after coming to the conclusion that there really was no point in staying any longer with the others in Jerusalem.

### b. Their discussion

"They talked together of all these things which had happened." We can hear Cleopas. He says to his companion, "Do you remember what He said when they nailed Him to that tree?" "How could I forget!" she says. "He said, 'Father, forgive them; for they know not what they do.' That was just like Him, wasn't it? How forgiving He was. Don't you remember how He told Peter once that he must forgive those who injure him seventy times seven times?" "Yes! And you should have seen Peter's face," Cleopas might have replied. "It was a picture. Can you imagine Peter forgiving somebody four hundred and ninety times for the same offense?" "No. But I can imagine Jesus doing it."

So they talked together of all these things that had happened. No doubt it was a very sad discussion they had. They recalled Christ's generosity, His gestures, and His gentleness. They talked about how genuine He was. They talked about His goodness, His grace, His glory. Had they known the old gospel hymn, it would seem they were doing just what it said:

> Fasting alone in the desert,
> Tell of the days that are past.
> How for our sins He was tempted,
> Yet was triumphant at last;
> Tell of the years of His labor,
> Tell of the sorrow He bore.

He was despised and afflicted,
Homeless, rejected and poor.[1]

They would recall His miracles, especially how He had raised
Lazarus. They would recall His parables. What wonderful stories He
told! They would recall the story of the good Samaritan, the story
of the rich fool, the story of the prodigal son, the story of the wheat
and the tares. "Never man spake like this man!" said Cleopas. "He
went about doing good," said his wife. "Remember how He dealt with
Zacchaeus?" said Cleopas. "And how He healed poor Malchus? And
now He is dead and buried, and it's all over." "What are we going to
do tomorrow, Cleopas?" she would say. "I don't know. I rather hope I
get arrested and crucified too." So we have set before us their misery.
Then comes their mysterious encounter along the road.

## 2. The two disciples and their mystery

The two disciples may have walked out on Jesus, but Jesus had no
intention of walking out on them. They might have been through, but
He was not. The meetings in the upper room might be dead and dull,
but a few hours alone with the Bible and with Him was going to turn
out to be quite a different matter. Our problem, of course, is that we
rarely give Him a chance to make the Book come alive to us.

### a. The stranger

They were plodding along toward a village called Emmaus. We do
not know for sure exactly where Emmaus was. We are told that it was
sixty furlongs from Jerusalem, about seven-and-a-half miles. They
had a long walk ahead of them, up hill and down dale, with Jerusalem
receding behind them, until they reached that turn in the road where
it would vanish behind the hills. There, perhaps, they would stop for
one last look. Then on again toward Emmaus.

They were deep in conversation and did not hear the hastening
footsteps behind them. Then suddenly they heard a hail. They stopped

and turned. Perhaps they are a little annoyed. When a couple are having this kind of emotional, nostalgic conversation, they do not welcome intruders. No doubt they did not want to talk to a stranger about the weather and the latest political outrage in their tortured land. They did not want to make small talk about the price of food or the beautiful scenery or the splendor of the setting sun. They wanted to go on talking to each other about Jesus.

But there was something about the exuberant friendliness and good fellowship of the stranger; something about his manner and his smile. They could not place it, of course, but there was something nostalgic about him. We have all met people like that. They remind us of someone, though we can't quite place it. But the look about the eyes, or the set of the mouth, or the mannerisms, seem familiar. And although the person is a complete stranger, we feel somehow as if we know them, because they are just like someone we do know. Perhaps that is the way it was.

They did not exclude the stranger from their conversation. They politely allowed him to join them. He said, "What manner of communications are these that ye have one to another, as ye walk, and are sad?" The word he used for "communication" should have arrested them then and there. It was the word *logos,* "the word." It was to become one of the greatest of all the Lord's titles in days to come, "In the beginning was the Word," John would say, "and the Word was with God, and the Word was God. . . . And the Word was made flesh" (John 1:1, 14). "Tell me about this *logos* of yours," the stranger said.

"And one of them, whose name was Cleopas, answering said unto Him, Art thou only a stranger in Jerusalem, and hast not known the things which are come to pass there in these days?" They stared at him. He must be a stranger indeed! He must be the only man in Jerusalem ignorant of what had been going on there for the past week.

Here then was the stranger. He was the man who knew nothing, but who knew everything. It is a sad thing when people look upon Jesus as a stranger. He is a stranger to many. Their eyes, like these two disciples of old, are blinded to the truth. They do not know Him. They would not recognize Him if they saw Him. They might know some things about Him, just as these two did. But they do not know Him. That was why Jesus joined them. He wanted to open their eyes. Now what did He do? Did He perform a miracle? He could have, of course. He could have said, "Let's stop for a bite to eat and I'll command stones to become bread." He could have summoned water from the rock and then changed that water into wine. Of course he could have. But He did no such thing. Faith must not rest in miracles. It must have a surer foundation than that. Instead, He drew their attention to the Scriptures:

### b. The Scriptures

First of all, they poured into His eager ears the whole sad story of their crucified hopes. They spoke to Him concerning "Jesus of Nazareth, which was a prophet." They said He was "mighty in deed and word before God and all the people." They told Him how the chief priests and rulers had delivered Jesus to be condemned to death, and how they had crucified Him.

"But we trusted that it had been he which should have redeemed Israel," they said. "And beside all this, to day is the third day since these things were done." They told Him the stories about a resurrection, now being spread by some of the women, whose testimony they discounted as worthless. They told him of the vision of angels that the women said they had seen, but they had written it off as of no account. One wonders how Jesus kept a straight face while all this was being said. He said nothing. He let them talk themselves out. Finally, they had said it was all over. Their much heralded Messiah was dead and buried and that was the end of it all.

When they had finally wound right down, they looked at Him to see what He would say. With what feelings He must have listened to their story. They obviously loved Him dearly. They evidently had trusted Him implicitly. How His heart must have burned within Him to hear them tell Him everything He already knew about himself. That is the very essence of worship, by the way. To tell the Lord Jesus all about himself and just how much we love Him and trust Him. To say to Him:

O Lord! when we the path retrace
Which Thou on earth hast trod,
To man Thy wondrous love and grace,
Thy faithfulness to God.

Faithful amidst unfaithfulness;
'Mid darkness only light,
Thou didst Thy Father's name confess
And in His will delight.

Unmoved by Satan's subtle wiles,
Or suffering, shame and loss,
Thy path uncheered by earthly smiles,
Led only to the cross.[2]

So they poured into His delighted ears their knowledge of Him,
their love, their trust, even their crucified hopes. And He silently listened to it all, drank it all in, and would have opened their eyes then
and there, except He had a better way. He was going to open their eyes
to the Scriptures before He opened their eyes to the Savior. For if we
would avoid crucified hopes again; if we would avoid walking out on
God's people again, just because the meetings are dull; if we would
avoid heading out on our own once more, out of fellowship with God's
people and with no future at all, useless to God and man, then our
faith must be grounded solidly on the Word of God. "Faith cometh
by hearing, and hearing by the word of God" (Rom. 10:17).

Nobody knew this better than Jesus. So He first gently rebuked
them for their folly and for their blindness to the Word of God.
"Ought not Christ to have suffered these things," he said, "and to
enter into his glory?

"And beginning at Moses and all the prophets, he expounded unto
them in all the scriptures the things concerning himself." They had
never heard anything like it before, the way He opened up their Bible
to them. He preached Christ to them from the familiar pages of the
Scriptures. They were amazed as He expounded to them the sufferings

and the glory of Christ embedded into every chapter, every verse, and every line of God's inspired Word.

He simply restored their balance. They had expected a militant Messiah, He showed them a meek Messiah. They had expected a Sovereign, He showed them a Savior. They had expected a Ruler, He showed them a Savior. They thought of a conquering Christ, He showed them a crucified Christ. The pages of Scripture burned and blazed with a light and a luster that outshone the burning brilliance of the setting sun.

He took them back to the *predictive types* that formed such a large part of their Bible.

He began, perhaps, with the promised seed. Perhaps He took them back to the Garden of Eden and showed them Adam and Eve standing in their guilt and nakedness. He reminded them of the very first prophecy, how the Serpent was to bruise the heel of the seed of the woman, but how the seed would triumph at last. He reminded them of the coats of skins provided for Adam and Eve at the cost of sacrifice, for only by the shedding of blood could their wretchedness be covered. He showed them God covering sin until such time as the Messiah could cancel sin. They likely said, "We never thought of that. Nobody ever told it to us like that before."

From there it would have been a short step to Abel's lamb and to God's utter rejection of Cain's bloodless sacrifice. "Ought not Christ to have suffered?" he said. And they, "We never saw it like that before." They looked at each other and looked at Him, their weariness and wretchedness now peeling away. "Tell us some more," they implored.

He went on, perhaps, to the story of Noah's ark. "Now how do you think Noah was saved from the wrath to come?" He might have asked. "He prepared an ark to the saving of his house." The ark represented a finished work of salvation. It was sealed against the storm. Then, when Noah and his family came into the ark, the door was shut and the storm of judgment arose. It broke in all its fury upon the ark, but not on them. Without the ark, they would have perished with the rest of the world.

Next, He likely would have taken them to Mount Moriah. He would have shown them father and son going up together to the place of sacrifice. And there, in meek obedience, obedience unto death, Isaac, having carried the wood to the site, was stretched upon it. The knife was raised and the fire was ready. But the story did not end there. For wonder of wonders, Isaac lived and found a bride.

And what about Joseph? Did they not see Christ in the sufferings and the glory in the story of Joseph? How he was his father's well-beloved? He went forth from the father to seek his wandering brethren, the children of Israel. He came to them, but was hated by them and sold for the price of a slave. He was handed over by them to the Gentiles. He was put in the place of darkness and death; and, in due time, he was brought forth and raised to the right hand of the majesty of the Pharaoh. He was then given a name above every name, that at the name of Zaphnath-Paaneah, every knee should bow and every tongue confess him as Lord (Gen. 41–45). Could they not see Christ in all of that?

And what about the Passover and the wave sheaf? Did not these things speak of Christ in death and resurrection? And what about the smitten rock, the serpent on the pole, and the offerings?

And what about David? Was he not rejected before he reigned? Did he not destroy him that had the power of death? And did he not at last, after many sufferings, come into his glory?

And what about Jonah? Was he not three days and three nights in the belly of the great fish, and did he not come forth in resurrection life to minister blessing to the Gentiles? How could they read their Bible and not see these things? What a Bible lesson that must have been! How those seven-and-a-half miles must have melted away!

From the predictive types, he must have turned to the *plain teachings* that formed so large a part of their Bible. He would have reminded them of the prophecy of the virgin birth (Isa. 7:14), the prophecy of His birth in Bethlehem (Mic. 5:2), the prophecy of the forerunner (Mal. 3:1). He would have reminded them of the prophecy of His rejection (Ps. 69:4), of His betrayal (Ps. 41:9), and of His being sold for thirty pieces of silver (Zech. 11:12). For it had all been foretold—the spitting (Isa. 50:6), the crucifixion (Ps. 22:16), His orphan cry (Ps. 22:1), the vinegar and the gall (Ps. 69:21), the gambling for his clothes (Ps. 22:18), and the piercing of His side (Zech. 12:10). So, too, was His resurrection (Ps. 16:10). "Ought not Christ to have suffered these things?" He said, "and to enter into his glory?" Thus it was that their very hearts burned within them.

The mystery of it all changed now. They were no longer occupied with the mystery of the stranger, they were occupied with the wonder of the Word and with the mystery of their own blindness and unbelief. Until at length, all too soon, the journey was over. They had arrived at Emmaus. And there the stranger bade them farewell and "made as though he would have gone further." But they had fallen in love with Him. They asked Him to come in. They wanted to hear more, and more, and more. Their faltering faith was flaming again. "For faith cometh by hearing, and hearing by the Word of God" and this stranger had so expounded the Word to their hearts that they wanted another Bible study right away.

## 3. The two disciples and their ministry

First their eyes were opened, then their hearts were opened, and then their mouths were opened. Jesus accepted their invitation to come in. He always does. He is waiting for us to invite Him in right now. Into our hearts first, and then into our homes. He is making as though He would go "further," so we must seize this moment of opportunity while it lasts. It might never come again. How much they would have missed if they had failed to invite Him in! So in He came and there, in that room of theirs, with the bread and wine on the table, He gave them a new vision, a new volition, and a new vocation.

### a. A new vision

He had come in to be their guest at their invitation. He never forces himself in. He never makes a move without being asked. They must have asked Him to bless their meal. They felt, we can be sure, that it would be fitting to do so. So He took the bread into His hands and blessed it. And in a moment, in the twinkling of an eye, they knew Him. And in that same moment, He was gone. He wanted them to rest on Him by means of the Word.

Perhaps it was the familiar gesture. They remembered Galilee; perhaps the feeding of the five thousand. Or perhaps they remembered his blessing the bread, just like that, only days before in the upper room. Perhaps they saw the nail prints in His hands. We simply know that they knew Him in the breaking of the bread. They remembered His words, "This do in remembrance of me" (Luke 22:19), and they remembered Him. They had a new vision.

### b. A new volition

"And they rose up the same hour, and returned to Jerusalem." Of course they did! They wanted to get back into the fellowship of God's people, so that very same night, they retraced every one of their wayward steps. They wanted to impart the blessing they had received to the others in their little fellowship. It is a mark of true conversion that we want to be with others who love Him.

### c. A new vocation

They burst into the upper room and said, "The Lord is risen indeed!" They found that Simon Peter had come into the same blessing they had. The Lord had appeared to him as well. They then "told what things were done in the way, and how he was known of them in breaking of the bread." Their *eyes* were opened! Their hearts were opened! Their mouths were opened. They sought to share with the saints just exactly how their own hearts had burned within them as they saw Christ first in their Bible and then at their table. What better proof of the reality of it all could there be than that? And then He appeared again, to them all, in the upper room. As He had promised, where two or three were gathered together in His Name, there He was in the midst of them.

## CHAPTER 20

# THE GREAT COMMISSION
*Acts 1:8*

1. They needed enlistment
2. They needed encouragement
3. They needed enlightenment
4. They needed enablement

THE CROSS WAS BEHIND HIM. The crown was before Him. Now heaven and home beckoned Him on the resurrection side of the grave. Over yonder, the standards of the Almighty were unfurled on the towers and turrets of the New Jerusalem. To the utmost bounds of the everlasting hills, they had trumpeted His triumph. "The Lord is risen indeed!" The angels who had kept silent vigil at the empty tomb had told their side of the wonderful tale. There had doubtless been a hearty laugh that rippled throughout the Celestial City, at the story of the guards, how with a howl of mortal terror they had run for their very lives.

There had doubtless been a round of applause for Mary Magdalene. One of the angels said, "She just looked at me and then right through me. Then she turned her back on me. It was priceless!" She wanted Jesus. Not Michael or Gabriel or any ranking member of the angelic throng would do. She just wanted Him.

Thus it was that the angelic host lined up on the walls of the heavenly city and mustered at the pearly gates. They were waiting for the

Lord to come home. Already a special angelic guard had been sent down to earth to provide Him with a suitable escort. But still He did not come.

The weeks went by. One week, two, three, four, five. For forty seemingly endless days, He continued to tarry in the environment of the tiny planet Earth. His own heart was hungry for home. He had been talking about it to His disciples even before He took the final turn in the road that led to Calvary's hill. "I go to the Father," He had said (John 16:17). "Whither I go, ye cannot come" (John 13:33). "I go to prepare a place for you" (John 14:2). He kept on talking about it. How He longed to exchange the Old Jerusalem for the New Jerusalem, the scene of His suffering for the scene of His glory. But still He tarried, coming and going, appearing and disappearing, watching and waiting and looking above.

The chief focal point, of course, especially at first, was the upper room. Whoever it was that owned the house where that upper chamber was located will be amply rewarded in heaven. He has managed to remain quite anonymous, both in the Gospels and in the book of Acts, and the room itself has no doubt returned to the rubble of the ages. It would be the greatest of all tourist attractions in Jerusalem, if only it remained standing, and if only we could know just where it was.

It was as familiar as home to the Twelve. There they were joined, before long, by the Lord's mother, no doubt brought by John. Then the Lord's half brothers, believers at last, drifted in and quietly took their place with the disciples.

We can well imagine that Peter played the host. "Yes," we can hear him say, "it was here that He observed the last Passover and inaugurated a new feast of remembrance. He sat right there, I sat here, John sat there, right next to Him. Judas sat over there. I remember how we sang the great Hallel. I really did not feel much like singing, but He sang as if He had not a trouble in the world. And there was Judas, singing along with the rest of us until, at last, he shoved away from the table and headed for the door. We all thought he was going out to give something to the poor.

"And that wall there—that was where He appeared when He

came to visit us on the resurrection day. He came right through that wall. We all thought it was a ghost. Then He sat at the table right there where you are sitting, Joses. He ate some honey and some fish and talked to us—then He simply disappeared. We had to pinch ourselves at first. But we got used to that kind of thing after a while."

More and more people arrived, those whose lives had been touched and transformed by Jesus during His earthly ministry, until at last there were about one hundred and twenty in all. Doubtless, Nicodemus was there, and Joseph of Arimathea, and Bartimaeus, and Martha, Mary, and Lazarus, and Mary Magdalene. Perhaps Zacchaeus was there. It would be nice to think that Malchus was there.

And still the Lord tarried, coming and going, appearing and disappearing. We have to ask ourselves, Why? Why did He tarry so long when He was so eager to go home? There were four things His disciples needed: *enlistment, encouragement, enlightenment,* and *enablement.* It was to impart these four things that Jesus stayed.

## 1. They needed enlistment

Jesus made known to them *His passion*. First and foremost, these men were Jews. They had been raised in the Jewish tradition. Their world had been centered in the Jewish temple. They had been raised in the local synagogues. The supreme authority was that of the Sanhedrin. None of them, so far as we know, had ever been outside the boundaries of their homeland, and a very small homeland it was.

True enough, they lived in Galilee and rubbed shoulders with travelers from various parts of the world, but as Jews, they were suspicious of strangers. Their dietary laws pretty well cut them off from the rest of the world. Indeed, Jesus himself restricted His own earthly ministry to "the lost sheep of the house of Israel." His own contacts with Gentiles were few and far between. It was not likely that, with such a background, they would have much of a world vision.

But that is exactly what they needed. They had to be enlisted for a program of global outreach. The very last words of Jesus, as His feet left the brow of Olivet were these: "Even unto the end of the world." Then the cloud wrapped Him around and they were alone.

In order to reach the world, Jesus enlisted the disciples for a mission to all mankind. To James, He might have said, "Not just Jerusalem and Judea, but also the twelve tribes scattered abroad." To Peter, He might have said, "Not just Palestine, Samaria, and Caesarea, but also to the strangers scattered abroad throughout all Pontus, Galatia, Cappadocia, Asia, and Bithynia. To John, He might have said, "You wanted once to call down fire upon Samaria. Well, so you shall. But you must see beyond that. You must see Ephesus, Smyrna, Pergamos, Sardis, Thyatira, Philadelphia, and Laodicea. You must take in all kindred and peoples and nations and tongues." In His mind's eye, the Lord Jesus, even as He stepped into the cloud, saw the eunuch from Ethiopia returning disappointed and disillusioned from Jerusalem, reading a book he did not understand about a person he did not know. He saw the man from Macedonia with outstretched hands from the dynamic European continent saying, "Come over and help us."

There was no doubt that these men needed enlistment. In all the generations from that day to this, people have needed enlistment for the cause of Christ, and never more so than today. Here we are two thousand years later, with still two thousand tongues to go before we can say that every person has at least a page or two of the gospel in their native tongue. We are losing the battle for the world by the sheer weight of the population explosion. Nor will it ever be done in our day. When the rapture of the church has occurred, God will have to save, seal, and send 144,000 Jewish evangelists to do the job we have not done. What an evangelism explosion that will be! Imagine 144,000 apostle Pauls let loose on the planet!

Then, too, the rising tide of nationalism is doing its best to slam the door on the gospel. Increasingly, laws are being passed against foreign missionaries, and nationals who profess Christ are increasingly subject to persecution. There is a tremendous resurgence of non-Christian religions; Islam, Buddhism, and Hinduism are not only tightening their grip on their own hapless millions, but they are expanding their reach. They have become missionary religions. One example is the startling fundamentalist movement within Islam. Another example is the proliferation of Hindu and Islamic cults in Western Europe and the United States.

Communism, it is true, has lost its economic appeal in Russia and the countries of the former Soviet Union. Communist countries have been forced to accept radical changes. But now nationalist movements are on the rise that promise to be just as radical as Communism ever was. We have a wide open and unexpected opportunity in many Communist lands at the moment, but it is an open question of how long it will last.

In the meantime, most Americans have little or no interest in what goes on outside their own country. In the United States, 150 times as much money is spent annually on gambling than on foreign missions. Nearly sixty times as much money is spent on alcohol. About fifty times as much is spent on tobacco. According to one survey, Americans spend twice as much on dog food as they do on foreign missions.

Or take a look at the larger English-speaking world. About 10 percent of the world's population speaks English. About 90 percent of the world's professing Christians come from the English-speaking 10 percent. When we look inside the church, we find a corresponding pattern of spending. About 96 percent of the church's income is spent on the 10 percent who speak English. Only 4 percent of the church's income is spent on reaching the 90 percent who do not speak English.

There is no doubt that we need enlistment. In 2004, the world's population was approximately 6.4 billion people, with more than 60 percent of them in Asia, where Islam, Buddhism, and Hinduism hold empire, and where Communism still reigns in China.[1] Surely there is a desperate need for us to feel afresh, for ourselves, the passion of Christ for the untold millions still untold.

We should remember that every book of the New Testament was written by a foreign missionary or by a convert or colleague of a foreign missionary. Every letter in the New Testament addressed to an individual was addressed to the convert of a foreign missionary. Every letter in the New Testament addressed to a church was addressed to a foreign mission church. The disciples were first called *Christians* in a foreign country. Of the original twelve disciples, all except two became foreign missionaries. Of those two, James was martyred for the faith in his homeland, and Judas of course became an apostate and a traitor and committed suicide.

It took time for the Lord's challenge to take root, but, before it was over, the early church took its enlistment seriously and profoundly affected the world of that day for Christ.

## 2. They needed encouragement

Jesus made known to them *His presence.* Evangelizing the world would have been an impossible task without Him. So, over and over again, during that monumental and exciting seven-week period, Jesus made it quite clear to the disciples that they were not being abandoned. He did not expect them to "go it alone." "I will not leave you [orphans]," He had already assured them (John 14:18).

The Lord's postresurrection appearances must have been very reassuring to the disciples. "Lo, I am with you always, even unto the end of the world," He told them (Matt. 28:20). That became Dr. David Livingstone's favorite text. In every crisis in his life, he fell back on it. When, thanks to the terrible hardships of pioneering in central Africa, he had been obliged to send his wife back to England, he wrote it down in his diary yet again, "Lo, I am with you." When, thanks to the gossiping tongues of the coastal missionary colony, he felt obliged to bring his wife back, despite all his better judgment, he wrote it down again. When she died as a result of those hardships and he was left desolate, again he wrote it down, "Lo, I am with you."

When he was surrounded by hostile savages, and his life was in the balance, he wrote it down again, "Lo, I am with you always, even to the end of the world." And he used to add his own postscript: "It is the word of a Gentleman of the strictest and most sacred honor, and that settles it."

So it was that the Lord Jesus sought to impress on His disciples His presence. They needed that encouragement so "he shewed himself alive after his passion," Luke says, "by many infallible proofs" (Acts 1:3). We are not called upon to preach a code or a creed, but a living Christ. It is not myth or make-believe that we preach, but hard, solid facts. Jesus Christ is a real person. He was crucified under Pontius Pilate; He was buried and He rose again. These facts are as hard, as adamant, as solid and real as the fact that Julius Caesar conquered Britain.

But before we can make Christ real to anyone else, He must first be made real to us. That is why the Lord Jesus took His disciples into His immediate presence for a period of forty days before returning to heaven. During that time He made himself real to them. With Mary Magdalene it was just the whisper of her name; with Thomas it was the challenge of his own unbelieving words; with the Emmaus disciples it was an exposition of the Scriptures, climaxing in that old familiar gesture when He took the bread, gave thanks, and broke it.

As a result, by the time He was finished with them, they were absolutely convinced of the reality of Christ. They had an unshakable conviction in the reality of *His resurrection, His rapture,* and *His return.* Nobody could shake them on those things. In the power of that reality, they went out to turn the world upside down—or rightside up might be a better way to put it.

### 3. They needed enlightenment

Jesus made known to them *His program.* He did not say, "Well, you men ought to know by now how it is done. You have a meeting and discuss the situation. Then you elect some likely candidates. After that you have a popular vote and choose a board and arrange for some committees, do things in an organized way. Do things by popular, majority vote."

That was just *not* the way it was to be done. They tried that and elected a man named Matthias to fill the empty space in the apostolate left by Judas. The Holy Spirit thereafter seems to ignore their choice and goes after *His* man, the apostle Paul.

The way to get the job done is to follow the principle for world evangelism that Jesus laid down, and the method of world evangelism used by Paul, the man the Holy Spirit chose. The Lord's master plan was very simple. You begin at Jerusalem. You enlarge operations to all Judea. You then cross your first frontier and evangelize Samaria. Then you go after the world.

That is to say, you begin in *your own community.* You begin at Jerusalem. You begin where you are, where you live. You are to be a witness there. Then you reach out to *your own country.* You reach your particular Judea. You evangelize your own country, city by city, and village by village. Then you reach out to *your own continent.* You cross the nearest national frontier and you evangelize the nearest alien culture, the one with which you are the most familiar. You evangelize your particular Samaria. And, as each new convert is discipled, he too begins the same process, until finally you reach the uttermost parts of the earth. We are already far back in the race.

Evidently something is wrong with our methods. In Romans 15:19, Paul could say that he had fully preached Christ all the way from Jerusalem to Illyricum. That is an astonishing statement. The words, "fully preached" could equally be translated, "I have fully evangelized." He could claim to have fully evangelized an area stretching fifteen hundred miles up through Syria, across Asia Minor, down into Greece, and up the Adriatic to present-day Yugoslavia. It took him just fifteen years to evangelize a long line of cities surrounded by thickly populated areas stretching for fifteen hundred miles. That could be represented in the United States by a line running all the way from Atlanta, Georgia, to Denver, Colorado.

It is impossible to visualize Paul selecting a small upriver village area, where no one else was working, and there building a mission station, seeking out Gentiles one by one, and gathering converts in ones and twos to his mission compound.

If Paul were here today, he would first find a nominally Christian church in a big city, and he would preach there until he was thrown out. By that time, he would have reached all those who were hungry for the truth. With these he would form the nucleus of a dynamic New Testament church. He would teach his converts the principles of victorious living, soul-winning, and New Testament doctrine. He would fire them up, send them out, and move on.

## 4. They needed enablement

Jesus made known to them *His power.* "Ye shall receive power after that the Holy Ghost is come upon you: and ye shall be witnesses." That is what impressed the ancient pagan world. The apostles were motivated by the highest kind of love, and accompanied by the highest kind of power. There is no other way to explain what happened on the day of Pentecost. Peter stood up, began to preach, reaching for the conscience of his audience. He did not even finish what he had to say, yet three thousand people were saved, baptized, and added to the fellowship. That was not Peter's work, that was the work of another person altogether: the Holy Spirit.

Notice what happened in the upper room before Pentecost. There you see a representative company of God's people, the nucleus of the church. These people loved the Lord and were living in obedience to the will of God. The Lord had told them to tarry in Jerusalem. They were tarrying in Jerusalem. They were in happy fellowship, one with another. They were making decisions relating to the affairs of the gathering. They were giving themselves over to prayer. They were searching the Scriptures and exhorting one another. They were rejoicing in a risen, raptured, and returning Christ. But they were powerless to witness.

They set before us a perfect cameo of thousands of local church congregations and millions of sincere Christians. They meet to enjoy good fellowship and to preach and pray and exhort. But nothing happens. The reason for that is very simple. We can no more convert a soul than we can create a star. Only the Holy Spirit can make Christ real to us and only the Holy Spirit can make Christ real to someone else. Indeed, we cannot even make Christ real to each other apart from the presence and power of the Holy Spirit.

Just then, Mary Magdalene, Joanna, Mary the mother of Jesus, and the other women came bursting in with the glorious news: "The Lord is risen!"

What happened? "Their words seemed to them as idle tales, and they believed them not" (Luke 24:11).

On the road to Emmaus, Jesus appeared to Cleopas and the other disciple. He unfolded the Scriptures to them in a form so memorable and so convincing that they felt their hearts burn within them. Yet they still did not recognize Him. Then He made himself known to them in the breaking of the bread. Overwhelmed with joy, they turned around and headed all the way back to Jerusalem. They burst into the upper room with the glorious news. But, says Mark, "Neither believed they them" (Mark 16:13).

Then, the Lord appeared in the midst of all ten of the disciples who were gathered in the upper room. First, He had to prove to them that He was not a ghost. Once they were all convinced, they tried unitedly to convince Thomas. "He was here, Thomas. He came through that wall there. He sat on this chair here. He ate some of that fish and this honeycomb. Then He vanished." Talking all at once and one at a time, it made no difference. Thomas said, "I will not believe."

It was not until after Pentecost that they were able to witness with soul-saving power. That is why they had to "wait for the promise of the Father" (Acts 1:4), for the promised coming of the Holy Spirit. They had to learn to live their lives according to the terms by which Jesus had lived His life. They had to wait for the coming of the Holy Spirit in power. Then they would have the same power that He had.

We do not have to tarry for Him anymore. He has already come. He makes himself available to us as we make ourselves available to Him. Our task is to make sure we are not grieving, quenching, or resisting the Holy Spirit. We need to claim the available filling and anointing of the Spirit. We already have received the baptism of the Spirit and the gift of the Spirit.

So we are no longer instructed to wait for Him. He is now waiting for us. He is waiting for us to seek cleansing, and in genuine yieldedness to accept His filling. Then we shall have all that the disciples had at Pentecost—all that we need to be witnesses to all mankind.

## CHAPTER 21

# SUCH A HIGH PRIEST
*Hebrews 8:1*

1. Such a powerful High Priest
2. Such a permanent High Priest
3. Such a patient High Priest
4. Such a perfect High Priest
    a. A Priest who is holy
    b. A Priest who is human
    c. A Priest who is helpful

THROUGHOUT THE GREATER PART of the Old Testament, we meet an order of priesthood based on ritual. Priests of this order had to be born into a special family. They had to be born into the tribe of Levi and into the family of Aaron. This specially chosen family had an absolute, divinely ordained monopoly on the priesthood. There were no exceptions. By the time of Christ, this priesthood was securely seated in its office by fifteen hundred years of truth and tradition.

It was, from beginning to end, a ritual priesthood. The Aaronic priests had to wear special clothes. They had to perform various ceremonies. They were governed by special laws. They were mediators of a ritual religion.

It was God-ordained, but, nevertheless, it was merely a *religion* that they administered and served. At every point in the worship process, the priests were inserted between the people and God. In actuality, it was all just an elaborate performance. The Old Testament ritual priest, of the tribe of Levi, of the family of Aaron, was simply a man dressed up to act a part in a great, orchestrated religion of rules and rituals, sacrifices and ceremonies, types and shadows. The whole system was incapable of removing a single sin. As the hymn writer has so perfectly put it:

> Not all the blood of beasts
> On Jewish altars slain,
> Could give the guilty conscience peace,
> Nor wash away the stain.[1]

The sinner came to the priests with his offering. The priests guided him through the various rituals specified for the particular kind of offering he had brought. Let us suppose he had brought a sin offering. He had to put his hand on the head of the sheep or goat, confess his sin, and then slay the sacrifice. He saw it burned outside the camp and went away feeling good, feeling that he had obtained absolution for his sins.

But before long, nagging doubts would arise. He would go back to see the priest. "Do you know," he would say, "I really don't *feel* any different than I did before. Are you sure that the blood of that lamb really took away my sin?" The priest, if he was thoughtful and honest, would have to say, "I suppose so. At least the law prescribes such-and-such a sacrifice for such-and-such a sin. We did what the law requires, so I suppose everything is all right." It was all so very unsatisfactory. How could the blood of bulls and goats really take away the guilt and stain of sin? David, in his penitential psalms, saw through it. But then David, his sins and guilt notwithstanding, was one man in a million.

Worshippers today who take their sins and his sorrows to the Virgin Mary, in the Roman Catholic religious system, have an even greater problem. Some years ago, I was in Vichy, France, a town famous for its spa waters. It is a busy health resort. Brooding over the town is the Church of Our Lady of Healing, dedicated to the Virgin Mary as the healer. A black statue of the Virgin is the church's central focus of worship. The statue is paraded through the city from time to time with pomp and ceremony. Plaques are built into the walls of the church by grateful Catholics who attribute their healing to Mary. The most unforgettable thing about that church, however, is the dome.

High up in the dome is a giant picture. Christ is in the shadows and Mary dominates the foreground. The picture is so painted that Mary's robe lights up when the sunbeams strike it through the stained glass windows. She is obviously the more important figure of the two. She stands triumphant, trampling a writhing serpent beneath her feet. On one side of the base of the dome is a quotation from John 3:16: "For God so loved the world, that he gave his only begotten Son." But that is not all. On the other side of the base of the dome, in letters that dwarf the Bible text, is the true message of Rome. It is a quotation from Saint Bernard that reads, "It is God's will that we receive all things through Mary."

Just think of what that means. All over the world, at any given moment, thousands upon thousands of devout Roman Catholics are reciting the rosary, counting their beads, and praying to the Virgin Mary. They are bombarding her with ten thousand prayers and petitions in a thousand languages and dialects. In order to hear them all, unravel them all, and take full note of them all, she would have to be omniscient as God is omniscient. In order to grant the countless requests and demands made upon her, at any given moment she would have to be omnipotent as God is omnipotent. Because these prayers are often made in shrines and churches, before her graven image, in ten thousand locations all over the world, to be present at each one of them she would need to be omnipresent as God is omnipresent.

But she is just a woman, after all; a very great woman, but a woman. Moreover, she confessed herself to be a sinful woman in need of a Savior. In her famous Magnificat she said, "My spirit hath rejoiced in God *my* Saviour" (Luke 1:47, emphasis added). She needed a Savior just like anyone else.

"If you want anything," says the Roman Church, "then go to Mary." But she is a powerless mediator. In fact, she is no mediator at all, for the Bible says, "There is *one* . . . mediator between God and men, the man Christ Jesus" (1 Tim. 2:5).

So, what we need, what the Old Testament Hebrews needed, what devout Roman Catholics need, what the Muslims, Hindus, and Buddhists need, what everyone needs, is a true priest, a true Mediator—what Job calls a *daysman* (Job 9:33), and what John calls an *advocate* (1 John 2:1). Thank God, we have just such a one in Jesus. We need no other.

There are four things we all need in a true priest. We need for Him to be *powerful, permanent, patient,* and *perfect.* Jesus meets all those needs.

## 1. Such a powerful High Priest

A priest without power is worse than no priest at all. Our Lord Jesus is a powerful High Priest. He is a priest for ever after the order of Melchizedek (Heb. 6:20).

That means that He is both a Priest and a King, something no priest of Aaron's line ever was or ever could be. Look at Hebrews 7:1–2. Underline the word *king.* For this Melchizedek, "*king* of Salem, priest of the most high God . . . to whom Abraham gave a tenth part of all; first being by interpretation *King* of righteousness, after that also, *King* of Salem, which is, *King* of peace." King! King! King! King! Jesus is a powerful King and a powerful High Priest.

Now turn to Genesis 14, where this priest-king Melchizedek is introduced. A tremendous battle had been fought and won, and the hero of the hour was Abraham. Years later, his exploits would be still remembered by the other notables in the land. They would confess, "Thou art a mighty prince among us" (Gen. 23:6).

Genesis 14 records the first battle in the Bible. It bears many of the features of the last battle in the Bible before the reign of God's true King of Righteousness and King of Peace. In Genesis 14 (as in Rev. 16), the kings of the East have mobilized and marched. They have poured across the Fertile Crescent and down into the Promised Land, led by Hammurabi of Sumer, whose fame is heralded to this day.

The kings of Sodom and Gomorrah have joined forces with the three other Jordanian kings, and the stage is set for the Battle of the Four and the Five. The invading army has been overwhelmingly successful. The five Jordanian kings have been handed a crushing defeat, loaded with chains, and treated as the spoils of war. Ahead of them are the slave markets of Mesopotamia or the executioner's axe.

It was now that Abraham makes his move to rescue his unhappy nephew, Lot, who has been carried captive with the other people of Sodom. Abraham mobilizes his men and marches, launching a surprise night attack on the victorious kings of the East, completely routing them, and putting them to flight.

He is now in a position to dictate whatever terms he likes to all the surrounding countryside. Overnight he has become a power to be reckoned with in the land. Instead of entangling himself, however, with the affairs of this world, he simply walks away from all the prospects of power and rule that were his, in order to place himself at the feet of Melchizedek.

That is how great Melchizedek was. He was the rarest of all Old Testament worthies, both a king and priest; but only Abraham had the spiritual discernment to know what mighty power Melchizedek had. He is called king of Salem, ("king of peace") and Melchizedek ("king of righteousness"). He was not only a king and a priest, he was "priest of the Most High God," not a mere pagan priest.

He was able to bestow something that no other king or priest in the Old Testament could bestow. He could bestow righteousness and peace. Righteousness is the *root* of a proper relationship with the Most High God. Peace is the *fruit* of a proper relationship with the Most High God. As king of Jerusalem, Melchizedek wielded *secular* power. As king of righteousness and peace, he wielded *spiritual* power.

Abraham, the "friend of God" (James 2:23) and "father of all them that believe" (Rom. 4:11), knew he needed the offices of this priest-king Melchizedek. He knew the value of such a one. So he came to sit at his feet. None of the Jordanian kings recognized Melchizedek;

none of the invading kings recognized him; but Abraham did. So we see the victorious Abraham sitting at the Lord's table, with the emblems of the Lord's passion before him, learning about God Most High, as "possessor of heaven and earth" (Gen. 14:19, 22). He rose up from that table to overthrow all the spiritual power of the enemy as represented by the king of Sodom.

Now we have such a High Priest, a King-Priest indeed. His name is Jesus! When the Lord Jesus lived on earth, He could not be a priest, because He was born into the wrong tribe and the wrong family. Though He was "over all, God blessed for ever" (Rom. 9:5), He never once ventured beyond the court of Israel. He never went into the temple. He never stood before the table, the lamp stand, and the golden altar of incense. He never lifted the veil and entered the "Holiest of all." He never stood before the sacred ark or looked upon the bloodstained mercy seat overshadowed by the golden cherubim.

The old Aaronic order, however, was abolished at Calvary. When God reached down from heaven and tore asunder the temple veil, He thus announced to Israel that the Old Testament ritual priesthood was henceforth null and void. There was a new High Priest, a King-Priest, a Priest after the order of Melchizedek. The apostle states this fact some half-dozen times.

Melchizedek of old was such a powerful high priest that Abraham, before whom the whole land trembled, came and knelt at his feet. And now, praise God, we too have such a High Priest.

## 2. Such a permanent High Priest

Aaron was not only a *ritual* priest, he was also a *replaceable* priest. The day came when he was stripped of his robes of office, his miter, his ephod, and his breastplate. They were taken off him and put on his son. It happened over and over again in the history of Israel's priests. They all died and were replaced in succession.

Here is an Israelite who has a favorite priest. He always goes to him. He feels the man knows his case, his weaknesses, his prevailing sins and shortcomings. One day he arrives at the tabernacle and asks for his friend, but is told that his friend is dead. Now he has to start all over again with somebody else. His priest is dead! It gives rise to uncomfortable thoughts. It reminds him that his priest was a sinner too. Not all the blood of beasts could keep him alive or raise him from the dead. Priests died just like everyone else.

That will never happen to us. Of Melchizedek, the apostle says he was "without father, without mother, without descent, having neither beginning of days, nor end of life; but made like unto the Son of God; abideth a priest continually" (Heb. 7:3).

Suppose we were to approach God one day, burdened with our sins, and say, "O God, I am a very great sinner. But I come to you in the precious name of the Lord Jesus Christ. He is my Advocate and my great High Priest, touched with the feelings of my infirmities," and God were to interrupt you: "Hold it! I am very sorry! You will have to find some other advocate. Your high priest is dead." Thank God, we shall never ever hear words like that. "He ever liveth to make intercession" for us, says the apostle (Heb. 7:25). We have such a High Priest.

## 3. Such a patient High Priest

Just before launching into the great theme of the Melchizedekian priesthood of Christ, the apostle says, "Every high priest taken from among men is ordained for men in things pertaining to God . . . who can have compassion on the ignorant, and on them that are out of the way; for that he himself also is compassed with infirmity" (Heb. 5:1–2).

The Lord Jesus can be patient with us in all our sins and shortcomings because He too is man. He has been on the earth. He has lived down here. He knows what it is like to live in a human body. He has faced the fiercest of temptations. He met and mastered Satan, and that on human terms. He knows what it is like to be tempted with "the lust of the eye, and the lust of the flesh, and the pride of life" (1 John 2:16). He "knoweth our frame; he remembereth that we are dust" (Ps. 103:14). He never sinned, but He knows what it is like to be tempted, to be fiercely tempted, to be "in all points tempted like as we are, yet without sin" (Heb. 4:15). Because He knows, He can be patient.

We have all tried, at one time or another, to minister to someone who says, "It is all very well for you. But you don't know what it is like. You have never had to face what I'm facing." But nobody can ever say that to Jesus. "Oh yes," He says, "I know all about it. I have been just where you are. I have been tempted with the very same things. I know what it is like to be tempted. I know what it is like to be poor. I know what it is like to be rejected and forsaken and betrayed. I know what it is like to be hungry and overcome with weariness; to have no roof over my head. I know what it is like to be mocked, to be spat upon and falsely accused. I know what it is like to weep my heart out. I know what it is like to suffer excruciating physical pain. I know what it is like to have my prayers go unanswered. I know what it is like to ask for a drink and be given gall. I know what it is like to be hated. I know what it is like to die." We have such a High Priest.

## 4. Such a perfect High Priest

"For such an high priest became us, who is holy, harmless, undefiled, separate from sinners, and made higher than the heavens" (Heb. 7:26). Think what this means. There are three things we all want in our great High Priest. We want a Priest who is holy, a Priest who is human, and a Priest who is helpful.

### a. A Priest who is holy

Picture, for a moment, the camp of Israel on the journey from Egypt to Canaan. The Hebrews have come to the frontiers of Moab. Down from the hills comes a man from Moab, a Gentile, a man under the curse of the law. He has seen the tribes spread out before him in perfect order, with the tabernacle in their midst. He has seen the fiery, cloudy pillar overshadowing the camp. He may even have heard of the prophecies of Balaam. He is filled with interest and curiosity. He draws near but is stopped at the gate of the court. He peers through and says to the man at the gate, "Who is that man in those gorgeous robes, the man in the garments of glory, with the fair miter on his head?" "That is the high priest," he is told. "Aaron, brother of Moses. He was Moses' prophet in the courts of Pharaoh, and now he is our priest in the courts of God."

"What day is this? Why all these crowds?" asks the Moabite. "This is the Day of Atonement," his Hebrew acquaintance replies. "I see two goats over there, and two rams and a bullock. What are they for?" the man asks. "They are for the ritual of atonement," the informant says. "This is the one day of the year when our high priest can go into the presence of God. He will go in there through that curtained door, which leads into the tabernacle. He will go in, taking with him the blood of one of those goats. He will go past the veil. He will sprinkle the blood on the mercy seat. Then he will come back out. He will confess our sins over the head of that other goat, which will then be led away into the wilderness."

The Moabite says, "How wonderful! But what about that big bullock over there? What is that for?" "Oh, that is for the high priest," he is told. "Before he confesses *our* sins, he has to confess *his own* sins. Before he goes into the Holy of Holies for us, he has to make sure that his own wicked heart has been properly atoned for."

There was something terribly disappointing about that. The biggest sacrifice, the costliest sacrifice, was for the high priest. Sin in the rank and file of the people was bad enough; and sin in the ordinary, everyday priests was even worse, but the blood of one goat could take care of all that. Sin in the high priest, however, was far more serious. It loomed much larger. One goat could take away all the nation's sins, but it took the blood of a full-grown bullock to take away the sins of the high priest.

Somehow, we expect better than that of God's high priest. We expect something better than that of Aaron, brother to Moses and Israel's first consecrated high priest. Well, if we do expect something better of Aaron, we are going to be very disappointed, because Aaron was a failure with his own family, not to mention the family of God. Two of his sons, priests in their own right, died under the direct judgment of God.

Aaron was a failure in other ways. He criticized Moses because he did not like Moses' wife. As a result, Aaron narrowly escaped being smitten with leprosy. He did worse than that. He made a golden calf and set it up as an idol the moment that Moses' back was turned. Again he only narrowly escaped the wrath of God. Worse yet, he blamed the people for his guilt in that matter.

There is something disappointing in this dismal record of priestly failure. We want a priest—a great high priest, indeed—but we want a priest who is holy, harmless, and separate from sinners. We want a priest who is as good as God is good, who is absolutely good. That's the kind of high priest we want—and hallelujah, we have Him.

### b. A Priest who is human

Now, as that man from Moab was talking to the man at the gate, we can picture another man coming along. He has listened with interest to this conversation. He has heard the Moabite express a wish for a priest who is holy. Now the second man speaks. He says, "That is all very well. Of course we need a priest who is absolutely holy, but there is something very cold indeed about mere goodness in the abstract. There is something even more frightening about utter, complete, and absolute holiness. To be perfectly honest, I find the thought of a priest who is utterly sinless, who is always right and never in the wrong, to be formidable, to say the least. I want a priest who is a little more human. I want someone who knows by experience what it is like to be touched with the feelings of our infirmities.

"I don't want a sinful priest. God forbid! But I would like to have a sympathetic priest. I would like to have someone who is thoroughly and truly human; somebody who knows what it is like to live in a human body and be tempted. I should like a priest who knows what it is like to live in a sin-cursed world; who knows what it is like to live in a human home; who knows what it is like to be cramped and crowded; who knows what it is like to have brothers and sisters who are not always nice. I would like to have someone who knows what it is like to go to school and rub shoulders with children who are mean and spiteful and quarrelsome. I would like to see him handle the class bully, for instance.

"I would like a priest who knows what it is like to have a sleepless night and who has to get up at five o'clock in the morning anyway. I would like a priest who knows what it is like to sweat at hard, manual labor in the hot, burning sun; who knows what it is like to be around people who curse and swear, and who cheat and steal and tell lies; who knows what it is like to be where life is raw and ugly. I want such a high priest. I want a high priest who is human." Well, thank God, we have such a High Priest.

### c. A Priest who is helpful

We watch as a third man joins the group. "I have been listening to you men, and I agree with both of you. I need a holy priest and I need a human priest. But I also want a priest who is helpful.

"I want someone who is not just a very good and blameless man. I want someone who is more than human. I want someone who is helpful. I want someone who can go into the presence of God for me. I don't mean just inside the veil of this goat-and-badger-skin tabernacle. I mean right into the presence of the Most High God in the Holy of Holies in heaven.

"I want a priest who can listen to all the ten thousand tongues, languages, and dialects of men, who can hear what everyone is saying to him, and who can unravel that Babel of voices. I want a priest who can even read our thoughts and the intents of our hearts. I want someone who knows me through and through and really understands me.

"That is what I want. I want someone who is more than a human being. I want someone who is not only a person but also God. I want someone who is wise beyond all, who is powerful beyond all, who is loving beyond all. I want someone who not only knows me, but who also loves me and cares for me.

"I want someone who controls all the factors of time and space; someone who can so utterly cleanse my heart from every taint and stain of sin that it is just as if I had never sinned.

"I want someone who can satisfy a thrice-holy God, someone who can silence Satan, and who can will my sin out of existence. I want someone helpful."

Thank God, we have such a High Priest. His name is Jesus. What more could we want than that?

## CHAPTER 22

# BEHOLD, HE COMETH
*Revelation 1:7-8*

1. The eventual triumph of Jesus (v. 7)
   a. His coming will be visible
   b. His coming will be victorious
2. The everlasting triumph of Jesus (v. 8)
   a. His omniscience
   b. His omnipresence
   c. His omnipotence

WHEN A SKILLFUL STORYTELLER writes a book, he does so in such a way that keeps the reader in suspense right to the end. If ever there was a sure hand at the spinning wheel where suspenseful stories are woven, it was the hand of Charles Dickens. A few years ago, I rediscovered Dickens. I had been forced to read him in high school, and then I thought him a bore and a windbag. I can remember plodding through the pages of *The Pickwick Papers,* thinking what an utter waste of time the whole things was. The Pickwick Club! I thought it was a club for lunatics. And as for Winkle and Wardle and Weller, and Jungle and Snodgrass, Dodson and Figg, well, the Victorian world might have taken them to heart, but for me they were a bunch of bores. But I have rediscovered Mr. Dickens, and a great storyteller he was, an absolute master of the art of suspense.

Take Uriah Heep, for instance, in Dickens's *David Copperfield.* What a loathsome, slimy, despicable character! We remember all too well the feelings of revulsion that gripped the soul of young David Copperfield when first he met this man and was obliged to shake his hand. The feel of that cold, clammy hand sent a shiver down his spine. David tells us, "I rubbed mine afterward, to warm it, and to rub his off. It was such an uncomfortable hand that when I went to my room it was still cold and wet upon my memory."

Uriah Heep, of course, is the villain of the story. David Copperfield is the hero, and beautiful Agnes is the heroine. We know how the plot slowly thickens. Dickens is a past master at drawing things out. We discover, to our horror and disgust, that Uriah Heep aspires to marry Agnes, and we shudder in fearful anticipation. It must never be!

We remember the occasion when David Copperfield invites Uriah Heep home for tea. "He sat with that carved grin on his face," Dickens tells us. "He said nothing at all. He stirred his coffee round and round, he sipped it, he felt his chin softly with his grisly hand, he looked at the fire, he looked around the room, he writhed, he stirred, and sipped again." He was in fine fettle. He had poor Agnes by the throat, for her dear father was in his clutches. He turned the screw. And so the story continues.

Then, when the tension becomes too great for us, we turn to the back of the book to see what will happen in the end. We want to see if the lovely heroine will, indeed, sacrifice herself to a fate worse than death, to become Mrs. Uriah Heep, in order to save her father's good name. What is going to happen? Will Uriah Heep succeed in his schemes? Will David Copperfield never wake up to her peril? We feel like saying, "Oh come on, Dickens! Out with it man!"

But there, that is how humans write books. They deliberately build toward a climax. They hold you in suspense as long as they can. The greater the tension, the greater the mystery, the stronger the sense of impending doom, the longer they can keep you dangling, hurrying on from page to page, the better. That is the very name of the game, when men write books.

Then God takes up His pen to write another of His books. Here it is, spread out before us, this brief but fascinating book of Revelation, which brings to an end the Word of God. We hurry on from page to page. We read of the growth of apostasy in the church, until at last the apostate church itself is seen as a great red harlot, wealthy beyond words, drunk with the blood of God's saints, riding a scarlet beast to her doom. We read of the breakdown of society. We discover that the inflationary forces already at work in our economy will end in a crash the likes of which has never before littered history's pages. We see the sudden surge of anarchy. We see old, established orders come tumbling down in ruins. We see the scarlet beast emerge, the incarnation of every form of vice and violence ever to plague this planet. We see men mobilized by the multiplied million. We read of war after war, of famine and pestilence and monumental deceptions, and of persecutions dwarfing all those in history. On and on it goes, crisis after crisis, plot and counterplot, scheme after scheme, all boiled and brewed in the cauldrons of hell.

But how is it all going to end? Well, John tells us on the very first page, in the opening paragraphs. It is going to end on a magnificent note: Jesus is coming again! The end is so good, so wonderfully, wonderfully good, that the Holy Spirit says, "Go ahead and tell them, John. Jesus is coming again! Write it down first: Jesus is coming again!" We breathe a sigh of relief. Everything will be all right. Jesus is coming again!

## 1. The eventual triumph of Jesus (v. 7)

There are two comings of Christ that are yet future: one for the church, and one for the world. Between these two comings lies the dark valley of the Apocalypse. John does not take time to distinguish between what we call the Rapture—the Lord's coming in the air to reclaim His own, and what we call the return—the Lord's coming to Earth *with* His own. John takes it for granted that we have already mastered Paul's two Thessalonian epistles, and that we have mastered these basic details. What John primarily has in mind in the book of Revelation is the second of those two comings. He has in mind the ultimate, eventual coming of the Lord Jesus to set up His kingdom on this scene.

### a. His coming will be visible

"Behold he cometh with clouds; and every eye shall see him, and they also which pierced him." He is coming with clouds. Some believe that those clouds are the clouds of the sky. It may well be. Clouds are worn by Him like royal robes.

When God summoned Israel out of Egypt, He marched before His people, every step of the wilderness way, wrapped in a cloak of cloud.

When Israel pitched the tabernacle in the wilderness, every peg and pin was formed and fashioned according to the blueprint mapped for Moses on the mountain. Then God came down and sat upon the golden mercy seat, upon the sacred ark, between the cherubim, behind the veil in the Holiest of all. There He sat, wrapped around in a cloud.

When the Lord took Peter, James, and John to Hermon's snow-clad height, He was transfigured before them. He spoke to His Father, for His eternal Father came down upon the mountain veiled in a shadowing cloud.

After His resurrection, the Lord Jesus took his embryonic church with Him, out of the city of Jerusalem, across the Kidron, up the slopes of Olivet, past Gethsemane, past Bethany, and on up to the brow of the hill. From there, He stepped into the sky, on His way back to the excellent glory from whence He had come thirty-three years before. As His feet left the earth, He flung a glorious robe of cloud around His rising form.

And when He comes again, to do battle with the beast, to claim this robbed and ruined vineyard as His own, and to "trample out the vintage where the grapes of wrath are stored," it will be with clouds. Then, as the hymn writer puts it:

His chariots of wrath,
The deep thunderclouds form.
And dark is His path,
On the wings of the storm.[1]

Some are convinced that these clouds are clouds of the sky. It may well be. Others are convinced that these clouds are not just water vapors, from which dart forth the lightnings of the thunderstorm, or from which are sometimes shaped the roaring column of the tornado. They think, rather, that these clouds are clouds of saints—those saved in other ages, in Old Testament times; those saved in the present age of grace; and those saved and martyred after the Lord breaks off diplomatic relations with the earth. According to this view, these clouds are clouds upon clouds of Christ's own people, coming back with Him to this tortured plane. They will be interested witnesses, come with Him to watch as He settles accounts with His foes. In any case, His coming will be visible. "Every eye shall see Him, and they also which pierced Him."

As a boy in school, I had to memorize the names and reigns of the kings and queens of England. I have long since forgotten most of them.

The teacher did his best to get these dates into our head by rote: William the Conqueror (1066–1087); William Rufus (1087–1100); Henry I (1100–1135). The list went on and on.

There was one king on the list, however, who always sparked the interest of even the dullest boy in school. That king was Richard I, Richard the Lionheart (1189–1199). And almost as interesting to us boys was John the Blackhearted, the graceless and unscrupulous brother of Richard the Great. But how we all loved Richard. He was a born leader, a brilliant general, the handsomest of kings, with all the Plantagenet good looks. He was the greatest fighter, the deadliest wrestler, the fastest runner, the finest poet, the courtliest knight of them all.

He ascended the throne when he was thirty-two. He was a true child of the age, a fearless fighter, and a vassal of the pope at Rome. He led the Third Crusade. His one great aim was to take to the East the most powerful and best equipped army that had ever crossed the seas. He left his kingdom in the grasping hands of John.

Now John was Richard turned inside out. He was selfish and cruel, crafty, shameless, shrewd, cynical, lustful, and false. He was not handsome like Richard. He was squat of shape and square of face. He had a hypnotic eye. He had a polished, suave, and sophisticated air, but he was a thoroughgoing tyrant. He had no gift for leadership, and no skill in statecraft. No sooner were Richard and his knights safely across the channel and on the way to the East than John began a plot to seize the throne. Richard's kingdom had fallen on very hard times.

Then news filtered back to England that Richard had been imprisoned, not by the generous Saladin, but by his old rival, Leopold of Austria. He was being held for ransom. *Well let him lie and rot in Austria*, thought John. *And good riddance to him.* Now the kingdom could be his. John sent letters, not to Austria but to France. Why should not France and England join forces? In John's opinion, the world of politics and power was well rid of Richard and his like.

In the meantime, the people of England suffered. They suffered under John, and they suffered under his chancellor, who abused his powers and rode roughshod over all. The common people groaned beneath John's heavy hand and prayed for the return of Richard and prayed his return might be soon.

Then one day, Richard came! He landed in England and marched straight for the throne. Around that glittering coming many tales are told, woven into the legend of England, along with the story of Robin Hood. John's castles tumbled like a row of ninepins. Great Richard laid claim to his throne and none dared stand in his path. The people of England shouted their delight. They rang peal after peal on the bells. The lion was back! Long live the king!

One of these days, a greater King than Richard will lay claim to a greater realm than England. Then those who have abused His absence; who have seized His vast estates; who have mismanaged His world, persecuted His people, and ignored His claims will be swept aside.

The kingdoms of this world will become instead the kingdom of God's beloved Son. The old hymn will come into its own:

> The heav'ns shall glow with splendor,
> But brighter far than they
> The saints will shine in glory,
> As Christ shall them array,
> The beauty of the Savior,
> Will dazzle ev'ry eye,
> For the crowning day is coming by and by.[2]

### b. His coming will be victorious

"Behold, he cometh with clouds . . . and all kindreds of the earth shall wail because of Him. Even so, Amen." We need to paint in some of the background to understand what has been going on down here. The forces of godlessness will seem to triumph. The world will crown at last a king, a man after its own depraved and dirty heart, a man the Bible calls "the Beast," "the Man of Sin," "the Son of Perdition," and "that Wicked One."

It will become a capital offense to have any God but him. Men will be forced to submit to the brand of the beast and publicly own him as their lord by wearing his mark. They will be compelled to worship him, to bow down before his image set up in bold blasphemy in the rebuilt temple of the Jews, and to worship this last universal Caesar and his openly acknowledged lord, Satan himself. The forces that will bring all this to pass are already at work in society. The only thing that holds them in check is the presence of the Holy Spirit in the church. The coming monster of wickedness, the Beast himself, could already be here. The mystery of iniquity, which will climax in his appearing, is already at work in the world today. In a coming day, all secrecy will be thrown to the winds, and iniquity will be openly, enthusiastically, and universally enthroned.

In the end, people will tire of the horrible excesses of the Beast. The eastern half of his global empire will break away from him and mobilize against him. The armies of the world will be drawn to Armageddon for the final bloodbath before the reign of Christ. That battle, however, will not be settled by a Western dictator, or by allied kings of the East. It will be settled by God. He will send back His Son to overthrow the forces of this world. Then the sin-maddened, demon-crazed men of the earth will find themselves face-to-face with God's beloved Son, the one they pierced, the one they have rejected for so long. They will look on Him, whom they cursed and crucified, the one they have so terribly despised. One word from Him, and down they will go in defeat, swept away by the Word of His mouth, ushered into the darkness of death to await their final meeting with Him at the great white throne. His coming will be victorious. But John has more yet to say.

## 2. The everlasting triumph of Jesus (v. 8)

"'I am Alpha and Omega, the beginning and the ending,' saith the Lord, which is, and which was, and which is to come, the Almighty." His everlasting triumph will rest upon the three great attributes of deity, which are His, and which are set before us here. It will rest upon His *omniscience*, His *omnipresence*, and His *omnipotence*. Let us consider how John puts these together.

### a. His omniscience

The Lord's omniscience lies hidden in the statement, "I am Alpha and Omega." The letters *alpha* and *omega* are simply the first and last letters of the Greek alphabet. The alphabet itself is an ingenious way of storing the accumulated learning, knowledge, and experience of the human race. It is the golden key that unlocks for us all the treasures of human wisdom and knowledge. All the poets, philosophers, scientists, and historians of the world have drawn on the letters of the alphabet to perpetuate their thoughts. They arrange them this way and that to form words. The poet takes them to create an epic, an ode, a hymn. The scientist takes them to write down a statement of fact. The novelist takes them to write *David Copperfield* or *King*

*Solomon's Mines* or *How Green Was My Valley*. The Holy Spirit takes them to write the Bible. The alphabet is the key to it all.

Jesus is the alphabet, the Alpha and Omega. He is the first and final source of all true knowledge and wisdom. He does not say, "I know the alphabet" or "I use the alphabet." He says "I AM the alphabet." He knows everything there is to know in earth or heaven or hell, for time and for eternity. In other words, He is omniscient. He cannot be deceived or disputed. He could not be when He lived on earth. He cannot be when He comes again. He will be the wisest ruler ever to sit on a throne.

### b. His omnipresence

Usually when we think of omnipresence, the ability to be everywhere at once, an attribute that belongs to God alone, we express it in terms of space. Here, it is expressed in terms of time. He says, "I am the beginning and the ending."

He is the ever-present one. He was present when the sons of God, the angel hosts, the cherubim, the seraphim, the highest archangels of glory, opened their eyes on the beauties of heaven. He was there when, as many astronomers believe, the "big bang" took place and when a hundred million galaxies sprang into being and rushed headlong into space. He was there when the mountains and seas were formed down here on planet Earth. He was present when the prairies were planted with grass, when the forests overspread the earth, and when life in its myriad forms appeared.

He was present at the marriage of Adam and Eve. He was present when the waters of the Flood drowned the world. He was present when Jerusalem and the temple went up in flames, fired by soldiers of Titus. He was there when Islam arose, and when Napoleon surfaced from the crimson seas of the French Revolution. He is present today, here and now, right where we are. He will be present at the moment of our deaths to either receive us into glory or to say, "I never knew you: depart from me" (Matt. 7:23). He is the beginning and the ending. He is omnipresent.

He is the one person in all the universe whom we cannot possibly escape. There is no place we can hide where He will not be. And when He sets up His kingdom and takes to himself His mighty power to reign, He will reign with all the assurance of one who has the ability to be everywhere at once.

### c. His omnipotence

"I am Alpha and Omega," He says, "I am the beginning and the ending, . . . [I am] the Almighty." That title, "the Almighty," occurs ten times in the New Testament, including nine times in the book of Revelation. The Septuagint (the ancient Greek translation of the Hebrew Scriptures) uses the word *Almighty* to translate the title "the Lord of Hosts." That title is first introduced in the Bible at a time of failure. It is used in 1 Samuel 1:3 where we read of Elkanah, the father of the little boy Samuel who later became the great prophet, that he "Went up out of his city yearly to worship and to sacrifice unto the Lord of hosts in Shiloh."

Everywhere there was failure. The judges had failed, the priests had failed, and there was no king in Israel. When finally a king did arise, he too was a failure. But God had not failed. He was "the Lord of Hosts." He was the Almighty.

When John takes up his pen to write the last few chapters of human history, again there is failure everywhere. The true church has been raptured to heaven. The apostate church left behind for judgment is evidence of failure. The nations have failed in every avenue of human endeavor and have now embarked on suicidal policies. Israel has failed, persisting in its two-thousand-year-old rejection of Christ. But God has not failed! Jesus is coming again and He is coming as the Almighty, the Lord of Hosts.

Oh, how different it will be from the way He came the last time. Then, He came in seeming weakness, came to be the Savior of men, came to suffer, to bleed, and to die. He who had all power in heaven and earth, the power to create galaxies, let men spit in His face and spike Him to a tree.

The miracle of His first coming was as much the miracle of power held back as it was of power unleashed. As the poet puts it:

> He might have built a palace at a word
> Who sometimes had not where to lay His head;
> Time was He nourished crowds with bread
> Who one crumb, for Himself, could not afford.
> Twelve legions, girded with angelic sword
> Were at His beck—yet He was bound and led
> Condemned alike by Jewish priest and Roman judge.
> He healed another's wound; His own side bled—
> Side, feet and hands with cruel piercings gored.
> Oh Wonderful! The wonders left undone
> Are scarce less wonderful than those He wrought.[3]

The everlasting triumph of Jesus. Calvary was man's answer to God's love. Men answered back by insisting, so far as they were personally concerned, "We will not have this man to reign over us." God's answer is patience. He waits. He woos. He remains silent. But one day He will break the age-long silence and speak again, terribly, in wrath. The long amnesty will be over. He will send back His Son to judge the world. "Behold, he cometh with clouds, and every eye shall see him, and they also which pierced him." What a day that will be! It will be a day of joy for all who love Him, a day of judgment for all who have rejected Him.

## CHAPTER 23

# THE GREAT WHITE THRONE
*Revelation 20*

1. The setting (vv. 11–12)
   a. The background
      (1) A terrible fact
      (2) A terrible figure
      (3) A terrible fear
      (4) A terrible fellowship
   b. The books
      (1) The book of the lost
      (2) The book of the Lamb
2. The summons (v. 13)
3. The sentence (vv. 14–15)

JOSEF STALIN RULED THE Soviet Union for twenty-five dreadful years. During his lifetime he was semi-deified. Historians claim it is unfair to compare him with Genghis Khan or Ivan the Terrible; they were children by comparison. Stalin was the greatest tyrant in world history, exterminating more people than any other despot in wars, planned famines, purges, mass deportations, and terror campaigns. He banished his wife's sister to a concentration camp for writing her memoirs about his earlier days. He was Asiatic, anti-Western, anti-European, and anti-Semitic. He killed ten million peasants in his drive to collectivize the farms of Russia. Ten million Ukrainians vanished from the earth during his purges, and another five million died of famine. Stalin's secret police shot and hanged thousands upon thousands of peasants, sometimes whole villages. Millions more were forced into slave labor camps to build railroads and canals, cut down forests, open mines, and gather harvests. He killed at least a million Communist Party members. He purged the entire leadership of the Red Army, killing off its leading generals and thirty thousand officers. All Red Army officers who had gained experience in the Spanish Civil War were simply brought home and shot. Some three million Jews vanished in Russia, the Baltic states, and Soviet-controlled Poland during and immediately after the Second World War. At the time of his death, Stalin was planning the systematic extermination of every surviving Jew in the Soviet Union.

Yet he died in his bed. He died with difficulty, slowly suffocating, but he died in bed. Even had he been tortured for fifty years, our sense of justice would not have been satisfied—but he died in bed. Our innate sense of justice cries out for punishment for this man. There has to be a hell if only for people like him.

Having said that, we need to remember that the grace and kindness and forgiveness of God is so great, and the work of Calvary is so complete, that had he repented, even Stalin might have been saved. Christ died for the ungodly, all the ungodly. But as best we know, Stalin died a comparatively easy death, but he died in his sins. The Bible tells us there is a hell for men like him.

But let us take another case. Her name is Sally. Her parents were missionaries from Latin America, home on furlough. Sally was just fourteen years old, just entering junior high, when this incident took place. A few days after the start of the school year, she found herself writhing and screaming on her bed. Perspiration covered her body and her tiny frame twisted in agony. Her neck jerked back with such violence that her mother seemed to feel the torture. Her piercing screams could be heard all over the house. Her eyes rolled or stared blankly. Her speech made no sense. Admitted to the hospital, she sank into a coma and remained like that for four days, yet her body was in constant motion. She kept babbling nonsense, "I'm an atom! I'm Methuselah! I'm in Jerusalem! I'm Jesus!" When her mother asked her if she knew her, she said, "Oh yes, I'm your mother." She had to be put into a locked room where she continued to writhe and twist in agony. Then the doctors diagnosed her trouble. Sally was experiencing the agonizing withdrawal from a drug-induced trip. She was a victim. Someone at school had slipped some LSD into her soft drink at lunch.

Nobody ever knew who did it. The young criminal concealed his or her identity too well for that—but God knows. As sure as God is holy, just and true, if that young villain does not repent and accept God's salvation, there is a day of judgment in store. God has a hell for people like that.

Nearly two thousand years ago, God's own Son, the Creator of the universe, came down to this sin-cursed planet and incarnated himself in human flesh. He came to offer us a more abundant life. People listened to Him for a while, then decided they did not like what He had to say about sin, about repentance, and about the need to be born again. So they conspired against Him. They gave Him a mock trial, scourged the flesh off His bones, crowned Him with thorns, and nailed Him up on a cross of wood. Then they stood around to watch Him, and even to mock Him while He died. That was two thousand years ago. Ever since then, God has been holding back His wrath, for God is a God of love. For two thousand years now, He has been offering people pardon and forgiveness and life forevermore. All He asks is that they lay down their arms of rebellion, come to His beloved Son, repent of their guilt and sin, and personally accept His Son as Savior and Lord. This great amnesty is still available today. But not for much longer. For one of these days, God intends to enter into judgment with this world for what it has done to His Son. Sooner or later, every person who rejects the Son will cross the hidden boundary between God's mercy and His wrath. For such a one there awaits the Great White Throne Judgment. For to reject Christ, to refuse Calvary, to trample underfoot the blood of Jesus and "to do despite to the Spirit of grace" (Heb. 10:29), is to face an outraged God at last. God has a hell for people like that. God has a great white throne upon which His own Son will sit to judge all those who die in their sins.

Let us look at what the Bible has to say about this coming judgment day and about the one to whom God has committed the final judgment of the lost.

## 1. The setting (vv. 11–12)

"And I saw a great white throne, and him that sat on it, from whose face the earth and the heaven fled away; and there was found no place for them. And I saw the dead, small and great, stand before God; and the books were opened." That is the setting. Let us consider the background and the books.

### a. The background

The Holy Spirit paints in four things for us to observe: a terrible fact, a terrible figure, a terrible fear, and a terrible fellowship.

#### (1) A terrible fact

There is, in the background, a great white throne—blazing, blinding, dazzling in its purity. It is white in color because white is the symbol of holiness. The awesome holiness of God is so dazzling that, according to the prophet Isaiah, the shining seraphim, the sinless sons of light, hide their faces in their wings before the fearful, burning majesty and holiness of God's throne. All they can think to say is "Holy! Holy! Holy!"

Guilty men brought face-to-face with such devastating holiness will have no place to hide. They will stand there, resurrected from their graves, naked and shivering in body and soul. All their fine sophistries and God-denying, soul-destroying philosophies will be gone. They say, "There is no judgment! Death ends everything! There will be a second chance for everyone! There is no God! Sin is an error of mortal mind! God is too loving and kind to judge people!" But all these feeble fantasies will shrivel up before one solemn, terrible fact: the great white throne.

The blusterings of Voltaire, the blasphemies of George Bernard Shaw, the God-hate of Karl Marx, the lying delusions of Joseph Smith, the deadly indifference of millions of others, will all vanish before the awesome fact of the great white throne of God.

### (2) A terrible figure

The terrible figure who sits on the great white throne will be recognized instantly by all, even though most have never seen Him before. They will recognize Him by the print of the nails in His hands, by the gaping wound in His side, by the marks of Calvary in His feet, by the brutal marks men printed in His flesh with hammer and nail, spear and lash, and crown of thorns. He will sit there and the mute evidence of His wounds will be all the judgment anyone will need.

When He lived on earth, He was the most approachable, the kindest, the most lovable of men. Women came to Him with their woes, little children climbed up on His knees, strong men left thriving businesses to become His devoted disciples. He went about doing good. He taught truth in a singularly memorable and undiluted form. He taught us a new name for God. God had been revealed in the Old Testament as Elohim, the Creator; as Adonai, the Sovereign Lord; as Jehovah, the God of Promise. Jesus taught them that God was also a Father—His Father willing to become their Father too.

But all that will be over the moment the judgment begins. The day of grace will end, and the Day of Judgment will dawn. And this same Jesus will sit—remote, terrible, and holy—on the great white throne.

Into the minds of each one will flood awakened memories. All will remember how they treated Him. Some will say, "I cursed Him. I used to take the name of Jesus Christ and add it to my oaths and blasphemies." Others will say, "I ignored Him. I heard about Him at my mother's knee, studied about Him in Sunday school, tuned Him out at church, and went out into the great wide world of sin and ignored Him." Still others will say, "I felt the tug of His Holy Spirit at my heart, but I sold Him for a godless friendship and for a few short years of sin." Some will say, "I wrote Him off. I never really gave Him the time of day. I persuaded myself it was all a religious myth, a profitable priestly farce."

But there He will be—real, solid, living, impassive, terrible to behold, with pierced hands and eyes that flash like a flame of fire—a terrible figure indeed.

## (3) A terrible fear

For the child of God, for the believing heart, to see the face of Jesus will be the crowning bliss of all. The hymn well says:

> When by His grace,
> I shall look on His face,
> That will be glory,
> Be glory for me.[1]

But, for the Christ-rejecter, that face will be the very first taste of hell. Before that face, the very heavens and earth will flee away, for sin has defiled both realms. Both now vanish from view. He will turn His face toward them and they will dissolve into their primeval atoms, explode into nothingness, and vanish away. At the end of the seal judgments (Rev. 6), men will call in terror on the mountains and hills to fall on them and to hide them from His face. At the Great White Throne Judgment there will be no such cry. There will no longer be mountains and hills. There will be no place to hide.

Oh that face! Men spat on that face, they punched that face, they pulled the beard from that face, they marred that face. Now the very ones who did those things, and all those who by their Christ-rejecting attitude have aided and abetted it and endorsed it, are forced at last to look upon it.

Nothing familiar remains. The heavens have gone. The old, familiar earth with its rivers, seas, and shores has gone. There is nothing left;

no place to stand, no place to flee. There is nothing but an appalling emptiness, a throne, a figure, a face, and a cramping fear. Again and again, the Bible warns us to fear Him. It tells us that "the fear of the Lord is the beginning of wisdom" (Ps. 111:10). Too late, men will stand in fear before that great white throne and before Him who sits upon it.

### (4) A terrible fellowship

"The dead," we read, "small and great, stand before God." What a picture: dead souls reunited with dead bodies, standing before God. The dead, newly arrived from the tomb, terrible to behold, riddled with guilt, tormented by conscience, standing before God.

The dead, small and great. There they are, little men and little women. People whose lives were filled with nasty little sins; snappish, selfish, petty little people. People who never amounted to anything. People whose very sins were small and drab and dowdy and mean and spiteful and groveling and vulgar and common and cheap. Great men and famous women. People who sinned with a high hand, with dash and courage and flair; who went in for wickedness on a grand scale; who lived flagrantly and with a certain diabolical flourish. But all dead now and on their way to being damned. A terrible fellowship, indeed. Such is the background of the Great White Throne Judgment.

### b. The books

God is a prodigious bookkeeper. He writes everywhere, on everything, all the time. When I lived in northern British Columbia, I worked as an accountant for a lumber company. On occasion I would go into the bush with an urgent message, or on an errand of some kind. I never ceased to be astonished at the ease with which a skilled woodsman could read the rings on a fallen tree. My boss could tell me the age of that tree, how it had been nourished by the soil, the years of heavy rainfall, the years of drought, what insect pests had flourished and in what years, even which way the prevailing winds blew in that area. It was all written down.

Or, to take another case, a man finds an old bone in a graveyard. He takes it to an anthropologist. He turns it this way and that, weighs it, tests it. He can tell the species, the sex, the age, the weight, the length, and maybe even the health of the person to whom that bone once belonged. It is all written down.

God keeps books. Anything man can do God can do better. We turn the dial on a box of wires, tubes, and circuits in our living rooms. Instantly, we pull out of the air sights and sounds that are throbbing through there all the time, unseen and unheard until the thing is turned on and tuned in. Then, instantly, we get sights and sounds—the news, a lecture, a convention, a movie. It is all there, pulsating through space, waiting to be translated from the unseen to the seen, from the silent to the audible.

If we can do these things, if we can record actions and conversations, if we can summon sights and sounds from afar and play them back at will, so can God. Only He can do it far better than we can.

Psychologists tell us that everything we have ever said or thought or done is all written down, etched deeply into our subconscious minds. All it takes is the right stimulus and back it comes. God keeps books. He keeps two kinds of books in particular: the book of the lost, and the book of the Lamb.

### (1) The book of the lost

"The dead were judged out of . . . the books, according to their works." In the Bible, salvation is always by *faith*, and judgment according to *works*. God will judge people by their record, by the things they have said and done and thought. He will judge their motives, their influence, their sins of omission as well as their sins of commission.

He will simply have to say one word: "Remember!" At once, all the guilty, uncleansed, unforgiven past will come marching back, as large as life. Things that people have forgotten, and things they can't forget no matter how hard they try. Their pasts will rise up like a wailing banshee and stalk to and fro before their very eyes. They will see men they have robbed, slandered, injured. They will see women they have exploited, shamed, wronged, and defiled. God will weigh not only their conduct and their conversation, but also their very character.

He will put them in the scales and weigh them alongside the perfect life of Christ. He will find them wanting. He will not even have to say it, they will know it instinctively, as the appalling conviction of personal guilt and sin comes home to their stained and blackened souls. They will be found to be guilty before God. Lost!

People say that all they want is a fair trial. That is what they will get. They'll say they were "doing their best." God will put the lie to that, for the book of the lost will be opened and that book contains the full, undoctored record of each life. It is a book that people are keeping themselves with every breath they breathe.

There is another book, however; the Lamb's book of life.

### (2) The book of the Lamb

In the Lamb's book of life, God writes the names of all the men and women and boys and girls who come to Jesus, the Lamb of God, for cleansing and salvation. It, too, contains the names of sinners, but the names of *saved* sinners.

Usually when I preach, there is someone up there in a back room, recording every word I say. What must I do to get that record expunged? It is really very simple. All I have to do is take a magnet and pass it over the tape. Then every word will be gone, expunged, cleansed. If Richard Nixon had taken a magnet to his White House tapes, he could probably have avoided a scandal. He could never bring himself to do that, however, so the whole record became public—all his secret conversations, all his swearing and duplicity. It damned him forever as a politician.

We have an even worse record. It is kept in God's great book, together with all the condemning evidence of time and place and word and deed and secret thought. However, to get that record expunged forever, all we have to do is bring our lives, with their guilty records, to Jesus. He will pass the mighty magnet of His holiness over that record, and His blood will cleanse it all. Then He will come into our hearts by His Holy Spirit and set up His own perfect record in its place. Moreover, He will write our names into the book of life. Whosoever has his name written there will never have to stand at the great white throne. Not to have one's name written there is to be forever cursed by the character and consequences of one's sins. That is the setting.

## 2. The summons (v. 13)

"And the sea gave up the dead which were in it; and death and hell delivered up the dead which were in them: and they were judged every man according to their works." As we have seen, there will be no place to hide. Our Bible begins with two great questions put to our first parents right after the Fall. "Where art thou?" and "What hast thou done?" Those same two questions will be repeated when the Day of Judgment dawns. They will be the last two questions ever asked of lost and guilty men.

God will call out, as He called out in Eden long ago, "Where art thou?" The dead will rise, every one of them. "Here I am, Lord!" will be the universal cry. Every dead person who has ever lived will be recalled by the mighty, omnipotent, omniscient power of Almighty God. The dust of the ages will be sorted out. Dust will hurry hither and yon, dust scattered and lost, but every bit of it known and marked by Him. Dust will gather to dust, bone will knit to bone. The flesh, the muscles, the nerves, and the sinews of the dead will be reshaped. Some will rise who died but yesterday, still lying in their satin coffins, in a perfumed, flowered funeral home. Some will rise who died in the early dawn of time. God knows them all and knows where they are. "Where art thou?" Back they will come, to the very last unredeemed man and woman of the entire human race.

And then the second question will be put to that vast assembled host of the raised and ruined dead. "What hast thou done?" Memories will leap to life. People will remember the sins of their childhood, sins of their forgotten youth. They will remember sins committed in the home, at school, and in the shop. They will remember sins committed under the broad light of day, and sins committed under shade and cover of night. "What hast thou done? What have you done with Jesus? Answer me that."

### 3. The sentence (vv. 14–15)

What a terrible sentence it will be! "And death and hell were cast into the lake of fire. This is the second death. And whosoever was not found written in the book of life was cast into the lake of fire." God wrote that. We may not like it, but we cannot alter it. Remember, too, that these terrible words will be spoken by the Lord Jesus. Throughout life, the Holy Spirit has urged people again and again to come to Christ. Jesus himself says, *"Come, unto Me."* But now He will utter the dread sentence, *"Depart* from Me, for I never knew you" (see Matt. 7:23; 25:41).

The lost will be banished from His presence. They will go out into the dark—alone. They will go to spend an eternity shut out from all that is pure and clean and good and lovely and wholesome. God does not want that to happen to people. It was to save people from this terrible doom that He sent His Son into the world. Jesus died a death of agony and shame on the cross of Calvary to provide a full and free salvation for all. But God will not save people against their will. In the last analysis, Jesus will not send people to a lost eternity; they will send themselves.

Here, for instance, is a man who has a disease. He goes to the doctor. The doctor diagnoses the problem and prescribes some medicine. He says, "Take this and you will recover." The man, however, does not take the medicine. Perhaps he does not like the doctor's personality, perhaps the medicine has a nasty taste, perhaps he does not believe his case is critical. For one foolish reason or another, he has refused to take the only medicine that can save him. He dies. It is his own fault. He has no one to blame but himself. He refused to avail himself of the remedy.

Men go to the lake of fire not because they are sinners. They go because they refuse the salvation God offers in Christ. Perhaps they do not like the preacher, perhaps they do not like to be told they are sinners. Perhaps they do not think their case is as desperate as God says it is. So people either choose to accept Christ as their Savior, or else they choose to face Him as their Judge. The choice is theirs.

## CHAPTER 24

# WORTHY IS THE LAMB
*Revelation 4–5*

1. The great discovery
   a. An unforgettable throne
   b. An unforgettable throng
   c. An unforgettable thrill
2. The great doxology
3. The great dichotomy
   a. The focal center of things
   b. The farthest circumference of things

"ALL SCRIPTURE IS GIVEN BY inspiration of God," and all Scripture "is profitable for doctrine, for reproof, for correction, for instruction in righteousness" (2 Tim. 3:16). The Holy Spirit says so. The divine dictum applies just as much to the Old Testament as it does to the New Testament. It applies as much to the details of the tabernacle and the details of Ezekiel's temple as it does to Psalm 23 or John 3:16. It applies just as much to the long chronologies as it does to the words of Jesus.

However, there are some sections of Scripture that do not have to be mined for their treasures. The moment we get into them, we strike it rich, for golden nuggets lie everywhere just waiting to be picked up. Revelation 4–5 is just such a section. This portion of the Bible seems to have been made of the very stuff of which eternity is made. It is a mountain of purest gold.

Paul tells us how once, years ago, he had been caught up into the third heaven and had seen and heard things "not lawful for a man to utter" (2 Cor. 12:4). That is, they were untranslatable. John had no such limitations. He made himself at home amid scenes of splendor and glory that would blind and dazzle most of us. But he kept his wits about him and he did something that Paul, for all his eloquence, could not do. We are indebted to John's writings for most of what we know about heaven. So let us at least get a glimpse for ourselves of what lies just beyond the range of our earthbound eyes and ears.

## 1. The great discovery

There is all the difference in the world between Revelation 4 and 5. In chapter 4, we see a throne, but it is a throne of government. In chapter 5, we see a throne, but it is a throne of grace. In chapter 4, we see heaven's Beloved, but we see Him as the Lord of creation; in chapter 5, we see Him as the Lamb of Calvary.

In chapter 4, we hear the glorious anthems that fill all heaven with praise and song, but here they sing, "Thou art worthy . . . for thou hast created" (v. 11). In chapter 5, we hear the glorious anthems that fill all heaven with praise and song, but here they sing, "Thou art worthy . . . for thou wast slain" (v. 9). In the one instance, it is the astonishing fact of His power that promotes the hallelujahs and hosannas of heaven; in the second instance, it is the astonishing fact of His passion that makes the high halls of heaven ring and resound.

But let us capture the scene before us. John has been caught up to glory, and at once he is surrounded by mystery and majesty. He is aware of three things: an unforgettable *throne*, an unforgettable *throng*, and an unforgettable *thrill*.

### a. An unforgettable throne

There is an awesome mystery about that throne. Everything is somehow similar to things with which we are familiar, but just the same, everything is quite different. For example, who ever thinks of God as a stone? God has revealed himself in many ways and by means of a variety of many symbols and figures of speech. He is the Rose of Sharon and the Lily of the Valley. He is the Bright and Morning Star and the Sun of Righteousness. He sits between the cherubim and accepts the praises of His people. He rides on the storm. He is a Shepherd; He is a man of war. He is the Creator, the Great I Am, the Lord of Hosts. He is from everlasting to everlasting. He is an Avenger, and He is a Redeemer. And, thought beyond all thought, He is a loving heavenly Father. But a *stone*? A jasper and sardine *stone*? There is something very mysterious about that. The jasper suggests hardness; the sardine speaks of fire and holiness.

Then, too, John saw the full circle of the rainbow in all its undimmed splendor. That was different, for it was not only a full-circled rainbow, it was also a rainbow of just one color—emerald green. He saw, too, the four living creatures, and certainly such creatures live on earth. Then, also, He was made aware of "the seven Spirits of God," suggesting the Holy Spirit in His plenitude.

So, there was John amid scenes of splendor that well-nigh defy description, yet all was familiar enough so that he could feel at home, and all was strange enough, different enough, that he was well aware that he was in another world.

But the thing that gripped him and riveted his attention was the throne. No matter where he looked, his eye came back to the throne. He mentions it seventeen times in two short chapters. He tells us of its mystery and of its majesty. Lightning played around the throne, and peals of thunder applauded its mandates and decrees. There, too, was the crystal stream flowing fast past the throne, and the high anthems of the heavenly hosts rang in upon it. John saw, in fact, the Supreme Court of the Universe, its high seat, its attendant ministers, and its awesome Judge. There will be no appeals against the verdicts and edicts of that throne, nor will any travesties of justice ever be associated with its righteous decrees.

John was about to see some terrible things—war, famine, earthquake, pestilence, and persecutions—horrors that crowd hard on each other's heels. He would see stars fall from heaven and demons surge up from the bottomless pit. He would see the great red dragon and hear it roar out his defiance. He would see the beast from the sea seize the planet and see wickedness ride high. Indeed it will seem for a while that Satan is going to win.

But before John was allowed to see any of that, he was shown the throne. There it stood in the calm before the storm, unmoved by rebellion, riot, and revolution. John learned that God is still on the throne.

### b. An unforgettable throng

The high courts of heaven are the home of the angelic hosts. We do not know how many individuals make up the ranks of the angels. They are countless, glorious in person, mighty in power, and of various order and rank. There are the angels and the archangels, the cherubim and seraphim, the thrones and dominions. There are also what the apostle calls "the spirits of just men made perfect" (Heb. 12:23), for the redeemed of all ages find their place in the throngs around the throne.

John was impressed by the four living creatures. These appear to be cherubim, those ancient guardians of *God's sovereign rights* in the universe. We meet them first at the gate of the garden of Eden where one of them stands with a flaming sword in his hand to keep Adam and Eve away from the tree of life. There they stood guard over God's rights as Creator. The fallen pair had raided the tree of knowledge. The cherub was there to make sure they did not raid the tree of life and live on forever in their sins, thus turning the earth into hell itself.

We meet them again in the tabernacle, where they had their special place in the Holy of Holies. The linen hangings were embroidered with their likeness, but the mercy seat was their special place. The mercy seat was made out of a solid slab of gold. From the same massive piece were fashioned figures of the cherubim. Their wings were outspread to overshadow the ark and the mercy seat. Their faces were turned inward and downward so that they were forever occupied with the blood sprinkled there. There they mounted guard over *God's redemptive rights*. There is no greater wonder among the ranks of the sinless sons of light who fill the high halls of heaven with their praise than the sight of that blood.

Now we meet them again in the glory. They take their stand alongside the throne. They have but one cry. It rings and reverberates around the great white throne and awakens the echoes of the everlasting hills: "Holy! Holy! Holy!" They uphold now *God's personal rights*. For God is thrice holy: Holy Father, Holy Son, and Holy Spirit. Nobody is allowed to forget it for a single moment. The chanting cherubim make sure of that.

John was impressed also by the four and twenty elders. All kinds of suggestions have been made as to just who these elders are. The most popular notion is that they are the twelve patriarchs and the twelve apostles, and that therefore they are the representative heads of Israel and the church. This cannot be true, however, because John himself would be one of the elders, if they represent the patriarchs and the apostles. How could he be in two places at the same time?

They are probably not human beings at all, but those angelic beings described by Paul as "thrones and dominions." They stand in contrast with the fallen angelic beings he elsewhere describes as "principalities and powers." The four and twenty elders have but one function—to worship, and to watch, as a kind of celestial jury, God's acts of judgment. They seem, then, to be an order of angels, the crowned royalties of heaven. They appear again and again in the Apocalypse.

As John stood there, he was caught up by the great volume of sound as the heavenly hierarchy, and the rank and file of the angelic hosts, and the redeemed of the children of men, poured out their anthems of praise. There was not a sad face or a sour note in all that mighty throng.

### c. An unforgettable thrill

Suddenly, a great cry rang through the celestial halls, for in the right hand of the one on the throne there was a book—actually, a scroll—sealed with seven seals. The scroll was the title deed of planet Earth.

Up from the throne there arose a cry. Up from the mountain, thunder riven it rang, up from the rocky steep. It echoed out along the sea of glass, sounding along the caves and crags of the everlasting hills: "Who is worthy to open the book, and to loose the seals thereof?" (Rev. 5:2). Now then! Let the man step forward who can claim to be a fit man to govern the globe—no matter what his rank or race; no matter what his clan or color; no matter what his name or fame. All that is required is that he be worthy. The cry was not, "Who is willing?"—else there would have been a stampede. The cry was: "Who is worthy?"

There was a deadly stillness, a terrible silence. Not a foot moved; every eye was abased as each man searched his heart. Oh the tragedy of it all! Of all the countless billions of people of Adam's ruined race, even among the ranks of the redeemed, there was not a man born of woman who was fit to govern the globe. No, not one! Not Elijah or Elisha; not David or Daniel; not Job or Jeremiah; not Moses or Malachi; not Abraham, Isaac, or Jacob; not Peter, James, or John. Not even the apostle Paul.

Over all that vast arena, there stole a palpable silence. The chanting cherubim ceased their song. The hallelujah chorus was stilled, and the harpers fell silent. Even the thunder ceased to roll. Like a deadening pall, the silence grew and spread and blanketed one and all. Until, at last, there settled down over the scene such a silence as had never been known in heaven.

Along with the silence came a deep sense of shame. Oh, the unmitigated shame of Adam's race. Not a single one of all its billions of people was worthy to take the scroll, loose the seals, sweep the planet clean of its vileness, and sit and reign from the river to the ends of the earth.

Suddenly, the silence was shattered by a sob. John said, "I wept much, because no man was found worthy to open and to read the book, neither to look thereon" (Rev. 5:4). That sob seemed to echo, too, like the crack of doom. The hosts of heaven picked up their ears.

There were those among their number all too familiar with sobs on this sin-cursed planet. But for someone to weep bitter tears in heaven? For sobs to sound out there? That was unmatched indeed.

John had made the great discovery. The human race was so fallen that it could not even govern itself. How true that is. In the two thousand years since John lived and ministered, things have not improved. The world as he knew it already had its long list of tyrants. He had learned as a boy in school about the Assyrians and the Babylonians, the Persians and the Greeks. His history books were filled with tales of what they had done to the world. And even if he had read nothing but his Bible, he would have known about the likes of those nations. Even as he penned the pages of the Apocalypse, he was a prisoner of Rome. The Roman Empire was vast, mighty, and splendid in so many ways. But it was also so ruthless and savage that it could only be depicted in Daniel and Revelation as a great wild beast.

The coming of Christ was to have changed all that. Instead of crowning Him, however, men crucified Him. God stayed His hand and allowed history to continue to run its course. Since then, empires have waxed and waned, kingdoms have risen to their peak of prosperity and power, and faded like the mown grass before the burning sun. The world has had its taste of Catholicism, colonialism, capitalism, and Communism. It is sick to death of oppressive governments on the one hand, and weak governments on the other. Man simply does not know how to govern the globe. There is no man worthy. That was the great discovery.

## 2. The great doxology

No wonder John's eyes brimmed with tears. No wonder they ran unbidden down his cheeks! No wonder the celestial songs were stilled. No wonder the cherubim, the elders, the glorious ones on high, stopped what they were doing to stand and stare. A man was *crying in heaven*. Finally, one of them could stand it no longer. He arose from his throne, came over to where the sobbing seer stood, and spoke. "Weep not!" he said, "Behold!" He bade John to look for the Lion, the

Lion of the tribe of Judah. The Lion of the tribe of Judah! Of course! How could he have forgotten Him, the one who was David's Son and David's Lord? That was the one, the one of whom the prophets had spoken. How could he have forgotten Him?

John now turned to look at the Lion. And in one of the most dramatic scenes in all the sweep and scope of human experience, instead of the Lion—instead of mighty mane and gaping jaw and claws of steel and glaring eyes—he saw a Lamb. A Lamb! A Lamb once slain.

There He was in the midst of the elders and in the midst of the throne. John had been looking right there but had been so busy with the sights and sounds of glory, so busy admiring the view, so occupied with taking in the startling landscape of the glory land, so occupied with the elders and the cherubim, so taken up with the throne and the throng, that he had missed Jesus altogether! But there He was "in the midst," where He always was. John should have known to look right there, for that is where Jesus always was when He lived down here. He was in the midst of the rabbis as a boy; in the midst of the thieves at Calvary; in the midst of the disciples in the upper room; and in the midst of His people in the church.

We feel like shaking John for being so blind—except that we often are guilty of the selfsame thing. As the old hymn puts it:

> If now with eyes defiled and dim,
> We see the signs, but see not Him;
> O may His love the scales displace,
> And bid us see Him face to face.[1]

The Lamb! He is called the Lamb only twice in the Old Testament, only twice in the Gospels, only once in the book of Acts, and only once in the Epistles. However, He is called the Lamb twenty-eight times in the book of Revelation. Once John sees Him as the Lamb, he cannot take his eyes off of Him. He sees Him everywhere, in everything, all the time.

"A Lamb as it had been slain!" There, clear to the eye, were the scars of Calvary. Moreover, the Lamb was a little Lamb, a title that is unique to the Apocalypse. In this book, Satan appears as a great red dragon. In this book, Satan produces his monstrous beast. In this book, men are mobilized by the millions against the true and living God and against the scattered and persecuted remnants of His people.

God's answer is a Lamb. A little Lamb! For "God hath chosen the foolish things of the world to confound the wise; and God hath chosen the weak things of the world to confound the things which are mighty; and base things of the world, and things which are despised, hath God chosen, yea, and things which are not, to bring to nought things that are" (1 Cor. 1:27–28). That is just like God.

Suddenly, the heavenly hosts sing a new song: "Worthy is the Lamb that was slain!" Once, a long time ago, they had sung the song of creation. They had seen God take countless stars and their satellites, toss them into prodigious orbits, hold them whirling and plunging on their way through space with such mathematical precision that we can foretell the occasion of an eclipse or the visit of a comet years in advance. The angels had clapped their hands, shouted for joy, and sung creation's song. They are silent now, for it is the redeemed who sing, "Thou art worthy . . . for thou wast slain, and hast redeemed us to God by thy blood out of every kindred, and tongue, and people, and nation" (Rev. 5:9). As the hymn puts it:

> Holy, holy, is what the angels sing,
> And I expect to help them
> Make the courts of heaven ring;
> But when I sing redemption's story,
> They will fold their wings,
> For angels never knew the joys
> That our salvation brings.[2]

So, at last, John hears it for himself, the great doxology that will ring out through all the ages:

> And when, in scenes of glory,
> I sing the new, new song,

'Twill be the old, old story
That I have loved so long.[3]

## 3. The great dichotomy

Now two groups come into focus, sharply divided one from the other. The great divide now appears; that great, fixed gulf, of which Jesus so clearly and solemnly warned.

We discover that the Lamb is to be worshipped by every created intelligence in the universe, without a single exception.

### a. The focal center of things

The sinless sons of light, whose songs had been stilled by a sinner's sobs, now pick up the new song in rapturous harmony: "And I beheld, and I heard the voice of many angels round about the throne and the beasts and the elders: and the number of them was ten thousand times ten thousand, and thousands of thousands; Saying with a loud voice, Worthy is the Lamb that was slain to receive power, and riches, and wisdom, and strength, and honour, and glory, and blessing" (Rev. 5:11–12).

Sometimes, in one of earth's stadiums, as some great champion comes forward to take the bat or kick the ball, the thousands watching begin to chant. It will begin over here, perhaps, but before long it is caught up by the whole vast crowd, a triumphant chant of praise and expectation. Just so here in Revelation. The chant begins, "Worthy is the Lamb! Worthy is the Lamb! Worthy is the Lamb!" until there, at the focal center, the chant is all you can hear: "Worthy is the Lamb!"

The voices rise higher and higher, louder and louder. The theme is eternal, inexhaustible, motivated by joy unspeakable and full of glory. The stars in their courses pick up the theme, the rolling thunder around the throne beats out the score, the glassy sea picks up the song and echoes it back to the everlasting hills. Heaven goes delirious with delight: "Worthy is the Lamb!" But there is more!

### b. The farthest circumference of things

"And every creature which is in heaven, and on the earth, and under the earth, and such as are in the sea, and all that are in them, heard I saying, Blessing, and honour, and glory, and power, be unto him that sitteth upon the throne, and unto the Lamb for ever and ever" (Rev. 5:13).

Every possible sphere! Every single tongue! All created orders and species! All will find tongue and voice. There will not be a dissenting voice in the entire universe.

The fallen angels will be forced to praise Him then. The countless hordes of demons and evil spirits; the four fallen angels now locked up in the Euphrates; the twice-cursed fallen angels, who are locked up in Tartarus; the evil spirits now incarcerated in the bottomless pit; Satan, the Beast, the False Prophet, one and all they will join the anthem of praise. They will have no choice. "Every knee should bow . . . every tongue should confess that Jesus Christ is Lord" (Phil. 2:10–11). They will be joined by wicked, Christ-rejecting sinners of Adam's race, adding their tribute from the regions of the lost. All, without exception, will be forced to sing His praise.

Everyone is going to praise Him, either at the *focal center* of things, or else at the *farthest circumference* of things. Out there, in outer darkness, where there is weeping and wailing and gnashing of teeth, even there in the dark dungeons of the damned, they will praise Him:

> Sinners in derision crowned Him,
> Mocking thus the Savior's claim;
> Saints and angels crowd around Him,
> Own His title, praise His Name.[4]

What a dreadful awakening that will be—to wake up in a lost eternity, knowing that having successfully refused to accept Jesus as Savior they still must acknowledge Him as Lord.

# Notes

## Chapter 1

1. The gospel of Mark overlaps almost entirely with the accounts recorded in Matthew and Luke (with the exception of only four verses). In fact, the entire gospel of Mark, with the exception of perhaps fifty-five verses, could be inserted wholesale into the gospel of Matthew. Consequently, we shall focus our present discussion on the independent accounts of Matthew, Luke, and John of the coming of Christ into the world.
2. Gordon Rattray Taylor, *The Biological Time Bomb* (New York: World, 1968).
3. C. B. Hardy, *Countdown* (Chicago: Moody, 1963), 8.
4. Henry F. Lyte, "Abide with Me," 1847.
5. Winston Churchill, *The Second World War* (New York: Houghton Mifflin, 1948), 35.
6. Isaac Watts, "Jesus Shall Reign, 1719."

## Chapter 2

1. George W. Robinson, "I Am His, and He Is Mine."
2. George W. Bethune, "There Is No Name So Sweet on Earth."

## Chapter 3

1. See Nathan Wood, *The Secret of the Universe* (Grand Rapids: Eerdmans, 1936).
2. Giles Fletcher, "Who Can Forget—Never to Be Forgot."
3. Christina Rossetti, "In the Bleak Midwinter."

## Chapter 6

1. Frederick Farrar, *The Life of Christ* (n.p., 1890).

## Chapter 9

1. Years ago, Simon Greenleaf, dean of the Harvard Law School, wrote a book titled *A Treatise on the Laws of Evidence*, which was a standard text in American law schools for one hundred years, during which time it ran though sixteen editions. When he was a mature lawyer of sixty-three, just seven years before his death, Greenleaf undertook to cross-examine Matthew, Mark, Luke, and John, to put them on the witness stand, to try them in an American court using the same rules of evidence used in courts of justice throughout the civilized world. He wanted to know if they were speaking the truth. He wanted to use the techniques developed by the law for exposing falsehood and for separating truth from lies.

   So he took their testimony as recorded in their Gospels, and subjected that testimony to the severest tests known to the legal profession. His findings are found in a book that runs to some 543 pages. His conclusion is that Matthew, Mark, Luke, and John are perfectly credible witnesses; that their testimony to the person and work of Jesus is true, unvarnished, and reliable.
2. Horatio R. Palmer, "Peace! Be Still!"
3. Robert Lowry, "Up from the Grave He Arose" (also known as "Low in the Grave He Lay").
4. Emma Campbell, "Jesus of Nazareth Passeth By."

## Chapter 10

1. I am indebted to D. M. Panton for these thoughts, "The Godhead of Jesus," *Dawn* magazine, 1923.
2. Charles Wesley, "Oh for a Thousand Tongues to Sing."

## Chapter 11

1. Daniel W. Whittle, "The Crowning Day."

## Chapter 12

1. Robert Lowry, "Up from the Grave He Arose" (also known as "Low in the Grave He Lay").
2. Frances Jane Crosby, "I Shall Know Him."
3. Esther Kerr Rusthoi, "When We See Christ."
4. Charles H. Gabriel, "O That Will Be Glory."

## Chapter 15

1. The Samaritans (whose sacrifices are a surviving relic of Jewish ritual) pierce their Passover lamb with a wooden spit, driven lengthwise through the lamb, and with a crossbar near one end. Thus their lamb, in imitation of Jewish practice, is impaled on a cross of wood.
2. Isaac Watts, "Not All the Blood of Beasts."
3. Horatius Bonar, "No Blood, No Altar Now."

## Chapter 16

1. William Shakespeare, *Macbeth,* Act 2, Scene 1.
2. J. Denham Smith, "Rise, My Soul! Behold 'Tis Jesus."
3. Samuel Taylor Coleridge, "The Rime of the Ancient Mariner."

## Chapter 17

1. John Newton, "In Evil Long I Took Delight."

## Chapter 19

1. Fanny Crosby, "Tell Me the Story of Jesus."
2. James George Deck, "O Lord! When We the Path Retrace."

## Chapter 20

1. The 2004 world population number comes from the Milken Institute 2005 Global Conference, www.milkeninstitute.com/presentations/slides/gc05._tapping_opp.pdf.

## Chapter 21

1. Isaac Watts, "Not All the Blood of Beasts."

## Chapter 22

1. Robert Grant, "O Worship the King."
2. Daniel W. Whittle, "The Crowning Day."
3. Poem by Richard Chenevix Trench.

## Chapter 23

1. Charles H. Gabriel, "O That Will Be Glory."

## Chapter 24

1. Charles H. Spurgeon, "Amidst Us Our Beloved Stands."
2. Johnson Oatman Jr., "Holy, Holy, Is What the Angels Sing."
3. A. Katherine Hankey, "I Love to Tell the Story."
4. Thomas Kelly, "Look, Ye Saints! The Sight Is Glorious."

# Hymn Index

# SCRIPTURE INDEX

# ALSO BY JOHN PHILLIPS

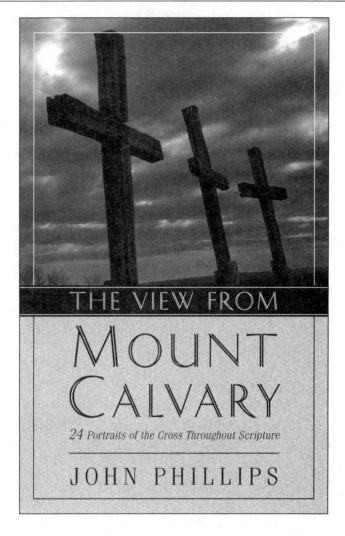

THE VIEW FROM

## MOUNT CALVARY

*24 Portraits of the Cross Throughout Scripture*

### JOHN PHILLIPS

**W**ithout Jesus, the Bible makes no sense. And without his atoning death on the cross, the Bible makes no difference. In *The View from Mount Calvary*, renowned Bible commentator John Phillips surveys the entire Bible and shows how its many sections, books, and subjects all revolve around the death of Jesus on Mount Calvary. Both *The View From Mount Calvary* and the follow-up *Jesus Our Lord* are excellent resources for communion services, Easter celebrations, and stirring devotional study.

**296 pages | paperback | ISBN: 978-0-8254-3376-4**